AF361611

**Praise for *Anatomy of a Duel: Secession, Civil War,
and the Evolution of Kentucky Violence***

"Divided loyalties in the border state of Kentucky manifested in personal combat as much as in formal recruitment by rival armies. In this rich exploration of a duel between a pro-Confederate citizen and a Union colonel, Stuart Sanders reminds us that Kentucky's culture of honor, masculinity, and personal reputation shaped expectations of public behavior well into the Civil War."—Aaron Astor, author of *Rebels on the Border: Civil War, Emancipation, and the Reconstruction of Kentucky and Missouri*

"In this excellent work, Stuart Sanders offers a compelling account of the tragic consequences of the code duello against the backdrop of Kentucky's Civil War. Given the current epidemic of violence in the land, *Anatomy of a Duel* also makes an important contribution to the sociology of violence in America."—James M. Prichard, author of *Embattled Capital: Frankfort, Kentucky in the Civil War*

"Sanders's work is a captivating and thorough examination of the intersection of politics, violence, and issues of honor in Kentucky's Civil War era. Viewed through the people and events of one of the state's last formal duels, this study reveals not only the complex issues of Kentuckians' loyalties during the Civil War, but also the changing nature of violence in relation to men's sense of personal honor. As an exploration of the ideological issues of the war and the far-reaching effects of such acts of violence on the Bluegrass State, Sanders shows that the Metcalfe–Casto duel cast a long shadow on Kentucky's history."—Andrea S. Watkins-Sutherland, coauthor of *Kentucky Rising: Democracy, Slavery, and Culture from the Early Republic to the Civil War*

"With *Anatomy of a Duel*, Stuart Sanders makes a much-needed contribution to the growing body of scholarship on Southern honor and the significant role it played in that society throughout the Civil War. By providing this excellent microhistory, Sanders gives us not only a fascinating forensic look into this particular event, but also a more complete picture of the complexity of Civil War Kentucky."—Timothy R. Talbott, Civil War scholar and battlefield preservationist

Anatomy of a Duel

ANATOMY OF A DUEL

Secession, Civil War, and the Evolution of Kentucky Violence

Stuart W. Sanders

A note to the reader: Several of the quotations printed in this volume contain racially insensitive language. Although actual slurs are elided, the original quotations are included to provide context for the events under discussion. Discretion is advised.

Scholarly publisher for the Commonwealth,
serving Bellarmine University, Berea College, Centre
College of Kentucky, Eastern Kentucky University,
The Filson Historical Society, Georgetown College,
Kentucky Historical Society, Kentucky State University,
Morehead State University, Murray State University,
Northern Kentucky University, Spalding University,
Transylvania University, University of Kentucky,
University of Louisville, University of Pikeville,
and Western Kentucky University.
All rights reserved.

Editorial and Sales Offices: The University Press of Kentucky
663 South Limestone Street, Lexington, Kentucky 40508-4008
www.kentuckypress.com

Library of Congress Cataloging-in-Publication Data

Names: Sanders, Stuart W., author.
Title: Anatomy of a duel : secession, Civil War, and the evolution of
    Kentucky violence / Stuart W. Sanders.
Description: Lexington, Kentucky : University Press of Kentucky, [2023] |
    Includes bibliographical references and index.
Identifiers: LCCN 2023014997 | ISBN 9780813198453 (hardcover ; acid-free
    paper) | ISBN 9780813198460 (paperback ; acid-free paper) | ISBN
    9780813198484 (pdf) | ISBN 9780813198477 (epub)
Subjects: LCSH: Metcalfe, Leonidas. | Casto, William T., 1824-1862. |
    Dueling—Kentucky—History—19th century. | Violence—Kentucky—
    History. | Kentucky—Social life and customs—19th century. | United
    States—History—Civil War, 1861–1865—Influence.
Classification: LCC CR4595.U5 S26 2023 | DDC
    394/.80976909034—dc23/eng/20230406
LC record available at https://lccn.loc.gov/2023014997

To my parents

Take, take my life that heaven gave,
And let my heart's blood stain thy sod;
But know ye not Kentucky's brave,
Will kneel to none but God?
> —"A Kentuckian Kneels to None but God" by
> Maysville, Kentucky, native Mary E. Wilson Betts

. . . one would think that more than three months'
imprisonment utterly without cause would be sufficient
to gratify the malice of a fiend.
> —William T. Casto to William A. Richardson,
> January 10, 1862

In one house lies a mutilated corpse. In another house
there is a dying man. The moral of the story is obvious.
> —The *New York Herald,* noting a violent altercation
> between A. M. Swope and William C. Goodloe

Contents

Introduction

On May 8, 1862, Union colonel Leonidas Metcalfe and William T. Casto, a secessionist civilian, fought a duel on the banks of the Ohio River just outside of Dover, Kentucky. Nearly a month earlier, twenty-three thousand Union and Confederate soldiers had been killed and wounded at the Battle of Shiloh in southwestern Tennessee. That engagement, which Mason County, Kentucky, native and Union soldier Jesse Hyde called "the hardest Battle that was ever fought in the United States," pulled the scales from the nation's eyes. After Shiloh, citizens and soldiers alike realized that the American Civil War would be long and violent. Yet, despite the carnage of the conflict raging around them, Casto and Metcalfe fought a negotiated, formal duel.[1]

The duel between Casto and Metcalfe was one of the last affairs of honor fought in Kentucky under the code duello, the rules that structured and standardized violent exchanges among upper-class white Southern males. Although dueling was illegal in the Bluegrass State, some elites, as historians Bertram Wyatt-Brown, Joanne Freeman, Dickson D. Bruce, Lorien Foote, Todd Hagstette, and others have explained, used the code duello to keep confrontations dispassionate and impersonal. With Americans killing each other in droves on battlefields in 1862, the idea of men following strict, formal guidelines to kill one another seems ludicrous today. For these two Kentuckians, however, both of whom were steeped in Southern honor culture, the duel was a way for one to redeem his lost honor and for the other to protect himself from future threats.[2]

Although honor pushed Casto and Metcalfe to the dueling ground, the affair is indelibly linked to the Civil War. Events and policies tied to the secession crisis sparked the fight between the two men, who at any other time might have been friends. Both were successful, upper-class

Kentuckians of privilege who lived thirty miles from each other. Both were enslavers. One was the son of a Bluegrass State governor; the other was an attorney and former mayor. The war, however, when mixed with the participants' sense of duty, honor, and egos, created an irreparable divide. Like the split between the North and South, the rift separating the two duelists could only, they believed, be resolved by violence. Therefore, as the Civil War raged around them, Casto and Metcalfe transformed the dueling ground into their own battlefield.

Union veteran Albion Tourgée, who became a noted attorney, politician, and civil rights activist, wrote that when remembering the Civil War, Americans should commemorate "only the causes that underlay the struggle and the results that followed from it." In looking at the Casto–Metcalfe affair, this book seeks to follow Tourgée's model to discover the causes and consequences of this duel. It examines why, during a time when Americans were slaughtering one another in open, brutal warfare, Casto and Metcalfe engaged in a formal process of negotiating and fighting a duel. In deconstructing this affair of honor, this book seeks to answer several questions: Why, during the Civil War, did they choose this violent method to settle their differences? How did society, the code of honor, and the Civil War push them to make this decision? Why was this not the last duel fought in Kentucky? And, finally, how did dueling and the application of violence evolve in the Bluegrass State after the Civil War? In answering these questions, this book views the secession crisis and the evolution of violence in Kentucky through the lens of the Casto–Metcalfe duel. It serves as a post-mortem examination of this violent confrontation.[3]

By analyzing how the secession crisis sparked the duel, the Casto–Metcalfe affair helps illuminate the bitterness that many Kentuckians held against one another after the breakup of the Union. Kentuckians were, of course, divided during the conflict, and the Bluegrass State was in an upheaval as the commonwealth contended with neutrality, secession, and civil war. The duel grew out of unionist policies that were meant to save the state. An analysis of its causes also provides a deeper understanding of the broader issues Kentucky faced during the initial stages of the Civil War.

An investigation of this duel also reveals how important September and October 1861 were to Kentucky's ultimate, unique attachment to the Union. In writing about that period, *Harper's New Monthly Magazine* explained, "The most important events of the month have occurred in Kentucky and Missouri." During that time, Union authorities consolidated their control over the commonwealth by any means necessary. They also sidestepped the issue of slavery, fearing that any hint of emancipation would drive the Bluegrass State—about 20 percent of whose population comprised enslaved African Americans—into the Confederacy. Unionists' efforts to control Kentucky included the suppression of newspapers, establishment of recruiting camps, and, most important to the Casto–Metcalfe affair, arrest of some of Kentucky's most important secessionists, including former governors and ex-congressmen. William T. Casto became caught in these events, which proved to be dragon's teeth buried in bluegrass soil. Well sown, they led to his duel with Col. Leonidas Metcalfe.[4]

Examining this affair of honor also provides an assessment of how Kentuckians used violence to resolve conflict. It shows how the public application of violence evolved in the state from the mid-nineteenth to the early twentieth century. After the Civil War, Kentucky gentlemen rejected dueling as a means of mitigating insults or slights of honor. Instead of carrying formal challenge notes, these men bore concealed weapons and resorted to impulsive public shootings or stabbings. With the demise of the code duello, violence among upper-class Kentuckians became deregulated. No longer did they fight in an organized, dispassionate way. Instead, by the 1870s, the use of violence to settle matters had become spontaneous, acts perpetrated with concealed weapons and fought on the streets of Kentucky communities.

There were also few consequences for this public violence. As historians Robert M. Ireland and James C. Klotter explain, killings done in public were frequently ignored by prosecutors and the courts. Consequently, the state essentially sanctioned elites' use of deadly force as a way of resolving difficulties. Ultimately, this honor-bound interpersonal violence, including street fights and murders, helped sully Kentucky's postwar national reputation.[5]

My father, who taught history at Washington and Lee University in Lexington, Virginia, for more than four decades, once told me a story about a Kentuckian who moved to town during the early 1900s. One day, this man traveled to the courthouse to settle a legal matter. When he walked toward the building, two local men began a raucous argument on the courthouse steps. The Kentuckian, who had left a culture where insulted men often pulled concealed knives or pistols and killed one another, took cover and waited for the bloodshed. When neither gunshots nor screams were heard, he emerged from his hiding place. To his surprise, the Virginians were shaking hands. The bewildered Kentuckian left the scene convinced that if these men had been arguing in the Bluegrass State, only one would have walked away alive. This story is emblematic of how white male Kentuckians often handled personal disputes after the Civil War. Because that change happened shortly after the Casto–Metcalfe duel, that affair of honor represents a time when dueling declined and spontaneous, public violence among elites began.

While the Casto–Metcalfe duel—and the dozens of others that took place in antebellum Kentucky—has mostly faded from public memory, modern Kentuckians can still hear reverberations from these past conflicts. For example, when attorneys and state officers (including the governor, public library trustees, the Kentucky Historical Society's governing board, and more) are sworn into office, they take an oath to uphold the US Constitution and the laws of the Commonwealth of Kentucky. They also swear that they "have not fought a duel with deadly weapons within this State nor out of it, nor . . . sent or accepted a challenge to fight a duel with deadly weapons, nor have I acted as second in carrying a challenge, nor aided or assisted any person thus offending, so help me God." As these officials take that oath, audiences usually chuckle. But, at a time when Kentuckians were dueling to uphold their reputations within their communities and to avoid public shame, this pledge served a grim purpose. By banning duelists and others involved in affairs of honor from political office, the state attempted to prevent members of the "bowie-knife-and-pistol-gentry" from killing one another and sowing disorder. Political ambition, they hoped, would negate a gentleman's desire to duel. While twenty-first-century residents no longer worry about gubernatorial candidates issuing challenges, this oath keeps the memory of these affairs of honor alive.[6]

As an attorney and politician, William Casto would have been familiar with that oath. As a soldier, Leonidas Metcalfe risked a court-martial if he dueled. For these two men, pledges and threats of punishment mattered not. Instead, the need to preserve their honor outweighed any potential consequences, including death. This fight, however, had complex causes that were deeply intertwined with the Civil War. Therefore, the duel illuminates a much broader story. It explains how, for many Kentuckians caught up in that conflict, larger events out of their control affected them on an incredibly personal level. For one of the principals in the Casto–Metcalfe affair, that outcome proved deadly. Further, it was said that the survivor "never expressed the slightest contrition for the part he had taken." Even though he had killed a man, the knowledge that he had defended his reputation against the larger backdrop of a national crisis soothed his conscience entirely.[7]

1

A Scene of Desolation

It was the light—a brilliant flash of white—that awakened the residents of Maysville, Kentucky, on the night of August 13, 1854. Anyone still sleeping had only a few moments of extra slumber, for the blinding brightness was soon followed by a roar that jolted the quiet town along the banks of the Ohio River. The resulting shockwave shook houses, threw people from their beds, knocked plates and glasses from tables, and pushed the mighty Ohio away from its muddy banks.[1]

With their homes lurching beneath them, residents soon heard a new sound: thousands of pieces of debris—rocks, wood, bricks, and dirt—fell from the sky, rattled rooftops, and smashed windows and doors.

In a few moments it was over. Silence descended as the final stones fell to the earth and the last shutter dropped from its hinges. The residents—some moaning, others crying, most coughing from the clouds of dust—spilled out of their homes, tripping over rubble and calling for friends, neighbors, and family members. Some feared an earthquake, perhaps a recurrence of the New Madrid Fault quakes of 1811 and 1812. Others believed that a massive bolt of lightning had struck their homes. The Godfearing residents of this town of four thousand inhabitants and a dozen churches contended that the end of the world was at hand and the angel Gabriel was calling them home. For all, however, it felt like a chapter out of the book of Revelations.

Survivors soon discovered that these were not the end times. Instead, twenty-seven thousand pounds of black powder had been stored in several brick buildings in a ravine just outside of Maysville. That night, more than eleven hundred kegs of gunpowder had erupted in a violent flash.[2]

Eyewitnesses described the blast, fired by "miscreants unknown" whose motives are lost to history, as "a vivid light, followed by a crushing

This 1853 engraving of Maysville and the Ohio River was made a year before the powder magazine explosion damaged the town. *Kentucky Historical Society, Frankfort, 2004.41.47.*

peal that shook the atmosphere with the concussion, and made the earth tremble." The blast terrified people for miles up and down the river, including those across the water in Aberdeen, Ohio.[3]

The explosion destroyed structures close to the magazine and damaged homes, churches, businesses, schools, and public buildings. Property damage across town was estimated to be nearly $200,000, or more than $6.2 million today.[4]

Surprisingly, there were few casualties. Several hogs and cows were killed, and one bovine head was "found some miles distant in a watermelon patch with the horns piercing [a] melon and pinioning it to the ground." Although it was reported that one "old lady subsequently died of fright," residents were fortunate that more people had not been killed. There was, however, one other loss. Mary Wilson Betts, a poet of some renown who had been born in Maysville in 1823, was lying ill less than a quarter mile from the center of the explosion. Although Betts survived the blast, about a month after the explosion, on September 16, 1854, she died of "congestion of the brain." She was thirty-one years old, and it was said that the explosion contributed to her demise. The following October, her husband also died.[5]

Among Betts's most famous works was "A Kentuckian Kneels to None but God," which honored Col. William Logan Crittenden, a Kentucky native executed during an 1851 filibustering excursion to Cuba. Crittenden, captured during the expedition, was told to kneel before he would be shot. He reputedly told his captors, "A Kentuckian kneels to none except his God, and always dies facing his enemy!" One stanza of Betts's poetic recounting of the incident reads:

Take, take the life that heaven gave,
And let my heart's blood stain thy sod;
But know ye not Kentucky's brave,
will kneel to none but God?[6]

At least one Maysville resident took that poem to heart. Eight years after the explosion, William T. Casto fought a duel near Maysville on the bank of the Ohio River to prove that he would never bow to any man or worldly authority. Although the Civil War raged around him, Casto sought a formal altercation to restore his honor and to achieve revenge against the man who had wronged him. This Kentuckian would kneel to none but God. His adherence to that principle—and the code of honor—changed the lives of many.

Born in Maysville on January 24, 1824, Casto was called "a lawyer and politician of some ability." His New Jersey–born father, Abijah Casto, was an early Maysville settler, successful grocer, and devout Baptist who freed his enslaved African Americans upon his death. At age seventeen, William, who had first been educated locally, entered what was then Yale College. A student with "a sensitive and rather reclusive turn," William graduated in 1845. He then entered law school at Transylvania University in Lexington, Kentucky. In 1849, two years after receiving his law degree, he unsuccessfully ran for the Kentucky legislature. Intelligent and well-read, Casto often lived on the wealth and goodwill of his father's estate. One writer from an adjacent town recognized Casto's lack of professional drive, calling him "a bachelor of good property and fine education, but one of that class of Kentuckians, too indolent to apply himself to any active calling, living in high style at the

The duelists: William T. Casto and Leonidas Metcalfe. *Kentucky Gateway Museum Center, Maysville.*

best hotels, and attending to a daily practice at *its* bar." This made Casto one of a class that historian Dick Steward calls "reputable *idlers* who came from respectable families and who placed themselves above the rest of society." Men like Casto had a haughtiness and sensitivity to insult that led one 1828 newspaper editor to refer to them as the "testy, touch-wood gentry, who are ready to draw a pistol if a cat should tread on their toe."[7]

Despite Casto's unsuccessful legislative race, he continued to chase political office. In 1853, he was elected mayor of Maysville, defeating his opponent by twenty-four votes. Reelected the following year, he resigned that November, shortly after the Maysville powder magazine explosion. Although his reasons for resigning are unknown, perhaps digging the town out of the dust and rubble was too much responsibility. Regardless, he moved to New Orleans to practice law. That southern sojourn, however, proved brief. Casto returned to Maysville and throughout the late 1850s was active in local Democratic politics. In January 1860, as sectional tensions over the spread of slavery reached a critical point, he served as a delegate to the Kentucky state Democratic convention.[8]

Slavery was on every delegate's mind, including Casto's. Unlike some attendees, however, he was not a large-scale slave owner. Instead, he enslaved one African American man, whom he leased out for work. This was not uncommon in his native Mason County. In 1860, 727 Mason County residents owned 3,772 enslaved African Americans, a little over five slaves per owner. Residents of Maysville, the county seat, also saw the slave trade firsthand. Slaves were brought into town to head into Kentucky's interior via the Maysville–Lexington road, and Maysville was also a port of exit for enslaved African Americans being sold to the Deep South. Like most of his neighbors, and most white Kentuckians, Casto supported the institution. In an August 1861 legislative election, he ran for the state senate as a Southern Rights candidate. However, he lost that race to the unionist nominee, 1,692 votes to 589. Maysville, like most of Kentucky, supported slavery but was also pro-Union.[9]

Unionist newspapers described Casto, "a portly man, florid, good natured and a prime favorite with his sporting friends," as "a notorious secession lawyer of Maysville." The redhaired Casto, who weighed two hundred pounds, never married. This was probably best, however, for the man's ill temper was known throughout town. A reporter once wrote, "Mr. Casto was a man of varied reading and cultured literary tastes. It was his misfortune to have a temper morbid and irritable, which rendered it impossible for him to associate pleasantly with those who differed with him in opinion, and he was too apt to treat dissent from his own views as a personal affront."[10]

As a Southern Democrat, during the 1860 presidential election Casto undoubtedly supported fellow Kentuckian John C. Breckinridge, a Lexington native and former US vice president. This race pitted Breckinridge against Northern Democrat Stephen A. Douglas; Constitutional Union candidate John Bell; and Republican Abraham Lincoln, also a Kentucky native. Although most Bluegrass State residents supported Bell, foreshadowing the state's conservative unionist stance during the Civil War, Lincoln won the national election. He did so, however, without the support of his native state, receiving only 1,364 votes in Kentucky. In Casto's Mason County, Bell won 1,305 votes, Breckinridge 799, Douglas 247, and Lincoln 26. Lincoln's national victory, however, put the South on the path to secession and civil war.[11]

An 1847 engraving of Maysville and the Ohio River. Steamboats and river trade helped the town thrive during the mid-nineteenth century. *Kentucky Historical Society, Frankfort, 2004.41.67.*

Maysville's location on the Ohio River made it a place of strategic importance during that conflict. Located sixty miles upriver from Cincinnati, nearly two hundred miles upstream from Louisville, and sixty-five miles north of Lexington, the town bridged the gap between northern and eastern Kentucky. Maysville also had a storied history. Ancient Indigenous cultures constructed mounds in the region and the remnants of structures, pottery, shells, and skeletons were found there throughout the nineteenth century. When Anglo settlers first arrived, they gave both their camp and a nearby creek that ran into the Ohio River the name Limestone. The camp soon became a destination as settlers traveled down the Ohio River and disembarked at the mouth of Limestone Creek. From there, they ventured into central Kentucky. Eventually, the town was renamed Maysville after the surveyor John May.[12]

As trade along the Ohio River grew, so did Maysville. In 1789, for example, at least thirty flatboats arrived daily, bringing eastern goods and people. The advent of the steamboat increased trade and created a local economic boom. In one month in 1831, for example, at least 155 steamboats landed there. According to historians Lowell Harrison and James C. Klotter, Maysville also became the "immigrant port of entrance" for central Kentucky. This traffic was soon aided by the Maysville–Lexington turnpike, one of the state's most important early roads. Begun in 1829 and fully opened six years later, it was the first macadamized (layered gravel) road in Kentucky. The turnpike undoubtedly boosted Maysville's economy, as goods could be shipped there via the Ohio River and then transported throughout the rest of the state. The road and the river were critical to the development of the region, and both certainly bolstered the grocery business operated by William T. Casto's father.[13]

By 1860, Mason County had 18,222 residents (with about 4,500 living in Maysville), which included 385 free Blacks, representing the fifth-highest number of free African Americans in the state. The county's manufacturing base, valued at $1,651,621, was assessed as the fourth highest in Kentucky. Agriculture was also strong, with cattle, hogs, mules, wheat, corn, hemp, and tobacco produced there for an easily accessible market. The town's location on the Ohio River and investments in transportation infrastructure kept the local economy thriving.[14]

Although the nation stood on the brink of civil war at the end of 1860, Maysville and Mason County were on solid footing. The community had rebuilt after the powder magazine explosion, and thanks to the Ohio River, businesses were prospering. While the town's location across from the Buckeye State tied many residents to the Union, some, including Casto, looked south. As a proslavery, states' rights Democrat, when Lincoln was elected and Southern states seceded, Casto hoped Kentucky would join them. The events of the secession crisis, however, spun Casto in a different, unforeseen direction. His honor and ego, wracked by those events, eventually pushed him to duel Leonidas Metcalfe.

2

All to Lose and Nothing to Gain

The duel between William Casto and Leonidas Metcalfe had its roots in the unionist response to the secession crisis in Kentucky. When the nation fractured, unionists feared that the proslavery Bluegrass State would secede. Therefore, they worked to consolidate their power across the commonwealth. These actions swept Casto into events beyond his control. Fears about Kentucky's possible secession, unionists' reactions to that concern, Casto's acerbic temper, and his adherence to the code of honor pushed Casto and Metcalfe to the dueling ground.

After multiple Southern states left the Union following the election of President Abraham Lincoln, Maysville, Mason County, and the rest of Kentucky considered their options. Like most of the commonwealth, Casto's hometown had strong connections to the Union. In November and December 1860, when South Carolina seceded, area unionists held multiple meetings in Maysville and surrounding communities. Although Kentucky was a proslavery state, the commonwealth ultimately rejected secession.[1]

Why did the Bluegrass State eventually support the Union? From an economic standpoint, it had strong ties to both regions, especially for communities along the Ohio River. Towns like Maysville shipped goods up to Indiana, Ohio, Illinois, and down to New Orleans. Although historian William Freehling writes that Kentuckians "traded far more with the North," economic concerns bound residents to both sides. Investments in Deep South cotton, ownership of Kentucky hemp farms that made bags or rope for the Southern cotton market, and other investments in the slavery-driven plantation system provided strong monetary incentives for some Kentuckians to support secession. The state's

13

location and family ties, however, linked many Bluegrass State residents to the Midwest, notably the southern portions of Illinois, Indiana, and Ohio. Before the Civil War, Kentuckians had flocked to these states, and when Lincoln was elected president, more than 120,000 residents of Indiana and Illinois had been born in Kentucky. This tie led to strong Democratic politics in southern Indiana and Illinois and connected many Kentucky families to the fate of midwestern states.[2]

National patriotism also reinforced the commonwealth's unionism. Hundreds of Kentuckians, including Mary Todd Lincoln's grandfather Levi Todd and Leonidas Metcalfe's grandfather John Metcalfe, had fought the British during the Revolutionary War. Later, another generation of Kentuckians picked up muskets against the Redcoats during the War of 1812. In fact, nearly 65 percent of that war's total casualties were Kentuckians, so the Bluegrass State lost more men than all other states combined. More than thirty years later, Kentuckians again rallied to the Stars and Stripes for the Mexican-American War, and prominent residents, including Henry Clay's son and namesake, became casualties. Noted national politicians also connected the state to the Union. Kentuckians Henry Clay and John J. Crittenden pushed for compromise in the US Congress while Richard M. Johnson and John C. Breckinridge became US vice presidents. Furthermore, thanks to Clay and Zachary Taylor, a Louisville resident, Kentuckians frequently ran for president. Among those politicians and other statesmen, historian Elizabeth Leonard writes, "declarations of 'patriotic love' for the nation became a dominant theme among the state's orators," which influenced Kentucky unionism. Moreover, when Kentuckians rallied to the Union during the 1828 Nullification Crisis, the commonwealth's governor was Thomas Metcalfe, the father of Col. Leonidas Metcalfe, who dueled Casto. This love of the nation and memories of past wartime sacrifices pushed many Kentuckians to embrace unionism during the Civil War.[3]

Other Kentucky unionists were simply pragmatic. They feared that if Kentucky seceded, the commonwealth would become a vast battleground. Confederate troops, they contended, would swarm into Kentucky and use the state as a geographic obstacle between the North and the South. Then, Kentucky would be torn apart. Unionist Samuel Starling worried, "I am sure that Kentucky is only a Union state for fear of the consequences of being the seat of war as a border Confederate State."[4]

Ultimately, Kentucky slavery and residents' faith in the US Constitution was a critical factor contributing to the state's unionism. As historians Aaron Astor, Jacob Lee, Patrick Lewis, Christopher Phillips, and others have argued, proslavery Kentuckians believed slavery would be better protected under the US Constitution than outside of it as part of the Confederacy. Unionists also believed that if Kentucky seceded, slaves would escape across the Ohio River and there would be no legal recourse or fugitive slave laws to force Northerners to return runaways. If Kentucky seceded, some unionists argued, not only would the border state become a vast battleground, but a host of enslaved African Americans would escape in the ensuing chaos without the legal means to have them returned. When considering secession, the slave-owning diarist Ellen Wallace wrote on April 19, 1861, Kentucky "has all to lose and nothing to gain by such a course but ruin." Kentuckian Robert H. Earnest agreed, worrying that "a once proud & prosperous country [would become] a pitiful mess of smoking ruins."[5]

In Casto's Mason County, residents' fears of slaves escaping and not being returned by Northern authorities were based on geography and a proximity to active emancipationists. Because Maysville sat on the shore of the Ohio River, and since antislavery advocates like the Reverend John Rankin lived in nearby Ripley, Ohio, local enslavers remained in a perpetual state of anxiety. During one week in early January 1860, for example, it was reported that more than thirty enslaved African Americans had fled Mason County. A newspaper reported that the slaves had been unable to cross the Ohio River; it was, therefore, assumed that the fugitives were hiding with free Blacks who lived in the region. Moreover, about a year and a half later, two escaped Maysville slaves were spotted in Cleveland, Ohio, on their way to Canada. Mason County residents also punished anyone who assisted freedom seekers. In 1838, for example, Ohioan John B. Mahan went on trial in Maysville for helping slaves escape.[6]

Slave rebellions also bolstered area enslavers' worries. Memories of the 1848 Doyle Conspiracy, in which the twenty-two-year-old Edward James Doyle led forty-two slaves out of central Kentucky toward the Ohio River, heightened white residents' anxiety. After a shootout, Doyle and the freedom seekers were eventually captured in Bracken County, west of Maysville. Doyle, sentenced to twenty years' imprisonment, spent the rest of his life in the Kentucky penitentiary, where he died from typhoid in 1863. The African Americans who sought freedom were returned to their enslavers.[7]

Local media reinforced residents' calls for a conservative unionism that believed slavery would be better protected under the Constitution. In March 1861, the *Maysville Eagle* reported, "This is no time for Union men to falter. . . . Let Kentucky be the last state to give up the Union. . . . Resolve that you will neither be preached, bullied, black-guarded, or *coerced* out of the Union, or driven from the assertion of your rights in it." The newspaper, therefore, called for unionism while urging Kentuckians to keep their "rights"—slavery—secure under the constitution. Mason County citizens evidently listened. Two months later, the *Fremont Daily Journal* claimed that "the Stars and Stripes float from nearly every building in town." A month after that, Maysville unionists held a torchlit procession through the streets to assert their support for the Federal cause. Moreover, in a congressional election that July, the local Union candidate, attorney and former state senator William H. Wadsworth, bested his secessionist opponent John S. Williams 12,230 votes to 3,720. Wadsworth, whose home on Second Street was heavily damaged during the 1854 powder magazine explosion, soon witnessed more destruction. He represented the district throughout the Civil War, became a Union colonel, and was an aide to Union general William "Bull" Nelson during the Battle of Ivy Mountain, Kentucky. John Stuart Williams, his opponent in the election, became a Confederate general.[8]

Conservative unionism had a tight grip on the region, and the area around Maysville soon emerged as a loyalist stronghold. In June 1861, one pro-Confederate resident wrote another Southern sympathizer that "The people here are mostly insane-foolish Union . . . The only real good Secessionists among the ladies as far as I have found here is my 'little Sweet' and she is enthusiastic on the subject." Unionism remained prevalent. Thomas Speed, a Union officer who wrote about Kentucky's devotion to the Federal cause, remarked, "Another interesting Union centre was the Maysville district. Chief among the unionists at the point was Hon. William Henry Wadsworth. Associated with him was Colonel Thomas M. Green, editor of the Maysville paper, and many other earnest Unionists." Green eventually played a significant role in the Casto–Metcalfe duel.[9]

Rallies, editorials, and these "earnest Unionists" did not trouble William Casto. The Maysville lawyer wanted—and apparently actively supported—secession. Although Kentuckians eventually enlisted into the Union army in higher numbers than they did into the Confederate service (there were approximately seventy-five thousand white and Black Union soldiers compared to thirty thousand Rebel troops), most residents simply sat on the fence. As historian William Freehling notes, "71 percent of Kentucky's white males of fighting age settled for inertia" and did not join either army. Despite these statistics, all Kentuckians were affected by the war, be it from economic consequences, the presence of troops, Union military policies, political upheavals, cavalry raids, guerrilla warfare, emancipation, or other factors. The onset of war changed the state. As one Henderson County farmer noted in May 1861, "the people once met to talk about Politics the crops &c they now meet for the purpose of drilling and preparing for the contest."[10]

Enlistment numbers in Casto's hometown of Maysville mirrored the rest of the state. During the Civil War, 1,202 white citizens and 105 Black residents from Mason County joined the Union army. These statistics place the county first in white Union enlistments among seven counties in that region. Some Mason County residents did, however, join the Rebel ranks, including at least twenty-nine men who served in the Second, Fourth, and Fifth Kentucky infantry regiments. Several of these men were killed and wounded at the Battle of Shiloh, while others became casualties at Murfreesboro, Chickamauga, Jonesboro, and other battles. Additional residents claimed that they wanted to join the Confederate army, yet family obligations kept them at home. In June 1861, one Maysville man wrote a Southern sympathizer that he wanted to travel to Virginia to enlist in the Rebel ranks, but he had to instead care for his younger brother and sister. He knew that his brother "would want to go with us and have a hand in the fun himself," but he was responsible for his siblings. Otherwise, he wrote, he "would have long since been with the Southern Army—and wish now that I could go." Because of local Confederate enlistments, unionists worried that surrounding communities would embrace the rebellion. In August 1861, for example, Leslie Combs, who served as the clerk of the Kentucky Court of Appeals, told Abraham Lincoln that nearby Cynthiana, less than fifty miles from Maysville, "is a dark hole of Traitors." Concerns about local secessionists remained a primary concern for local unionists during the first year of the Civil War.[11]

By April 1861, seven Southern states had seceded from the Union. Following South Carolina's lead, Mississippi, Florida, Alabama, Georgia, Louisiana, and Texas all joined the Confederacy. On April 15, after South Carolina forces fired on Fort Sumter in Charleston Harbor, Lincoln called for seventy-five thousand troops to suppress the rebellion. Viewing this as presidential despotism, tyranny, and coercion, by June 1861, Virginia, Arkansas, North Carolina, and Tennessee had also left the Union.[12]

When Lincoln issued his call for soldiers, Kentucky was among the states expected to provide troops. The response from the commonwealth's governor, Beriah Magoffin, was swift. "I say, emphatically," Magoffin responded, "Kentucky will furnish no troops for the wicked purpose of subduing her sister Southern States." Although most Kentuckians supported the Union, Magoffin, an attorney from Harrodsburg, was a Southern sympathizer. In his September 1861 address to the legislature, Magoffin said Lincoln's call for troops "was, in my opinion, illegal," and "I did not then doubt that the real object of it was the prosecution of an unconstitutional war of coercion against the South." The governor's response was a blow—yet not a shock—to Kentucky unionists, who had hoped to see the Bluegrass State support the federal government. Several of these Kentuckians likely recalled the inscription on the stone that Kentucky had sent to be part of the Washington Monument in the District of Columbia: "Under the auspices of heaven and the precepts of Washington, Kentucky will be the last to give up the Union." Overt unionism, however, would have to wait.[13]

Magoffin's reply did not push the Bluegrass State into the Confederacy. Instead, as both sides jockeyed for control, Kentucky declared armed neutrality. Some residents hoped a neutral stance would allow the commonwealth to forge a compromise between the warring North and South. The state had a long history of seeking solutions, from the leadership of Henry Clay and the Compromise of 1850 to Senator John J. Crittenden's Crittenden Compromise before the war. Others, however, feared that secessionists simply supported neutrality to bide their time and gather strength. But, as Union officer R. M. Kelly wrote, both sides sought "to gain time." Delay, secessionists believed, would improve their

Governor Beriah Magoffin of Kentucky was a Southern sympathizer who opposed Federal recruiting efforts during the state's period of neutrality. *Library of Congress.*

chances of pushing the state into the Confederacy. Kentuckians John L. Helm and E. M. Covington explained, "The policy of Kentucky was to adhere to a strict neutrality. In that determination those who feel that it is the interest of Kentucky, on final separation of the States, to be united with the Southern States, have persisted in a rigid adherence to neutrality. Thus acting, the public opinion was being molded to the point of a final union with the Southern States." Many unionists, however, believed neutrality was tantamount to endorsing rebellion. In considering Kentucky's neutrality, one Pennsylvania resident wrote, "In a contest like the present one, there can be no middle ground. . . . Neutrality, when the Government is threatened, by traitors is virtual treason." Therefore, loyalists in Kentucky worked to consolidate their power and to elect a legislature that sympathized with the federal government.[14]

Most Kentuckians understood that it would be difficult for the commonwealth—wedged between the warring sides—to maintain neutrality. The state was too tempting for the contending armies to ignore. Yet, a violation of Kentucky's neutrality would have disastrous consequences for residents. Ellen Wallace of Hopkinsville explained, "The neutrality of Ky. at this time is I fear only like the omenous calm before a great storm. We look to the future with anxiety and fear, least our state may become the battle ground for conflicting armies." In Maysville, however, some supported neutrality. On May 28, 1861, H. M. Pearce wrote Governor Magoffin that "the youths of the city of Maysville" had organized "a company for the protection of the Neutrality of our state." Pearce, who said he was captain of the company, asked Magoffin to send him a sword and belt to make him look and feel more official.[15]

The political course of the Bluegrass State largely hinged on legislative elections, held in August 1861. Advocates for both sides crossed the state, giving speeches at rallies and picnics and on courthouse steps. This included Casto, who unsuccessfully waged a state senate campaign. A week before the election, unionists had been confident. With some Kentuckians having already traveled south to join the Confederate army, Orlando Brown wrote, "*We* are losing no votes, while the *secession* voters are moving off to Virginia, to Tennessee, or to the Devil." When the votes were counted, the devil had his due; unionist candidates won a majority across the state, giving them control of the Kentucky House of Representatives: seventy-six Unionist seats to twenty-four States Rights seats. The Unionists also secured the state senate, twenty-seven seats to eleven. To show their support for the Federal cause, when the legislature convened in early September, members passed a resolution to fly the US flag over the capitol building. It was an unmistakable message that control of the General Assembly was in unionists' hands. Casto, who lost his election, likely cringed when he read about the Stars and Stripes flapping over the statehouse.[16]

With the General Assembly under unionists' control, they continued to consolidate their power. President Lincoln had authorized a lieutenant in the US Navy, William "Bull" Nelson, to establish a Union recruiting ground in central Kentucky. Once unionists gained political control, Nelson began organizing new soldiers.

Like Casto, Nelson was a native of Mason County. Born outside of Maysville on September 27, 1824, Nelson had studied at local schools and at an academy in Vermont before attending the US Naval Academy at Annapolis, Maryland. He saw active service on a ship during the Mexican-American War and by 1855 had risen to the rank of lieutenant. When the secession crisis erupted, Nelson was an ordnance officer at the Washington Navy Yard. Because of his imperious temper and hulking size—he stood some six feet, four inches tall and weighed more than three hundred pounds—he quickly earned the nickname "Bull."[17]

Federal authorities knew Kentucky was a proslavery state with a secessionist governor and a divided populace, so Nelson was first sent there to analyze the state's political climate. "Never in my life have I seen any thing like the excitement there is here," he reported in April 1861. "The people have absolutely gone mad." As both sides argued over secession, Nelson assured his superiors, "You can tell the President that I think Kentucky can be held still—but it will require exertion." On April 22, the officer urged the administration to arm loyal Kentuckians. Although the Bluegrass State officially declared neutrality the following month, Nelson correctly surmised that Kentucky would "be true to her colors in the long run."[18]

Nelson, in fact, used Maysville as a base to enforce Kentucky's loyalty. To support Bluegrass State unionists, the Lincoln administration shipped muskets—called "Lincoln guns"—into the commonwealth. As the key Federal officer in the region, Nelson played a critical role in getting the weapons into the right hands. Because of Maysville's strategic location on the Ohio River, Nelson sent many of the Lincoln guns to Hamilton Gray, a prominent local business owner who distributed the weapons across the state. A liquor merchant and banker, Gray was a bold unionist who bravely took a public stand for having the guns brought through Maysville. In 1861, he ran a notice in local newspapers, taking credit for their distribution. Nelson, who prided himself on personal courage and bombast, must have loved Gray's nerve. Once the muskets were under Gray's control, the firearms were sent deeper into Kentucky via the Maysville–Lexington Road. Speed Fry, for example, a Danville lawyer and merchant who eventually became a Union officer and hero of the Battle of Mill Springs, Kentucky, ordered seven hundred muskets from Gray to distribute in central Kentucky. These successes initially enamored unionists to Nelson. Joshua Speed, one of Lincoln's key Kentucky advisors, told the president that the officer was doing great work in the state: "No one can serve us better than Captain Nelson." He added, "He is true, active, vigilant, a Kentuckian himself—with a large acquaintance with an air & manner well adapted to this region." Maysville secessionists like Casto bristled at the knowledge that their community had become the point of entry for many of the Lincoln guns that helped enforce unionism throughout the Bluegrass. In June 1861, one of them wrote another Confederate sympathizer, "There are about 2000 of those cursed Lincoln guns up in this part of the state. But hurrah for the Southern Confederacy—and I hope old Kentucky will soon join with her for the Union has gone to—Pluto."[19]

With the guns distributed, Nelson began recruiting. In August 1861, as soon as unionists secured the state legislature, Nelson established Camp Dick Robinson, a recruiting ground in Garrard County, south of Lexington. Named in honor of Richard Robinson, who owned the property, the recruiting ground likely encompassed more than five hundred acres. As the state was still officially in a position of armed neutrality, Governor Magoffin complained to Lincoln that the camp violated Kentucky's sovereignty and insisted that it be removed. With a lawyer's touch, the president noted that it did not disturb the Bluegrass State's neutrality because Kentuckians—not Federal troops—were gathering there. Although Lincoln acknowledged that "some arms have been furnished to this force by the United States," he maintained that "this force consists exclusively of Kentuckians, having their camp in the immediate vicinity of their own homes." Prominent Bluegrass politicians, the president said, had expressed their support for the camp. Furthermore, he added, "I do not believe it is the popular wish of Kentucky that this force should be removed beyond her limits, and, with this impression, I must respectfully decline to so remove it." When Lincoln had called for troops after the fall of Fort Sumter, Magoffin had sharply refused. Now, when Magoffin asked for Lincoln's assistance in removing Camp Dick Robinson, the Kentucky-born president threw out a barb of his own. Asking why the governor would object to a force working to maintain the federal government, Lincoln wrote, "It is with regret I search, and cannot find, in your not very short letter any declaration or intimation that you entertain any desire for the preservation of the Federal Union." The camp remained, and multiple regiments were ultimately recruited there. Several military campaigns were also initiated from Camp Dick Robinson, including the fight at Wildcat Mountain in Laurel County in October 1861 and the Battle of Mill Springs, fought near Somerset in January 1862. Without a doubt, the establishment of Camp Dick Robinson was a critical action that assisted the unionist consolidation of power in Kentucky.[20]

While unionists rejoiced at Lincoln's stand to keep Camp Dick Robinson, their celebrations were short-lived. On August 30, 1861, Kentuckians seethed when Maj. Gen. John C. Frémont, the commander of the Federal Western Department, issued a proclamation regarding freed slaves belonging to Missouri secessionists. This sent proslavery Kentuckians into a tailspin of panic and anger. Frémont's proclamation solidified secessionists' fears that Black Republicans were plotting to destroy the institution. It also weakened Kentucky unionists' argument that slavery was better protected under the US Constitution. Others contended that Frémont's edict would spur slave insurrections in the commonwealth. Joshua Speed immediately wrote Lincoln that Frémont's proclamation "will hurt us in Ky—The war should be waged upon high points and no state law interfered with." He added, "All of us who live in slave states whether Union or loyal have great fear of insurrection—Will not such a proclamation read by the slaves incline them to assert their freedom? And the owner whether loyal or not & the whole community suffer?" Kentucky native Brig. Gen. Robert Anderson, the Union hero of Fort Sumter who had become the Federal military commander of the commonwealth, told the president that Frémont's proclamation "is producing most disastrous results in this State." Anderson wrote, "If this is not immediately disavowed and annulled, Kentucky will be lost to the Union." Lincoln understood the danger of Frémont's act: "I was so assured, as to think it probable, that the very arms we had furnished Kentucky would be turned against us. I think to lose Kentucky is nearly the same as to lose the whole game. Kentucky gone, we can not hold Missouri, nor, as I think, Maryland. These all against us, and the job on our hands is too large for us. We would as well consent to separation at once, including the surrender of this capitol." Understanding that emancipation could drive Kentucky into the Confederacy, Lincoln revoked Frémont's proclamation. Casto and other Maysville secessionists, furious over Frémont's edict, surely hoped that the act would propel the Bluegrass State into the arms of the South. It was not, however, to be.[21]

Frémont's actions sowed paranoia among Kentucky unionists. They also made the commonwealth's Northern neighbors fear that the Bluegrass State was on the brink of rebellion. Indiana's Governor Oliver Morton wrote Thomas Scott, the US assistant secretary of war, "At the risk of being considered troublesome, I will say the conspiracy to precipitate Kentucky into revolution is complete. The blow may be struck at any moment, and the southern border is lined with Tennessee troops, ready to march at the instant the Government is ready to meet them. If we lose Kentucky, God help us." This paranoia, which multiplied once Confederate armies entered Kentucky, contributed to the arrest of Casto and others. Unionists decided that they needed to quell the possibility of internal insurrection and thereby worked to rid the state of people who were aiding the Confederacy.[22]

Governor Morton had reason to worry about Confederate troops lurking along the state's southern border. In early September 1861, Rebel forces led by Maj. Gen. Leonidas Polk seized Columbus, Kentucky. A strategically important location on the Mississippi River, Polk took Columbus because he feared that Union troops led by Brig. Gen. Ulysses S. Grant were planning to advance across the river from Belmont, Missouri. When Governor Magoffin questioned the move, Polk responded, "A military necessity . . . required me to occupy this town." In response, Grant seized Paducah, Kentucky, located at the confluence of the Tennessee and Ohio Rivers. The next day, Anderson moved his

Governor Oliver Morton of Indiana frequently worried that Confederate troops would invade the Hoosier State from Kentucky. *Library of Congress*.

headquarters from Cincinnati to Louisville to demonstrate that Federal forces were not going to abandon Kentucky without a fight.[23]

With Rebel troops pouring into the state, the unionist legislature acted. On September 11, the Kentucky House of Representatives adopted a resolution ordering Magoffin to demand that Confederate forces leave Kentucky. That body failed to pass a resolution telling US soldiers to also leave the state. The Kentucky Senate adopted the resolution, which the governor promptly vetoed. His veto, however, was overridden. Magoffin may have been a Southern sympathizer, but he was also a man of duty. Therefore, he followed legislative wishes and asked the Confederates to withdraw. Instead of leaving, the Rebels advanced. On September 18, Kentucky-born Brig. Gen. Simon Bolivar Buckner took Bowling Green, in southcentral Kentucky, for the Confederacy. Shortly thereafter, Brig. Gen. Felix Zollicoffer similarly seized the Cumberland Gap in Eastern Kentucky. This prompted Federal soldiers from Ohio, Indiana, Illinois, and other midwestern states to move into the commonwealth. The state's neutrality was in tatters, and Hopkinsville resident Ellen Wallace proclaimed, "Federal and Confederate troops are pouring into Kentucky on every side."[24]

The Confederate presence was knee-buckling for some unionists. Governor Morton of Indiana, who constantly feared a Rebel horde knocking on his southern border, wrote Lincoln that losing Kentucky would make winning the war "immeasurably" more difficult. "Her central position, the character of her people, her power for good or evil almost make her the turning point of the contest," Morton wrote. While the Hoosier executive worried about Southern soldiers, the Kentucky legislature formally cast their lot with the Federal government. On September 18, as Buckner advanced, the General Assembly ended neutrality and officially threw the state's support to the Union.[25]

The legislature tried to reassure Kentuckians that binding the state's fate to the Union would not remove constitutionally protected rights, namely slavery. Lawmakers knew that the state contained Southern sympathizers, but, they insisted, no rights would be infringed on. Legislators also wanted to assure slave owners that they should not fear meddling Federal commanders like Frémont. Therefore, the legislature issued a proclamation stating, "No citizen shall be molested on account of his political opinions, that no citizen's property shall be taken or confiscated because of such opinions, nor shall any slave be set free by any military commander, and that all peaceable citizens and their families are entitled to, and shall receive, the fullest protection of the government in the enjoyment of their lives, their liberties, and their property." Although the resolution offered calming words, it was wholly dependent on Federal military policy. It also rested on the actions of Union army commanders who had the power to determine which secessionist citizens were acting peaceably and which were aiding the Confederacy. Those who were deemed to be antagonistic to the Federal government—including Casto and several others in Maysville—would soon lose their liberties.[26]

3

When Men Talk Politicks Now They Whisper

Kentucky's neutrality had been a three-month shadow, a naïve, paper-thin wisp of hope that collapsed under internal and external pressure. Bluegrass State politicians would not forge another compromise between warring sides. Instead, with troops led by Maj. Gen. Leonidas Polk in Columbus for the Confederacy and Brig. Gen. U. S. Grant in Paducah for the Union, the legislature aligned the state with the Federal cause. When neutrality ended, soldiers from both sides advanced into Kentucky. By mid-September 1861, Confederate forces had established a defensive line across the southern portion of the state, from Prestonsburg and Cumberland Gap in the east though Bowling Green (seventy miles north of Nashville) and on to Columbus on the Mississippi River. Union commanders, watching enemy troops inch northward, worked to secure railways, bridges, telegraph lines, and strategic communities north of the Confederate position. As Federal officers recruited men and organized regiments, fears of Rebels operating behind their lines spurred authorities to act against suspected secessionists.

As the contending sides squared off, military actions and strategic maneuvers replaced politicians' resolutions. On September 19, a skirmish erupted at Barbourville, in eastern Kentucky. That same day, Union troops marched northward from Camp Dick Robinson and secured Lexington. On September 21, Federal authorities established recruiting grounds in Pendleton and Nicholas Counties. Brig. Gen. Robert Anderson, the Union military commander of Kentucky, then called for additional recruits. "No true son of Kentucky can longer hesitate as to his duty to his State and country," Anderson proclaimed.[1]

The Kentucky-born Anderson, who had become a national hero while commanding the Union garrison at Fort Sumter, took command

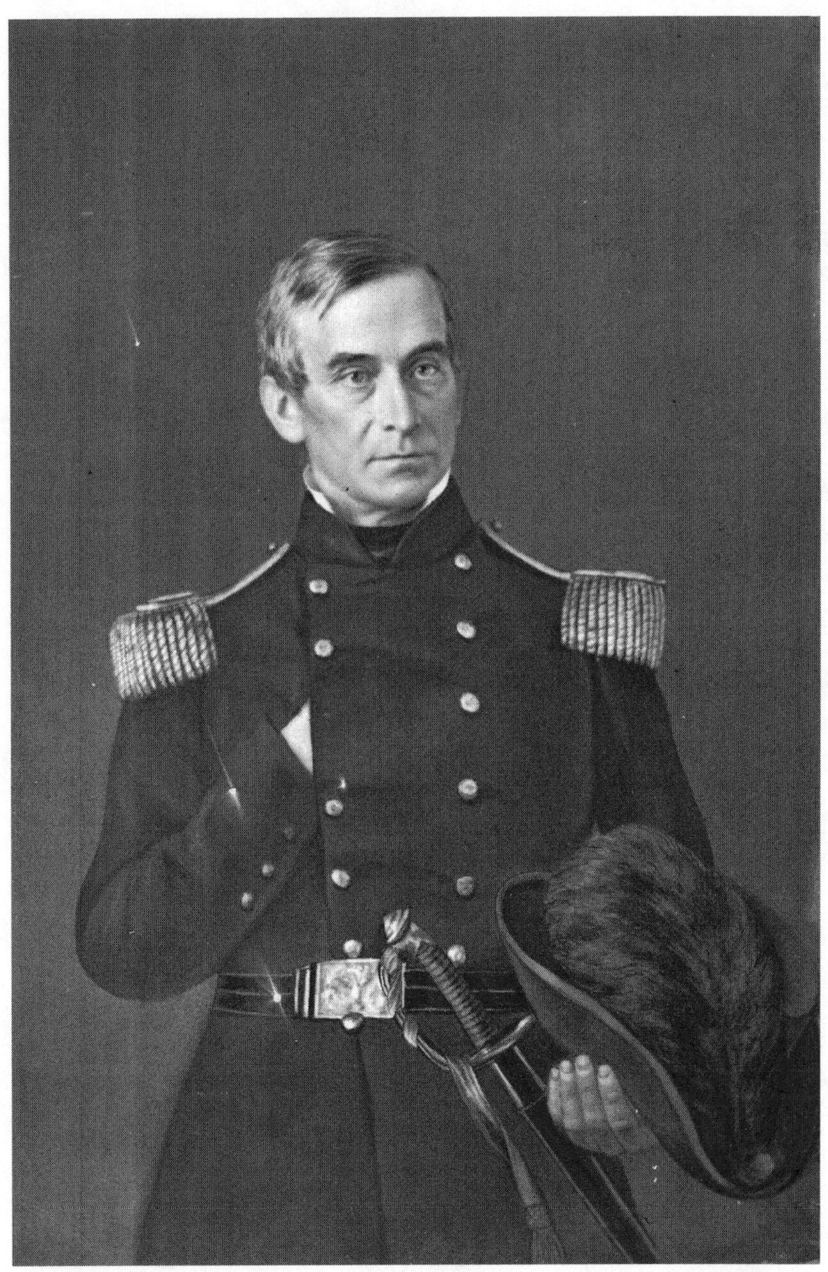

Brigadier General Robert Anderson was the hero of Fort Sumter who became the Union commander of the Bluegrass State. *Library of Congress*.

of Kentucky on September 21. Anderson, playing a balancing act in a divided state, pushed a conciliatory policy toward Southern sympathizers because he hoped to convince them to join the Federal cause. Anderson tried to set secessionists' minds at ease while warning those who sought to subvert Union war aims. Three days after taking charge, Anderson issued a proclamation stating "that no Kentuckians shall be arrested who remains at home attending to his business and does not take part either by action or speech, against the authority of the General or State Government, or does not hold correspondence with, or give aid or assistance to, those who have chosen to array themselves against us or our enemies." Anderson had reason to worry; the day after he issued his proclamation, it was reported that at least one thousand secessionist Kentuckians had traveled to Prestonsburg, with some continuing to Virginia. This exodus of Southern sympathizers, coupled with recruits gathering in Eastern Kentucky and unionist anxieties about the safety of Lexington and Louisville, enhanced fears about Confederate insurrection. "Every neighborhood was in confusion," John Porter of Butler County explained. "It was not infrequently the case that persons on their way to join the federal army were met by others on their way to enlist in the cause of the South."[2]

Although unionists had secured Louisville, Lexington, and most of Kentucky north of Bowling Green, fears for the state's safety generated paranoia behind their lines. Lincoln's friend and advisor Joshua Speed of Louisville helped define these concerns as early as September 1. He wrote the president that Kentucky faced "traitors & enemies at home and a disciplined army from Tennessee advancing." The next day, Joseph Holt, a prominent unionist who worked diligently to keep Kentucky loyal, also informed the president that "the traitors in that state are preparing to carry her out of the Union by a coup de main." When Grant took Paducah less than a week later, unionists' dread of a strong secessionist presence behind their lines was reinforced when troops saw "numerous" Rebel flags flying across town. The Federals had more to fear than banners. Col. Thomas Bramlette of the Third Kentucky (Union) Infantry Regiment informed his superiors, "There is an unusual stir in all the adjacent counties, either for preparation or from fright." On September 8, Ellen Wallace wrote in her diary, "The cloud of war is getting thick over Ky . . . when men talk politicks now they whisper." In early September 1861, Kentuckians were on edge.[3]

Unionists feared that the state was on the verge of falling into Rebel hands. Moreover, they were terrified about a potential insurgency by pro-Confederate civilians lurking behind Union lines. Governor Oliver Morton of Indiana told Lincoln "that a conspiracy is on foot to precipitate the State into revolution and civil war. . . . The secession element in Kentucky is large daring and desperate and will risk everything to accomplish its purpose." This worry—a fear reinforced as Rebel banners flew, Southern armies advanced, and secessionist Kentuckians marched southward to join the Confederate army—reached its apex in mid-September. One Kentuckian believed that "a crisis in Kentucky's position will probably occur in the next five days." Rumors persisted that secessionists were gathering at various points and that they would seize arms from unionist militia. On September 24, another loyal Kentuckian reported, "The secessionists were very busy running around this vicinity last night with guns." In towns throughout Kentucky, Federal authorities worked to dilute Confederate influences. In Owensboro, for example, they confiscated secessionist flags, convinced "a strong disunion sentiment is manifest in the place." Soon, as Casto and others learned, Union authorities would do more than take Rebel banners.[4]

To Kentucky unionists, Confederate sympathizers often appeared out of nowhere. John W. Tuttle wrote, "The Secession fever seemed to be contagious and epidemic. Men of sound mind and principles would go to bed at night violent unionists and without any apparent cause, wake up the next morning rabid secessionists. We unionists could not understand it and did not know whom we could trust or what calculations to make upon the permanency of our following. Those things for a time seemed to all go one way." Of course, with neutrality finished and much of the state in Union hands, secessionists were unlikely to voice their opinions too loudly, lest they face the wrath of the Federal government or their loyalist neighbors. Therefore, the abrupt political conversion of a friend or family member could seem unexpected.[5]

Unionist anxieties continued throughout late September, and officials dreaded a Rebel coup. The speaker of the Kentucky House of Representatives, John Fisk, told a Union officer, "The capital is thought to be in danger." Fisk thus asked for three hundred troops to defend Frankfort. Unionists also feared that the State Guard, Kentucky's militia unit that initially enforced the state's neutrality, was confiscating gunpowder and lead to arm secessionists. It was even reported that disloyal members of the militia were "tearing up lead pipes" to cast bullets. This paranoia was compounded because Federal authorities were woefully unprepared for any Confederate advance. On September 20, Anderson told Lincoln that only three thousand "untried troops" were available to defend Louisville. In addition, Southern soldiers were said to be better trained and equipped. Informing the president that Brig. Gen. Simon B. Buckner was reputedly moving on Louisville with seven thousand Confederate infantry, twelve hundred cavalry, and twenty-one artillery pieces, Anderson warned, "The men are said to be remarkably fine looking and well armed. Kentucky is intensely unprepared for such an invasion." Luckily for Anderson, these rumors were baseless.[6]

During this period, unionists continually worried that Louisville—the state's commercial giant on the Ohio River just south of Indiana—was in danger. At one point, Governor Morton delayed sending troops to the city because he had heard that ten thousand Rebels were advancing. Later, to protect Indiana's southern border, Morton deployed three thousand Hoosiers there. "Louisville is considered in great danger this morning," he told Anderson, "and many doubt whether it can be saved." That same day, the Union's Brig. Gen. O. M. Mitchel was "greatly excited" that Louisville would be attacked. Soon, rumors of a joint advance spread. Buckner was reportedly moving on the city while Brig. Gen. Felix Zollicoffer was advancing on Lexington or Frankfort for the Confederacy. External fears only heightened worries about internal threats. Secessionists—or even men who supported neutrality—became more dangerous. With "secession fever" mounting, Union authorities concluded that they had to remove Rebel elements from their lines. Therefore, to save Kentucky and to consolidate their power, by late September Union authorities began arresting prominent pro-Confederate civilians and spiriting them to out-of-state prisons without warning, formal charges, or trial. They would break their influence and frighten others who might consider aiding the Southern cause. "Ky. poor Ky." one Kentuckian wrote, "how my heart bleeds to think what she is suffering & is to suffer." Soon, Casto joined the multitude of sufferers.[7]

The Federal crackdown on secessionist civilians in Kentucky began in mid-September 1861. Initially, many of the arrests happened at the local level. Home Guard units, who were unionist militia, spurred on by loyalist calls for arrests, confined citizens who were reputedly traveling south to join the Confederacy. In several instances, prominent Kentuckians were among those seized. As unionists worked to control the state and arrest noted secessionists, Ellen Wallace lamented, "The flames of civil war are already beginning to consume the people and their rights."[8]

These arrests created paranoia. On November 1, for example, a farmer from Henderson County feared he was in the crosshairs. "Came home at night with Considerable fears of being arrested for a supposed offence," he informed his diary. Nine days later he still worried. "Coming home this morning I felt truly like a fugitive and a wanderer although I have done no crime although I have committed no offense that should ever trouble a man in a free and enlightened country yet under a despotism as tyrinical as that of any foreign despot could be I may be driven from the quiet and peacefull pursuits of this life to mingle in this unholy and unrighteous war if so I shall do my best on the side of freedom," he explained.[9]

While citizens worried, some Bluegrass unionists advised their commander in chief to take drastic measures to rescue the commonwealth. On September 2, Joseph Holt wrote Lincoln, "The movement is a most critical one for Kentucky." Holt claimed that the Rebels planned to force Kentucky into the Confederacy and added that "a *prompt & decided* movement" was needed to "save the state." Some local authorities took heed.[10]

Home Guard units saw themselves as the first line of defense. As there was little authoritative supervision of these citizen-soldiers, the militiamen, armed with their "Lincoln guns" and gripped with fears that the state was falling into Rebel hands, detained suspicious citizens with impunity. Although many Home Guard members were overzealous, some Kentuckians were indeed on their way to enlist into the Rebel ranks. Kentuckian John Lafferty, for example, related that at least 125 secessionists met two miles north of Cynthiana and marched southeast to Prestonsburg, where they mustered into the Confederate service. In another instance, a Union officer reported that fourteen men from Clark County were arrested on September 24 as they traveled to join the Rebel army. They were armed with "six pistols, two bowie-knives and four guns." While these confinements may have prevented a handful of men from reaching Southern lines, some Federal authorities worried that arbitrary arrests would push civilians into the Confederacy. Therefore, many of the men confined by unionist militia were released after swearing an oath of allegiance to the Union. In Wayne County, for example, Home Guard units arrested Confederate sympathizers and hauled them before a local judge, who made them swear a loyalty oath. While trusting in oaths of allegiance may seem antiquated to modern sensibilities, violators could find themselves on the wrong end of a firing squad or a hangman's noose. In addition, as historian Aaron Astor explains, "for most Kentuckians . . . loyalty oaths treaded heavily upon honor-bound conventions of public performance." For secessionists, Astor adds, the oaths could be "deeply humiliating and caused considerable consternation." Kentuckians bound by Southern honor culture found that the difficult choice between taking a loyalty oath or going to prison was influenced by one's social standing, self-worth, and the need to avoid shame. As Casto discovered, oaths and incarceration challenged all three.[11]

Authorities seized multiple suspected secessionists. On September 10, for example, J. L. Pruett, the brother of a Kentucky legislator, was arrested in Missouri and forced to dig trenches in St. Louis for the Union army. Upon hearing of his confinement, the Kentucky House of Representatives circulated a petition asking for his release. U. S. Grant also urged Pruett's freedom, and the Kentuckian was eventually sent to Grant's headquarters at Cairo, Illinois. Kentucky Home Guard units were equally vigilant. Militia in Marion County arrested Harrodsburg resident J. W. Robards on September 18 and sent him to Louisville. Although Robards hired a lawyer and was supposed to go on trial in October, he was instead hustled away to an out-of-state prison. Robards swore that he was a Union man and was unable to carry weapons because of "white swelling" in his limbs. Taken to Indiana and then Fort Warren in Boston Harbor, Robards took the Union oath of allegiance and was released from custody on November 28. Other Kentuckians were released from Fort Warren about the same time, including residents of Oldham, Mercer, Nelson, Marion, and Fayette Counties. These men had likely been accused of aiding the Confederacy, traveling south to join the Rebel army, or encouraging others to enlist. Kentuckian William Grubbs and fifteen others, for instance, were confined for trying to recruit men for the Southern service. Sent to Fort Lafayette in New York and then to Fort Warren, they, too, were released in late November after taking the oath.[12]

While many of these men returned to their communities and led quiet, unassuming lives, Robards took a different track. While he was confined in Fort Warren, Robards's friends and family worked to secure his release. One Kentuckian told Secretary of State William Seward that the twenty-one-year-old Robards "is ignorant" and that he "supported his mother and two sisters as well as he could by working at farm work for wages." He added that Robards "has little intelligence and no politics. In no respects a dangerous man." Released after taking the oath of allegiance, Robards violated his pledge and joined the Second Kentucky (Confederate) Cavalry Regiment under John Hunt Morgan, Kentucky's most famous Rebel horseman. Captured and confined at Camp Douglas in Illinois for a time, Robards returned to the Confederate army and served until the end of the war. After the conflict, he became a noted contractor in Harrodsburg, excelling in concrete work. His later life, however, took an ominous turn. During the war, Robards had been injured in the eye. After a failed operation, family members concluded that the ocular trouble had "affected" his mind. Others agreed when, in 1909, the seventy-year-old Robards stormed into a local newspaper office. He was evidently "a dangerous man." Pistol in hand, he accused the editor of having inappropriate "intimacy" with one of Robards's family members. Robards then opened fire. One bullet struck the editor in the shoulder, ranged down his arm, and exited near his elbow. The wounded editor pulled a revolver from his desk and shot Robards in the head, killing him. Robards was not the only secessionist arrested in 1861 who became embroiled in the postwar violence that clung to Kentucky like a shroud.[13]

Although some Bluegrass State civilians were clapped in irons and shipped to the northeast, General Anderson tried to rein in Home Guard units by giving clear expectations for how secessionist Kentuckians should be treated. Anderson believed that a conciliatory policy would prevent civilians from joining the rebellion. On September 24, he issued a proclamation that residents did not have to fear arrest if they were peaceful. They would also avoid confinement if they did not support the Confederacy (by action or speech) and did not "correspond with, or give aid or assistance to, those who have chosen to array themselves against us as our enemies." Regardless, arrests continued. Two days after Anderson's proclamation, Union authorities seized Harry Bedford and Larkin B. Towles of Bourbon County and took them to

Camp Dick Robinson. The next day, authorities again clarified their policy, stating that "no one will be arrested for mere opinion's sake. All peaceable citizens, of whatever opinion, will be protected if they do not engage in giving aid in any manner to the enemies of our country." Three days after this clarification, authorities arrested J. R. Curry, the county judge of Harrison County, Sheriff William P. Graves of Harrison County, and Andrew Jackson Morey, the editor of the *Cynthiana News.* Charged with "affording aid and comfort to the enemies of the government," they were initially jailed at the Newport Barracks before being sent to Camp Chase in Ohio. Morey later took up the pen—and pistol—to fight against what he perceived as unionist tyranny. It is likely that the politically active Casto, who lived forty-five miles from Harrison County, knew these arrested men.[14]

Because there were still fears that the Confederates would seize Kentucky, many unionists did not approve of Anderson's catch-and-release policy of arresting secessionists, confining them for a few weeks, and then allowing them to take the oath and go home. Anderson, however, defended his conciliatory stance. "I think that a judicious use of the pardoning power upon the parties taking the oath will do much good," he told Seward. Others claimed that the arrests were a waste of time and effort. "They are very inferior men," unionist S. C. Hawley said about those who had been arrested. "They are not conspirators and have no influence in society. I think we can fill our forts and prisons with much better men who are much more dangerous than they."[15]

While secessionists complained about the arrests, the number of men confined was low, considering that a civil war was raging. According to historian Mark E. Neely Jr., from the beginning of the war until February 15, 1862, the time when Secretary of State Seward oversaw "internal security," Federal authorities arrested 864 civilians. Of these, 49 were Kentuckians. Neely notes that in 1860, the Bluegrass State comprised 5 percent of the North's population, yet Kentuckians made up 8.4 percent of the total men arrested. Neely's statistics show that the Lincoln administration— notably Seward—used arrests to control secessionists in the border states. At least 42.8 percent of the arrests made through mid-February 1862 were carried out in Kentucky, Maryland, and Missouri. Seward recognized that this policy was effective in breaking the will of secessionist civilians. When asked if the administration was arresting the correct

US Secretary of State William Seward oversaw the arrest of many secessionist civilians in border states, including Kentucky. *Library of Congress.*

Bluegrass State residents, Seward reputedly said, "I don't care a d———n whether they are guilty or innocent. I saved Maryland by similar arrests, and so I mean to hold Kentucky." Moreover, when asked what he would do if the Kentucky legislature or the public condemned this action, Seward spat, "I don't care a d———n for the opinion of Kentucky." He wanted the state to remain in the Union, and he would lock up as many civilians as it took to ensure the commonwealth's loyalty. Robards, for example, was one of the men who fell into Seward's crosshairs. Robards was charged with trying to enlist men into the Confederate army and, it was reported, he was confined "by order of the Secretary of State."[16]

Seward did not care for the opinion of Kentucky legislators, but Bluegrass politicians certainly worried about each other. When Seward's orders spirited away secessionist Kentuckians, unionist lawmakers were usually silent. One notable exception was their petition for the release of J. L. Pruett, the St. Louis ditchdigger. On September 22, 1861, however, civilian arrests hit closer to home. That day, two Home Guard officers, Lt. Col. S. P. Barbee of Boyle County and Quartermaster James F. McKee of Mercer County, arrested three legislators in Harrodsburg, the county seat of Mercer County. Senator John L. Irvan of Murray; Representative George W. Ewing of Logan County; and Representative George W. Silvertooth, who represented Fulton and Hickman Counties, were on a leave of absence from the legislative session. Traveling south through Harrodsburg, the local militia confined them, claiming that the lawmakers were traveling to Confederate lines. Kentucky politician Brutus J. Clay wrote his wife, "The highways are watched in all directions & all suspicious persons arrested. I hear that three members of the legislature who were starting for Louisa [in Eastern Kentucky] . . . were arrested near Harrodsburg and are now in confinement. This country is in a dreadful state of commotion in every direction."[17]

The militia threw the lawmakers into the local jail, and word soon reached the state capital that the three politicians had been confined. Although dozens of Kentuckians were languishing in out-of-state prisons, the legislature jumped into action when unionists arrested three of their own. The General Assembly formed an investigative committee comprising state senator W. B. Read and representatives John B. Huston, and John M. Elliott. On September 24, the committee arrived in Harrodsburg, where the members found their colleagues under the lock and key of the local Home Guard. When questioned, the Home Guard officers said that they suspected that Irvan, Ewing, and Silvertooth were "co-operating with the rebel party of Kentucky." They also believed that the men had left the legislative session without a proper leave of absence and assumed that authorities had issued arrest warrants for them. The committee returned to Frankfort and reported, "The arrest and detention were not made upon any legal process, but seemed to have grown out of suspicion alone, engendered by the excitement of the unhappy condition of our State and country." Had the committee paid attention to the scores of Kentuckians already locked away, this should not have been a surprise. The committee added, however, that "the military force making the arrest appeared to be somewhat irregular in their organization, and wanting in a general controlling power." Again, an overzealous and unchecked Home Guard unit confining men who were traveling south should not have startled investigators. Similar arrests were occurring across the state. The committee did report with relief that Irvan, Ewing, and Silvertooth "received kind attention and treatment" while imprisoned at Harrodsburg.[18]

The arrests did raise attention to the unchecked martial enthusiasm of the Home Guard. According to Neely, this was not unusual. Local militia arrested many of the civilians who were detained during this period. He writes that 43 percent of arrests occurred outside of the authority of Seward and the US State Department and that many confinements could be blamed on the "overzealousness on the part of some local authorities." Kentucky was no exception, as local militia units' political zeal blinded them to citizens' rights. They would do what was needed as opposed to what was legal.[19]

The General Assembly hoped to check the Home Guard's unbridled authority. After hearing the committee's report, the legislature offered a resolution calling the arrests "illegal, unwarranted, and . . . disapproved." They added that "the arrest of any citizen of this State, except for sufficient cause and in accordance with law, meets our condemnation." Fortunately for Irvan, Ewing, and Silvertooth, the legislative delegation's visit was enough to ensure their release. The Home Guard "cheerfully discharged said gentlemen, and have aided them on their road to their homes." Other Kentuckians, confined in Newport Barracks, Camp Chase, Fort Lafayette, and Fort Warren, were not so fortunate. Their calls for freedom fell on deaf ears. William T. Casto soon met a similar fate.[20]

While Irvan, Ewing, and Silvertooth were among the most prominent men arrested, they were not the biggest prey snagged by the Home Guard. Unionists had arrested dozens of middling Kentuckians, such as J. W. Robards of Harrodsburg and several newspaper editors. They also

James B. Clay was the son of noted Kentucky politician Henry Clay. Union authorities arrested James while he was allegedly traveling southward to join the Confederacy. *National Archives and Records Administration.*

confined well-known officials, like the county judge and sheriff of Harrison County. Federal authorities, however, sought to trap a more prominent secessionist. If unionists could grab a man of renown—a noted politician or a member of a distinguished family—secessionists would understand that no one was safe from their grasp. Southern sympathizers of all classes would learn to be quiet or face confinement. As S. C. Hawley contended, most of the arrested secessionists had been "very inferior men." On September 26, however, a man with the most prominent surname in the state stumbled into their grasp.

When the Civil War erupted, few Kentuckians held the storied Bluegrass pedigree of James B. Clay, son of Henry Clay, the renowned Whig politician who had served as Speaker of the US House, US Secretary of State, and who had run unsuccessfully for president three times. Although James lived, as historian Lindsey Apple contends, "in the shadow" of his father, he was successful in his own right. Born in November 1817, James attended Transylvania University before working at a "Boston counting house." He became an attorney and managed multiple business ventures, including a farm in Missouri and real estate investments. He also ran Ashland, his late father's estate in Lexington, which James had purchased in 1853. While James found success as a farmer, the true family business—politics—beckoned. James served as US minister to Portugal, held a seat in the US Congress, and was a delegate to the Washington Peace Conference, which had hoped to find a compromise to end the sectional crisis before the Civil War. When the conflict erupted, the Clay family fractured. Four of Henry Clay's grandsons served in the Confederacy while two fought for the Union. James Clay also leaned toward the South. During the secession crisis, a diarist wrote, he gave speeches "in defense of the Southern Rights Party."[21]

Like his father, who fought several duels, James also had his own affairs of honor. He once considered challenging George Prentice, the influential editor of the *Louisville Journal,* because several articles in Prentice's newspaper had disparaged both James and his father. Clay told a friend, "I have gotten myself into a terrible difficulty with the Editor of the Louisville Journal." He blamed it on the fact that he gave a speech "in opposition to the Know Nothing Party [which Prentice supported] and in defense of your Catholics & of the cause of liberty." After exchanging notes, Prentice told Clay, "I do not wish to kill you, and I am very clear in the opinion that my article affords you neither just cause nor a rational pretext for killing me." Prentice said he would neither duel nor follow "the etiquette of duelists in telling you so." Therefore, the fight never happened. Later, Clay nearly dueled Roger Hanson, a Bluegrass lawyer and politician who became a Confederate general, when they squared off for a seat in the US House of Representatives, which James won. Then, while holding that seat in February 1858, Clay and Gen. William Collum of Tennessee nearly dueled. Collum had struck Clay after James made a joke that had insulted the Tennessean. At the chosen dueling ground on February 24, US senators John J. Crittenden of Kentucky and Robert Toombs of Georgia intervened and secured a truce. Collum apologized and averted the duel.[22]

Although those squabbles were behind him, James Clay soon faced a harder struggle. On September 26, 1861, the Home Guard arrested him on the road between Richmond and London, Kentucky, while reputedly traveling toward Brigadier General Zollicoffer's Confederate army. James was armed with "two pistols and a shotgun." Union authorities named Clay "the ringleader" of a group of fourteen men bound for Rebel lines. They whisked him away to Camp Dick Robinson, roughed him up, put him in shackles, and then paraded him through the streets of Lexington. By marching Clay through his hometown, unionists sent a clear warning to residents about their power and authority. They then transported him to Louisville.[23]

Upon hearing of Clay's arrest, unionist newspapers rejoiced. The *New York Times* called Clay "a traitor worth having" and added, "His treacherous tread profanes the soil that HENRY CLAY'S patriotism hallowed." Having Clay in chains was not enough, the paper argued. The editors also hoped that Ashland, Henry Clay's estate, which James owned and operated, would be confiscated to become a monument to the Great Compromiser's memory.[24]

Like many unionists, Gen. Robert Anderson believed Clay's arrest would quiet secessionists. If authorities could seize Henry Clay's son, then they could confine anyone. "I shall not resist it thinking that this course & his being placed under heavy bail for conspiracy if not treason will produce a good effect," Anderson wrote Lincoln. Seward, however, wanted more. Simply having Clay skulking about under the burden of bail was not enough. He told Anderson, "Disregard the habeas corpus and send the prisoner under guard to-night to Indiana and forward them direct to Fort Lafayette." This, Seward contended, was "by direction of the President." Seward did not want Clay to fall under the control of local authorities. Instead, as he did in several instances, the secretary of state wanted the writ of habeas corpus—which would have

In suspending the writ of habeas corpus, President Abraham Lincoln said, "Are all the laws, *but one*, to go unexecuted, and the government itself go to pieces, lest that one be violated?" *Library of Congress.*

brought Clay's case in front of a judge—ignored. To ensure this, he rushed prisoners out of state as rapidly as possible to circumvent their rights. Seward did not believe that these cases would be handled properly in divided Kentucky and did not want to risk local judges freeing secessionists or placing them under "heavy bail." He wanted them in a prison cell, far from the Bluegrass. Sending these Rebels into exile, Seward believed, sent a clear message, even if it was illegal to do so.[25]

Lincoln and Seward had previously suspended the writ of habeas corpus in parts of Maryland to keep secessionists there under control. Although Chief Justice Roger B. Taney of the US Supreme Court had ruled that only the US Congress, and not the president, had the right to suspend the writ, the Lincoln administration continued sending prisoners away without hearings. In July 1861, Lincoln justified his actions by asking, "Are all the laws, *but one* [habeas corpus], to go unexecuted, and the government itself go to pieces, lest that one be violated?" For the administration, the preservation of the Union superseded executing the writ of habeas corpus. In the Bluegrass State, however, the General Assembly attempted to intercede. A proposed resolution in the Kentucky House of Representatives from September 23, 1861, called the suspension of the writ "when done by the President, or any subordinate executive or military officer of the United States . . . unauthorized by law, and are dangerous assumptions of power." The legislature was powerless to stop Federal authorities from ignoring the writ, and Kentucky secessionists found themselves bound for out-of-state prisons.[26]

In the case of James B. Clay, however, others intervened before Seward could exile him. Kentuckians James Guthrie and James Speed, two of Lincoln's unofficial advisors, counseled Anderson to keep Clay in Kentucky and not send him to Fort Lafayette. Anderson, who continued to embrace conciliation, followed their guidance. A judge issued a writ of habeas corpus, and, as Seward had feared, a jury released Clay on the grounds that there was not enough evidence to show he was traveling with the intent of joining the Confederacy. Clay was released on a $10,000 bond and returned to Lexington. While he kept a low profile during the months following his arrest, he later contacted Seward on behalf of two men who had been detained with him. "I presume it is somewhat unusual for you to receive a letter from one who has been himself accused of conspiracy and treason against the United States," Clay wrote. He asked Seward to intervene on behalf of the men, but it is unlikely that the secretary of state, still smarting over the Kentuckian's release, did this favor for him.[27]

Although some Federal officers had hoped a conciliatory policy would bring secessionist Kentuckians back into the fold, by September

1861 the presence of Rebel troops in the state created anxiety about pro-Confederate civilians being located behind Union lines. To counter this threat, unionist soldiers and militia began arresting suspected secessionists. Dozens of Kentuckians—including average citizens, legislators, and even Henry Clay's son—found themselves detained. Although Clay was eventually freed, the policy of confining alleged Rebels continued. Eventually, the strategy led to the arrest of a former governor and set the stage for the duel between Leonidas Metcalfe and William Casto.

4

Beyond the Reach of Law or Liberty

Although the courts initially foiled Seward's plan to confine a noted Kentucky secessionist, James Clay's escape did not deter unionists. Instead, they nabbed another man of prominence: former Kentucky governor Charles S. Morehead. This arrest showcased unionists' strength and helped check the actions of rebellious Kentuckians. On September 19, 1861, Union authorities in Louisville arrested Morehead; Reuben Durrett, the editor of the *Louisville Courier;* and Martin W. Barr, "the news agent of the Southwestern Telegraph company." While local home guard units seized random travelers on their way to join the Confederate army, federal authorities were more intentional. They targeted Southern sympathizers whose detainment would make a public impact and deter others from supporting the rebel cause.[1]

Barr was the least known of the three arrested men. Unionists charged Barr, seized at home and taken to jail, with using "his position as a telegraph agent of the Associated Press to advance the insurrectionary cause." Barr's detainment illustrates that the arrests were strategic. Authorities were working to cut off secessionists' ability to communicate beyond Kentucky, thereby hindering pro-Confederate elements in Louisville from linking their efforts to other out-of-state secessionists.[2]

Barr was transported to Fort Lafayette in New York Harbor without a hearing or trial. On October 15, the telegrapher wrote a friend proclaiming his innocence. "I have been prudent and conservative," he wrote. "I have violated no law . . . I have been snatched from my house in the night. A writ of habeas corpus has followed me. I am here beyond the reach of law or liberty or juries." Barr added sadly, "Write me whenever you have leisure. I am lonesome."[3]

Learning from Clay's botched arrest, Seward ignored the right of habeas corpus and rapidly sent detained men to out-of-state prisons. The secretary of state, however, was not seeking long-term confinement for "insignificant men." Instead, he wanted to send a message. He also hoped to avoid legal entanglements and trials—he had a war to worry about, after all. Therefore, he wanted lesser-known prisoners like Barr to spend a few weeks under confinement before offering them freedom if they took the Union oath of allegiance. Seward wanted to break the men quickly, as in modern "shock probation." He hoped to terrify them into stopping secessionist activity by threatening them with long prison terms without representation or trial. In many instances this worked. In others, it drove the men to join the Confederacy. In Casto's case, it pitched him to the dueling ground.

Efforts to detain Morehead, Barr, and Durrett were aided by the inaction of the Kentucky General Assembly. On September 24, legislators proposed a resolution calling for an investigation "into the causes" and "by what authority, and for what purpose" the men had been seized. The House of Representatives had no interest in pursuing an investigation of three accused secessionists, and the resolution was defeated, fifty-two votes to seventeen. Although the legislature ignored the arrest of a former governor, they did pass broader proclamations urging the federal government to leave citizens alone. While legislative investigations had previously helped politicians detained by local home guard units, proclamations did little to help Kentuckians targeted by federal authorities, who simply ignored the edicts.[4]

Some Kentucky secessionists recognized that the arrests were an effective scare tactic. Leland Hathaway of Mount Sterling, who avoided home guard units as he slipped away through Pound Gap into Virginia, wrote that arrested men had few options: "There was no exchange for the mere political prisoner and his only avenue of escape was to swallow anything in the shape of political dope [oaths of allegiance] that the bigoted and fanatical Gatrap chose to force down his throat and to submit to such terms of restriction or banishment as pleased those arbitrary and petty despots."[5]

On December 30, Barr was told that he would be released if he took the oath of allegiance. He initially refused, claiming that he was "illegally taken" and that justice would prevail. As time passed, however, he tried to negotiate. He asked to be exchanged for "some disaffected telegrapher" who was being held in the South. Union authorities simply wanted him to take the oath, go home, and sit out the war quietly. When Barr asked for an exchange, some unionists suggested that they should release him, since the telegrapher was "worthless and his detention a useless expense to the Government." When authorities reminded Barr that he needed to take the oath to be freed, he again tried to bargain. He asked to be exiled to Canada, where he promised to stay for the war's duration. Finally, on March 17, 1862, after nearly six months in confinement, and weary of negotiations with an insignificant prisoner, authorities paroled Barr.[6]

Morehead's arrest was more complicated. As Kentucky's former chief executive and a well-known politician, Morehead was not a "worthless" prisoner. US Marshal A. H. Smead had arrested him in Louisville for "being actively engaged in stirring up and promoting rebellion." Smead informed President Lincoln that he had seized Morehead, Barr, and Durrett "upon the Charge of aiding & abbeting the rebels." Therefore, the marshal wanted the men to remain in confinement. Upon sending them across the Ohio River, "the effect of these arrests has had a beneficeal Effect here & it would be disastrous to have them released." To avoid a writ of habeas corpus, authorities spirited Morehead, Barr, and Durrett to Jeffersonville, Indiana, where they were detained in a hotel. On the same day the arrested men were taken across the Ohio, the Kentucky legislature passed a resolution stating that authorities should not bother citizens for speaking out against the government. Within twenty-four hours, Morehead, Barr, and Durrett were on their way to Fort Lafayette in New York Harbor.[7]

Confederate authorities believed that these arrests would benefit them. They hoped that as Kentuckians remained confined and newspaper headlines screamed about tyrannical federal policies, the popularity of the Union cause would decline. On September 20, the day after Morehead's arrest, Brig. Gen. Simon Bolivar Buckner wrote his commander, Gen. Albert Sidney Johnston, that, "News relative to public feeling rather cheering. General Anderson has arrested ex-Governor Morehead and other prominent Kentuckians and sent them to [the] Indiana penitentiary." Buckner and other Southern soldiers hoped that public outcry would support their efforts and, ultimately, would guide the Bluegrass State into the Confederacy.[8]

Former governor Charles Morehead was among the most prominent pro-Confederate civilians from Kentucky to be arrested during the Civil War. Morehead was eventually imprisoned in Fort Lafayette in New York Harbor. *Kentucky Historical Society, Frankfort, 1914.32.*

This, however, was not to be. Instead, Morehead's arrest, made immediately after the end of Kentucky's neutrality, showed Kentuckians that no one was safe from the long arm of unionist control. The governor's confinement had a quieting affect; if the Federals could detain a former governor, then they could strike at anyone. This was especially needed after James B. Clay had slipped from unionists' grasp. Federal authorities now sent a clear message to rebel sympathizers. In arresting Morehead, they took a secessionist politician of prominence. In seizing Barr, they confined a telegrapher who had access to communications and intelligence. And, in taking the newspaper editor Reuben Durrett, they stifled secessionist dissent in Kentucky's largest city.

With Morehead's detention, Union authorities had finally seized a noteworthy symbol of secession in Kentucky. Born in Nelson County on July 7, 1802, Morehead attended Transylvania University in Lexington and graduated from that school's law department. After practicing law in Christian and Franklin Counties, he served in the Kentucky General Assembly and was the state's attorney general. He then returned to the legislature and was speaker of the house for several terms. In 1847, he was elected to the US Congress as a Whig, where he served alongside Abraham Lincoln. In Washington for two terms, in 1853, he returned to the Kentucky legislature. After the Whig party collapsed, Morehead ran as the American Party (Know-Nothing) nominee for governor and won by 3,500 votes. As Kentucky's chief executive, Morehead supported education, training for teachers, and prison reform. Although the Whig party was gone, he continued to work for internal improvements, including the expansion of railroads. When his gubernatorial term ended, Morehead practiced law in Louisville. He stayed politically active, and his statewide prominence was evident when he served as a pallbearer at Henry Clay's funeral. In 1860, Morehead owned 13 enslaved African Americans in Louisville and 180 more on a Mississippi plantation, which bound him to the Deep South. That year, he supported John Bell, the Constitutional Unionist candidate, for president. Upon Lincoln's election, Morehead served as a representative to the February 1861 Washington Peace Conference. Three months later, he was a delegate to a border state convention that met in Frankfort, Kentucky, that also attempted to find a peaceable solution to the secession crisis. Despite his later arrest, Morehead was initially considered an advocate for the Union. In November 1860, one writer to the *New York Times* counted him among politicians who would "proclaim in thunder tones [Kentucky's] unshaken devotion to this Union, her unabated dread of disunion, and her utter antagonism to the alleged right, duty, policy, or possibility of secession of any State." On September 19, however, he was arrested for treason. Although a judge had issued a writ of habeas corpus, Seward immediately sent Morehead to Fort Lafayette. Unlike James Clay, Seward would not let this quarry slip from his net.[9]

Upon Morehead's arrest, the *New York Times* tied the governor's alleged disloyalty to his connections to the Southern plantation economy: "He is a gentleman of a commanding appearance, and rather courtly in his manner, but rather too gracious and insinuating for perfect sincerity." Although Morehead had given pro-Union speeches across the South before the war, the newspaper said that he exhibited vacillating "white-feather Unionism" because of his "fine cotton plantation on the Mississippi. . . . There was none finer in the State of Mississippi; and there were slaves to work it." Therefore, the *Times* argued, Morehead's unionism shifted as he sought to protect his own economic interests. By September 1861, those business pursuits landed him in the secessionist camp. The *Times* scoffed at Morehead, suggesting he "may be a traitor, but he is not a hearty one. He is one by necessity. Neither is he a dangerous man. He is a good feeder, a fair drinker, a lover of cushioned chairs." The stress of Morehead's confinement, surely exacerbated by the negative press coverage, put his wife on the verge of a mental breakdown.[10]

Because of Morehead's prominence, Lincoln received multiple letters urging the governor's release. Others called for his continued confinement. Leslie Combs asked the president to keep Morehead locked away, calling him "the most specious, plausible, dangerous of all our Kentucky traitors." Letter-writers to Kentucky newspapers concurred. One Kentuckian wrote the *Louisville Daily Democrat* that Morehead was "an active and dangerous enemy to the peace and loyalty of this state." The writer added, "Kentucky has a heavy account against Mr. Morehead." Others, however, rushed to his defense. Former US vice president John C. Breckinridge, then a senator from Kentucky, complained about Morehead's confinement. He lamented how, "without indictment, without warrant, without accusation," Morehead was dragged from his home and taken out of state. Breckinridge certainly had his own political biases; eventually expelled from the senate, he became a Confederate general and the Rebel secretary of war.[11]

Before Morehead reached Fort Lafayette, Union authorities fed him at the Astor House in New York City, giving him one last

Multiple secessionist civilians from Kentucky were imprisoned at Fort Lafayette, "the American Bastille," in New York Harbor. *Library of Congress.*

sumptuous meal before shuttling him out to the fort on September 25. There, all comfort ended. The US secretary of state, secretary of war, and other military authorities had confined nearly one hundred men in the fort, where they lived in spartan conditions.[12]

Having gained influential friends during his decades of public service, Morehead hoped that political connections would set him free. On December 15, 1861, he wrote Senator John J. Crittenden, another former Kentucky governor, asking him to contact Lincoln on his behalf. Morehead told Crittenden that he could not take the oath of allegiance. If he swore fealty to the Union, Morehead said, his entire Mississippi cotton plantation, worth a staggering $400,000, and his 180 enslaved African Americans "would thereby be subject to confiscation" by the Confederacy. He also told Crittenden that conditions in Fort Lafayette were less than ideal: "I have read of prison-life in history and in romance, but I declare to you that I remember nothing which can compare with the inhumanity and loathsomeness of Lafayette." He told Crittenden that he had never been formally charged and expressed indignation at being "dragged out of bed after midnight by the marshal of my own State, with a band of sixteen armed ruffians, with a warrant charging me with giving aid and comfort to the enemy. . . . I was forcibly carried across the Ohio River." Crittenden could not immediately secure Morehead's release, and the former governor was transferred to Fort Warren in Boston Harbor. Conditions at Fort Warren were considerably better, and Morehead was likely pleased with the change of scenery and increased comfort.[13]

As an attorney and former state executive, Morehead was infuriated at the Lincoln administration for seizing citizens and speeding them away to out-of-state prisons without trial. "The despotism claimed and exercised by Mr. Lincoln and his subordinates of arresting and incarcerating in remote prisons any man or woman at his mere arbitrary will and discretion, without the accusation of any crime, and without the possibility of being heard in defense, is too horrible to need a serious refutation, in a community accustomed to the enjoyment of constitutional liberty," he later wrote. Others agreed, and the legislature finally acted. In December 1861, the Kentucky General Assembly passed a resolution calling for the release of Morehead and other imprisoned Kentuckians.[14]

Morehead blamed Lincoln for his predicament, but the president claimed ignorance. On October 4, Lincoln told Seward he did not know about Morehead's arrest and that Seward should heed the counsel of James Guthrie and James Speed, two Kentucky politicians. If Guthrie and Speed believed Morehead and others should be released, Lincoln said, Seward should set them free. Lincoln claimed "the Kentucky arrests were not made by special direction from here." While overzealous home guard members indeed made numerous arrests, Seward played a hand in multiple incarcerations. According to historian Mark Neely Jr., the Federal response that arrests had "not been directed by this Department" was "an excuse often used to minimize Washington's responsibility for military arrests of civilians."[15]

On October 25, Guthrie, a former US secretary of the treasury and president of the Louisville and Nashville Railroad, wrote to Lincoln that releasing the former governor would not harm the Union cause in

Kentucky. Several weeks later, Crittenden contacted Seward and urged Morehead's release. Crittenden told the secretary of state that Morehead had medical problems and needed to go to New York for an operation. George Prentice, the unionist editor of the *Louisville Journal* who had backed Morehead as a Know-Nothing candidate in the 1850s, also pled for Morehead's freedom. Prentice reminded Lincoln "there are no formal charges against him" and that although Morehead supported the Confederacy, "he has committed no crime against the Government for which any court in the nation, civil or military, would think of sentencing him to imprisonment." Knowing Morehead's financial ties to Mississippi, Prentice asked Lincoln to release the former governor without requiring him to take the oath.[16]

Prentice told Lincoln that Morehead had been "one of the dearest of my personal friends for nearly thirty years." Although Morehead favored the South, Prentice said, he also loved the Union. Morehead was initially against secession but had been angry with the administration's policies. Prentice believed that Morehead's imprisonment "can do no good; I think his release may do some." The editor feared the governor's incarceration "would be the ruin of his amiable and excellent family," and added, "Strongly as I am opposed to his recent course, I would rather give a portion of the brief remnant of my life than to have his confinement protracted."[17]

Lincoln, who understood Prentice's influence on public opinion, must have listened. On January 6, authorities released Morehead on the condition that he enter neither Kentucky nor any seceded state. He was not required to take the oath of allegiance, which saved his plantation from Confederate confiscation. Upon his release, the *Lexington Observer and Reporter* explained that although Morehead was not loyal to the Union, "we do not think he has ever said or done anything for which he should have been deprived of his liberty." Unionist Kentuckians despised secessionists, but many wanted to ensure that citizens were treated fairly under the law. Morehead immediately slipped away to Canada. Four months later, he wrote Crittenden, "I do believe that these arrests, if not stopped, will lead to a guerrilla war all over the state." Although an insurrection over confinements never materialized, the arrests did lead to violence. In Casto's case, hostility would be played out on the dueling ground.[18]

On the night authorities arrested Governor Morehead, they also detained Reuben T. Durrett, the editor of the *Louisville Courier*, a prominent Southern rights newspaper. Born in Henry County, Kentucky, in January 1824, Durrett attended Kentucky's Georgetown College, graduated from Brown University in Rhode Island, and then finished law school in Louisville. In 1852, he married Elizabeth H. Bates of Cincinnati. He then served one term on the Louisville City Council. Following this post, he purchased half of the *Courier* and served as its editor for two years. By 1860, he was a successful businessman who enslaved eleven African Americans, four male and seven female, ages two to forty years old.[19]

During the secession crisis, Durrett penned pointed editorials aimed at the Lincoln administration. While he courted attention, he never expected his prose to reach the highest levels of the federal government. On September 9, 1861, Charles Fishback of Indianapolis sent Seward several of Durrett's articles. He said that he sent the pieces, which condemned the Lincoln administration, "merely to inquire if it is not about time the editor were an occupant of Fort Lafayette or some other suitable place for traitors? The people are getting tired of sending their sons to fight rebels while such as this editor, more mischievous by far than if armed with muskets, are allowed to furnish aid and comfort to the enemy unmolested." Nine days later, the United States Postal Service deemed the *Courier* hostile to the federal government and banned it from the mails. The following day, authorities arrested Durrett for "having written and had published in that paper editorials of most treasonable character."[20]

Durrett maintained his innocence. As in Morehead's case, a judge in Louisville issued a writ of habeas corpus but federal authorities ignored it. Instead, the newspaperman was hustled off to Indiana and then to Fort Lafayette. Like Morehead, Durrett found the conditions there deplorable. But that, of course, was the point. "I was compelled to sleep upon a bag of straw half a foot shorter than myself without a pillow or blanket until I could secure endurable bedding from friends in New York," Durrett complained. "The food given me there was raw pork, tough beef and bread (the bread was good) served upon a board table which the dirty cook swept with the same broom with which he brushed the floor." Like Morehead, Durrett was also transferred to Fort

Warren. Although conditions were better there, his incarceration was too much for his wife, Lizzie, who suffered a nervous breakdown. It was reported that she was "in a truly pitiable condition; and her mother's (Mrs. Caleb J. Bates) state is not much better."[21]

Some influential Kentuckians urged Lincoln to keep Durrett behind bars. "The Courier under this man's editorial management has done everything to incite the people of Kentucky to take up arms against the General Government," Joseph Holt wrote. He added, "His arrest has rejoiced the hearts of the Union men" and releasing the editor would "be a fatal mistake."[22]

Leading citizens of Louisville, including George Prentice, Hamilton Pope, Bland Ballard, W. F. Bullock, James Guthrie, and others, asked Lincoln to free Durrett. While they told the president that the *Courier* was "a very offensive newspaper," they argued that Durrett had not penned the treasonable editorials. He was "a harmless man."[23]

Surprisingly, one of the strongest advocates for Durrett's release was George Prentice, editor of the *Louisville Journal*. Prentice wrote several letters to Lincoln, including one in which he claimed Durrett "will do no possible harm & his worthy wife is fast going *mad*." Louisville residents must have been shocked that Prentice had argued for Durrett's freedom, because the men were enemies. Yet, Prentice could not resist insulting his adversary. Prentice told Lincoln,

> Mr. Durrett has been and I presume still is a bitter personal enemy of mine but I am extremely anxious for his release. He is a secessionist, but he has never done any harm in our community. He couldn't do any harm if he would. He is not without talent, but he has no influence, and his discharge could not be productive of the least possible injury to the Union cause. But the strongest reason why I wish his release is that his wife, a most estimable woman, is on the very verge of delirium on his account. I do believe in my heart that if he be kept from her many days she will go utterly and hopelessly mad.[24]

Despite their mutual hatred, Prentice tried several channels to secure Durrett's release, including writing Seward. On October 2, 1861, Seward told Prentice that since Morehead, Barr, and Durrett "were arrested and sent to Ft. Lafayette by order of the military authorities of Kentucky it would be improper for me to intervene." This, of course, was a lie, because it was Seward—not Kentucky military authorities—who had ordered Morehead and others sent to Fort Lafayette to avoid writs of habeas corpus and the courts. In doing so, Seward had deceived one of Kentucky's most powerful citizens.[25]

Few of Louisville's nineteenth-century residents were as notable as Prentice. His *Louisville Journal* was the most influential newspaper in Kentucky and was a widely read newspaper of record. From Whig politics during Henry Clay's era, Prentice stirring up passions during the 1855 Bloody Monday nativist riots in Louisville, and the editor's staunch unionism, Prentice and the *Journal* molded public opinion. Historian E. Polk Johnson called the newspaper "a very tower of strength to the cause of the Union in Kentucky." Prentice's friends found him genial and kind, yet he was a ferocious editor who pulled no punches. One doctor who knew him wrote, "His castigations were a trick of the trade. He never spared his enemies or political opponents. He took delight in unveiling the most secret histories of their lives. No moral anatomist or surgeon ever wielded a sharper knife, or more keenly exposed the vital organs." It is no wonder that Prentice found himself involved in personal entanglements. But, the doctor recalled, "He was utterly fearless, if not reckless." In one instance, a "rival editor" sent Prentice a threat. Prentice simply responded, "Tell Mr. Hughes I will be down as soon as I have loaded my pistols." The doctor added, "It is hardly necessary to add that the offended gentleman was not there when Mr. Prentice reached the front door."[26]

As a vocal and sometimes controversial editor, Prentice was not afraid to make enemies. Although political differences frequently put him at odds with others, the root of the animosity between Prentice and Durrett was a business rivalry between their two newspapers. Their hatred, however, had reached its pinnacle long before Durrett's arrest. This occurred when the two editors exchanged gunfire on the streets of Louisville.

In July 1857, Prentice wrote an editorial accusing John Milton Elliott, then a congressman from Kentucky, of being a drunkard. In response, the *Courier* published an anonymous article charging Prentice with alcoholism. It also called Prentice an abolitionist and "an

George D. Prentice was the editor of the *Louisville Journal*. He had a street fight in Louisville against rival editor Reuben Durrett. Prentice later lobbied for Durrett's release from prison. *Library of Congress*.

imported wooden-nutmeg Yankee." This led to a venomous correspondence between Durrett and Prentice, who eventually met in front of G. D. Hinkle's law office on Jefferson Street in downtown Louisville. There, the two men argued before pulling handguns. Hinkle, an innocent bystander, was wounded, and Prentice suffered "a slight wound in the fleshy part of the leg, below the knee." Durrett escaped unscathed. Despite their animosity, Prentice actively worked to secure Durrett's release from Fort Warren.[27]

Prentice had surprised many by asking for Durrett's freedom, but the editor's plea was ineffectual. Durrett remained incarcerated. On December 2, 1861, he tried his own emotional appeal. He wrote Seward, "The peculiar disposition of my wife renders her incapable of bearing these troubles. I am advised that she is breaking down with her load of grief and now [lies] prostrate upon a sick bed." Durrett then questioned the secretary of state about the reasons for his arrest. "What let me ask have I done to deserve all this or to make it necessary thus to torture into lunacy or death my poor wife? I myself know of no treason that I have committed." Durrett believed that "personal and political enemies" had encouraged his arrest (he likely included Prentice on this list) and that "the Federal Government in my case has been made a mere tool to work out private hate against me." Seward must have believed Durrett was sufficiently broken. Three days later, Seward ordered Durrett's release if he took the oath of allegiance and agreed to not enter any seceded state. Durrett took the oath on December 9 and was promptly set free. Perhaps Prentice's plea had not been so ineffectual after all.[28]

5

The Soul of the Rebellion

When Union authorities arrested James Clay, Governor Charles S. Morehead, Reuben Durrett, and other Kentuckians, William T. Casto surely read the news with disbelief and disgust. Stories of fellow Kentucky secessionists being plucked from their homes and transported to distant prisons without charges or trials must have angered him, an attorney with Southern sympathies. Casto's attention, however, was soon called to Union activity closer to home. On September 21, 1861, Federal authorities replaced William "Bull" Nelson as commander of Camp Dick Robinson, the Union recruiting ground south of Lexington. Nelson promptly returned home to Mason County, where he established Camp Kenton three miles from Maysville.

When Nelson constructed his new base of operations, loyal residents became more vocal about their unionism. That month, a man named Key, who owned a farm a half-mile from Maysville, hosted a Union barbeque. Thousands attended, watched a military parade (with Nelson reviewing the troops), and listened to speakers, including the Reverend W. B. Carter and Horace Maynard, influential East Tennessee unionists. Despite the construction of Camp Kenton and overt displays of unionism, paranoia about neighborhood Rebels ran rampant. When reporting on the barbeque, the *Cincinnati Daily Press* warned, "In the mean time, the rebels, from all accounts, were furbishing up their arms, running their spoons into bullets, and, with as little noise as possible, collecting at the various points of rendezvous, preparatory to active operations." This concern ramped up activity at Camp Kenton and a new company of Union recruits from the area gathered there for training. Additional Federal troops soon arrived, including four hundred soldiers from Ohio, whom residents greeted warmly. While reviewing recruits was a good public relations move, Nelson had more important

A native of Mason County, Kentucky, William "Bull" Nelson ordered the arrests of William T. Casto and other Maysville secessionists. Casto's confinement was the cause of his duel with Leonidas Metcalfe. *Library of Congress.*

strategic tasks before him. From Camp Kenton, he was charged with driving Confederate forces from Eastern Kentucky. To protect his rear before embarking on this campaign, Nelson first decided to stamp out the most prominent secessionist sympathizers within his lines; he ordered Col. Leonidas Metcalfe to arrest Casto and other supposed Rebels for "fomenting treason and disturbance in Eastern Kentucky."[1]

Metcalfe was the right man for the job. As one of the area's most prominent unionists, he was a staunch early loyalist and a soldier with a strong sense of duty and personal honor. Nelson's order put Metcalfe on a mission to cleanse secessionists from his home region. Born on March 9, 1819, at "Forest Retreat," his parents' home thirty miles southwest of Maysville near Carlisle, Kentucky, Metcalfe was the last of eight children born to Thomas Metcalfe, whom voters elected governor of Kentucky when Leonidas was nine years old.[2]

Leonidas's father had given him a sense of obligation to community and country. Thomas Metcalfe was born in Fauquier County, Virginia, in 1780, to a Revolutionary War officer who had moved the family from the Old Dominion to Nicholas County, Kentucky. One of sixteen children, Thomas became, in his teen years, an apprentice to his elder brother, a stonemason. This education, hewn among tools rather than books, earned the future politician the nickname "Stonehammer." Thomas became an able mason, and examples of his work still survive. He built the foundation of what is now Kentucky's Old Governor's Mansion in Frankfort and helped construct courthouses in Carlisle and Green Counties. He also laid the foundation for Forest Retreat, his Nicholas County home.[3]

Thomas served in the Kentucky legislature from 1812 to 1816. He took a break from his legislative duties during the War of 1812, raised a company of soldiers, was that unit's captain, and fought at Fort Meigs in Ohio. During his political career, Metcalfe became friends with many Kentucky luminaries, including Henry Clay and John J. Crittenden. In 1819, Kentuckians elected Metcalfe to the US Congress. As a federal legislator, historian Frank M. Mathias writes, Thomas was "a friend to the common man and promoter of western democracy." In 1828, he became governor of Kentucky, winning by approximately seven hundred votes. As governor, he supported internal improvements, including the construction of the Maysville–Lexington Road, which ran by Forest

Trained as a mason, Kentucky's Governor Thomas Metcalfe was known as "Stonehammer." *Kentucky Historical Society, Frankfort, 1939.7.*

Retreat. Two years earlier, he had called the road "the beginning of a good work in our State—a work which being National in its character, is calculated to benefit in an eminent degree, not only the citizens of Kentucky, but of many other States belonging to the confederacy." Following his gubernatorial term, Metcalfe served in the state senate. In 1840, he became president of the Kentucky Board of Internal

Improvements. Eight years later, legislators chose him for the US Senate. After one term, he retired to Forest Retreat.[4]

Thomas was a slave owner who, like Henry Clay, supported emancipation and the colonization of freed slaves to Liberia. However, his financial self-interest outweighed those opinions. Instead of sending his own chattel property to Africa, he put them to work. According to one nineteenth-century history of Nicholas County, Metcalfe "owned a large number of slaves, three of whom were plasterers by trade, and [they] made a good deal of money for the [governor]."[5]

Leonidas Metcalfe learned Southern honor culture from his father. While Thomas was in congress in 1827, a South Carolina congressman named George McDuffie challenged "Stonehammer" to a duel. Metcalfe had written something that insulted McDuffie. In the ensuing public correspondence, Metcalfe wrote that if McDuffie was offended, "his remedy as a man of honor and bravery, was obvious." Furthermore, Metcalfe, said, alluding to the war of words, "Opprobrious epithets are not the weapons with which men of honor should settle their controversies. I will not descend to them." Instead, he used arms. As the challenged party, Metcalfe picked the weapons: rifles at thirty yards. McDuffie asked to use pistols, which Metcalfe refused. Negotiations then stalled. It was reported that McDuffie's second complained that Metcalfe would not "give his friend satisfaction with the ordinary weapon" (pistols, which were typically used in duels), so "it would be unavailing to continue the correspondence." McDuffie had evidently sustained an earlier arm injury and it was difficult for him to "manage such a heavy piece of ordnance." The Utica, New York, *Western Recorder* contended, however, that "the real reason probably was, that this old Kentuckian understood the gun too well; having no doubt been accustomed to shooting bears, wolves, and panthers, all his life, and could hit his game when and where he pleased." The duel was never fought, and the following year, Metcalfe returned to Kentucky to begin his gubernatorial term. McDuffie later became governor of South Carolina, so the episode highlights how affairs of honor did not hinder Southern politicians' political careers. Historian Roger Lane concurs: "As the habits of formal dueling at the one end of the white social spectrum and informal brawling at the other were generally ignored by the law and applauded by the bystanders, a violent reputation became something like a qualification for public office."[6]

In 1827, George McDuffie of South Carolina nearly fought a duel with Thomas Metcalfe when they both served in the US Congress. *Library of Congress.*

Leonidas Metcalfe's father, Kentucky's Governor Thomas Metcalfe. Metcalfe County was named in his honor. *Kentucky Historical Society, Frankfort, SC1272.F2.005.*

Thomas Metcalfe died from cholera at Forest Retreat on August 18, 1855, and was buried in the family cemetery at his home. Metcalfe County was named in his honor, and, as historian Frank Mathias contends, "Metcalfe must be ranked as one of the better governors of his era."[7]

While "Stonehammer" had little formal education, his political connections and wealth allowed him to educate his children. In 1836, Leonidas entered the US Military Academy at West Point, but he did not graduate. In 1841, he married Nancy Lemons Thatcher of Bourbon County. Their marriage was blessed with four children, but Nancy died in September 1852. Seven months later, Leonidas married Sara Victor, and they had five children together.[8]

Just as his father had joined the military during the War of 1812, Leonidas also answered the call to serve. When the Mexican-American War erupted, he joined the Third Kentucky Infantry Regiment, which included John C. Breckinridge (who became US vice president and the Confederate secretary of war), Thomas L. Crittenden (son of John J. Crittenden and a Union major general), Thomas H. Taylor (a future Confederate general), and Walter C. Whitaker (a Union general). In September 1847, Maysville residents welcomed Metcalfe's company to town. The mayor greeted them "with the welcome due to those who go to give their all to their country." Fourteen years later, other Maysville residents would not see Metcalfe's presence in such a positive light.[9]

Although Metcalfe went to war, he became ill on the journey and was left in Jalapa, Mexico. His regiment traveled on without him. During this time, his father sent him advice. "The life of a soldier is at least, but a hard one," Stonehammer wrote. "You must obey, if you expect to be obeyed. Stand firmly up for the just rights of your company; but encourage no insubordination. You can do more with your men, by commanding their love and respect, than by acts of hardship or of tyranny—but this you will soon learn, without my advice." Leonidas was ill during much of the war and therefore was frequently absent from his regiment.[10]

Upon his return from Mexico, Metcalfe farmed in Nicholas County and practiced law. In 1860, he was forty-one years old, owned $24,000 in real estate, and held $14,000 in personal property. He also enslaved five African Americans, three male and two female, ages twelve to fifty years old. At the time, Nicholas County had a population of just over 11,000 residents, including 1,614 slaves and 365 slave owners. This was the second lowest number of slaves and enslavers within a seven-county region surrounding Nicholas County. There were also 155 free Blacks living around Carlisle. Within a few years, Metcalfe, his ideology shifting because of the Civil War, became virulently antislavery. During the 1860 presidential election, however, he supported his former regimental comrade, the Southern Democrat John C. Breckinridge, who won the county with 988 votes. Constitutional Union candidate John Bell (who won most counties in Kentucky) secured 690 votes, while the Northern Democrat Stephen A. Douglas took twenty-six votes. Only one resident in Nicholas County voted for Abraham Lincoln. Metcalfe likely voted for Breckinridge because of their acquaintance during the Mexican-American War. As the son of a notable politician, Metcalfe knew the importance of political connections and patronage.[11]

During the secession crisis, however, Metcalfe was a vocal unionist. Although this placed him in the crosshairs of pro-Confederate Kentuckians, Metcalfe was not one to be toyed with. One reporter described him and his reputation: "He was about five feet ten inches high, with slightly stooping shoulders when a careless ease, flat chested, without an ounce of surplus flesh upon his wiry frame, weighing certainly not 140 pounds, with actions quick and nervous. His forehead was low and not very broad, eyebrow prominent and knit, hair dark and sprinkled with gray, his complexion pale and skin clinging close to the cheek bones, compressed lips, and a cold-steel blue eye, the pupil of which perceptibly contracted under excitement." The reporter added that Metcalfe was a "rugged customer," and "he was the last person in the world with whom a man of sense would have sought wantonly to trifle." Known to be a fighter and an excellent rifle shot, Metcalfe had inherited toughness from his father.[12]

On July 15, 1861, as Union authorities worked to secure Kentucky, Garrett Davis, the state's US senator, wrote Secretary of War Simon Cameron on Metcalfe's behalf. Metcalfe wanted to fight for the Federal cause and was quick to have supporters pass his name along to authorities. Davis told Cameron that Metcalfe was a governor's son and had commanded troops during the Mexican-American War and that he wanted the authority to raise a Union regiment. "He is a man of capacity, energy & courage, & entitled to your fullest trust," Davis wrote. Thanks to Davis's endorsement, Metcalfe became one of the first Union recruiters in Kentucky. Shortly after the senator wrote Cameron, Bull Nelson

A Mexican-American War veteran and an early Kentucky unionist, Colonel Leonidas Metcalfe dueled William T. Casto in May 1862. *Kentucky Historical Society, Frankfort, SC1272.F2.003.*

beseeched Metcalfe, "Use your powerful influence aiding the raising of men for the Brigade." Nelson told Metcalfe that although their efforts were "progressing rapidly," they needed to raise troops quickly "for a political reason." Nelson added, "I have seen the old fogies in Lexington, they are very weak but they will be compelled to come up to the scratch in the long run." On July 18, Nelson told Salmon P. Chase, a former Ohio governor and the US secretary of the Treasury, Metcalfe "can raise a good regiment in his section of the State & I recommend him to do so."[13]

When Nelson began shipping "Lincoln guns" into Kentucky, some of the first firearms went to Metcalfe, who oversaw muskets sent to Nicholas County. The weapons arrived in Maysville at night. Metcalfe, along with a driver and two other men, hauled the guns toward Carlisle in a wagon. News of their approach spread, and Nicholas County secessionists gathered to stop the wagon. Several men were chosen to meet Metcalfe before he reached town. When they found him on the road, they told him that the guns were not welcome. If he continued his journey, they said, seventy-five men would meet him and prevent him from reaching Carlisle. With "an oath," Metcalfe replied that if seventy-five men showed up to block him, "seventy-five would never go back to Carlisle." He drove on. Although there were only four unionists in the wagon, no secessionists tried to block their path. The guns were taken to Metcalfe's house, where they were distributed to local loyalists.[14]

By the fall of 1861, Metcalfe was leading an irregular Kentucky cavalry regiment that had yet to be formally organized. He was under Nelson's command, but Metcalfe soon found that following Nelson's orders could be problematic. Nelson ordered Metcalfe to seize horses owned by a Mr. McKrell in Mason County. Nelson had heard that the man planned to sell the mounts in the South. Metcalfe seized the horses, but McKrell used the courts to abrogate the unionists' authority. In doing so, he also sued Metcalfe for damages, including broken fencing. The case was finally resolved in 1864, when a war-weary jury decided that Metcalfe was simply following orders and was not liable for damages.[15]

Another one of Nelson's directives ultimately placed Metcalfe in harm's way. Determined to clear secessionists out of the Maysville region before moving into eastern Kentucky, Nelson ordered Metcalfe to arrest Casto and other alleged Mason County secessionists. On October 2, 1861, Metcalfe led two hundred soldiers into downtown

Maysville. After forming ranks, squads of soldiers were dispatched to arrest Casto and the other disloyal men. These "active secessionists" included Casto, former US congressman Richard H. Stanton, George W. Forrester, James H. Hall, B. F. Thomas, Isaac Nelson, W. B. Tolle, and William Hunt. The soldiers appeared at Casto's home and arrested him for being "an ardent secessionist" allegedly working to aid the rebellion. They also accused Casto of "being one of a clique of rebels there who were fomenting treason and disturbance in Eastern Kentucky."[16]

On securing Casto and the other men, Nelson reported that he had "arrested several traitorous scoundrels who were engaged in fitting out men for the Southern army, subscribing moneys, getting up nightly drills and doing the manner of things usual among the secessionists." He added, "Their arrest has relieved the community here of an incubus the most depressing." Nelson apparently hoped to snag more Maysville Rebels, but several were tipped off and slipped away before they could be confined.[17]

Union soldiers escorted the prisoners through town to the Ohio River, where they were put on the steamboat *Hazel Dell* and taken to Cincinnati under the escort of Deputy US Marshal William Davis. Nelson neither sent proof of the men's disloyalty nor proffered any formal charges. On reaching Cincinnati, authorities lodged the prisoners in the Broadway Hotel. There, Maysville prisoner Richard Stanton "sent for Hon. George E. Pugh and Major J. K. Hallam, acquainted them with the nature of the case, and requested they would provide that they should have a hearing." The men would soon discover, however, that under Seward's watchful eye the wheels of justice would not turn. Although a judge issued an order for a writ of habeas corpus, Union authorities blocked the writ's enforcement.[18]

The irascible Nelson likely beamed when he heard that Metcalfe had arrested Casto. Once, when Nelson was recruiting troops at Camp Kenton, he and Casto argued. In their exchange, Casto "grossly insulted" Nelson, reputedly telling him that a secret group of pro-Confederate Kentuckians would soon get Nelson and his men. This act surely placed Casto at the top of Nelson's list of area secessionists targeted for detention. While vigilant unionists were pleased to hear of the arrests, the confinement of the Maysville residents did anger some Kentuckians. The *Louisville Daily Courier* complained about Nelson and his order, calling him "Lincoln's supple tool in Kentucky, who, during the last three months, has been the means of accomplishing more evil than he could be able to atone for if he lived to the age of Methuselah." In another editorial, the *Courier* complained that the arrested Maysville men were "victims to the tyranny of the Northern invaders of our soil. For no crime, for no violation of law, for *thinking* that the South is right and the North wrong in this war, they have been torn from their families and sent *out* of the state." These complaints did little to stop civilian arrests. In October 1861, authorities arrested seven other citizens, including five from Harrison County, one from Mason County, and one from Metcalfe's native Nicholas County. Taken to Maysville, they were placed on the steamer *Bostona* and sent to Cincinnati for confinement. Shortly after these arrests, unionists in Maysville held a rally that included speakers Joseph Holt, John J. Crittenden, and future US vice president Andrew Johnson. Local loyalists, at least, were celebrating.[19]

After watching Casto and the other secessionists steam away down the Ohio River, Metcalfe forgot about them. He moved on, continuing his work on behalf of Kentucky unionism. For Metcalfe, coordinating the arrests was all in a day's work; he executed the order and moved on to other duties. In fact, a Union camp had been established on his farm in Nicholas County, and he likely supervised recruiting there while he was in the region. Within several weeks, he was leading troops under Nelson in Eastern Kentucky, where he struck Hazel Green in Wolfe County and captured thirty-eight Rebels. From Hazel Green, the Federals pushed on to Jackson, but the Confederates had departed. On November 8 and 9, Metcalfe fought at Ivy Mountain and Piketon (present-day Pikeville), where he led two companies of approximately 140 men. Union soldier Winchester Rudy related that after the fight at Piketon, where the Confederates retreated "double quick," Metcalfe led a scouting party to hunt down the Rebels. Shortly thereafter, he went to Breathitt County and promoted unionism.[20]

Metcalfe was recognized as a "gallant officer," in December 1861, and his unionist neighbors in Nicholas County pled for his return. It was reported that a group of Confederates had visited a unionist at Carlisle, destroyed his property, and tried to kill him. Residents wanted Metcalfe, who had gained a good reputation among area loyalists, to lead a cavalry regiment to protect them. While Metcalfe worked for the nation, Casto, brooding far away in a Federal prison, thought about revenge.[21]

While Casto focused on vengeance, the other Maysville men set their sights on freedom. The prisoners consistently proclaimed their innocence, stating that while they had supported Kentucky's neutrality, they supported neither secession nor the Confederacy. Richard H. Stanton became the most vocal of the Maysville prisoners. He also emerged as their de facto leader.

When Bull Nelson established Camp Kenton outside of Maysville, he immediately set his sights on Stanton. "He is the soul of the rebellion in this part of Kentucky," Nelson said. Born in Alexandria, Virginia, on September 9, 1812, Stanton was the son of a bricklayer who was also a veteran of the War of 1812. Educated locally, Stanton read law and became an attorney. In 1833, he married Asenath Throop. Two years later, the family moved to Kentucky. Ultimately settling in Maysville, Stanton edited the *Maysville Monitor* until 1842. He then practiced law for seven years, was elected to the US Congress as a Democrat, and held that seat for three terms. Stanton's most memorable legislative contribution was naming the State of Washington. When Congress considered the future Washington Territory, the name "Columbia" was initially proposed. Stanton, however, wanted to honor the nation's first president. "We have never yet dignified a Territory with the name of Washington," he said. "I desire to see, if I should live so long, at some future day, a sovereign State bearing the name of the father of his country." He argued that the United States already had the District of Columbia. Therefore, what could have been called "Columbia Territory" was named after the first president.[22]

Stanton served in congress with Kentuckians Henry Clay, Linn Boyd, Humphrey Marshall, William Preston, and John C. Breckinridge. Jefferson Davis, the future Confederate president, was in the US Senate at that time, representing Mississippi. After six years in Washington, Stanton returned to Maysville and became a highly regarded attorney. He wrote several legal books and, with Casto, Isaac Nelson, and others, was actively involved in the local Democratic Party. In the 1850s and 1860s, he owned one slave. On the eve of the Civil War, he was a forty-eight-year-old county prosecuting attorney with $6,100 in real estate and $2,500 in personal property. During the 1860 presidential election, he supported John C. Breckinridge. When the Civil War erupted, Stanton claimed to support Kentucky's neutrality and said he simply wanted

Union and Confederate troops to stay out of the state. It is likely, however, that he pushed neutrality to provide time for secessionists to maneuver the commonwealth out of the Union. Regardless of his stance, rebellion was a family affair. His son, Henry, who had moved to Memphis in 1860, raised Rebel troops, served the Confederacy under Brig. Gen. John Stuart Williams, and became adjutant for several Southern generals. After the war, Henry became the poet laureate of Kentucky. His father, the arrested Richard Stanton, was recognized when the town of Stanton in Powell County was named in his honor in 1852.[23]

While some Kentuckians gave Stanton accolades, Bull Nelson hurled invectives. "This man Stanton is the head of secession in Northeast Kentucky," he roared. "He is the depositary of money for fitting out men from this and adjoining counties for the Southern army. He was actively engaged at the time of his arrest in establishing and maintaining nightly drills of armed traitors." Nelson added that Stanton actively corresponded with Confederate authorities, allowed Rebel officers to stay in his house, and helped send 250 recruits to Southern lines. Therefore, Stanton needed to "be removed further from the scenes of his villainies." After arresting Stanton and transporting him to Cincinnati, Nelson remained unsatisfied. "He is too close to us still," he spat. "He is a man of wonderful intellectual energy, personally truculent and cowardly but morally a very Cataline. His arrest has struck secession dumb here." Stanton was still too close to home, but Nelson believed he had met his objectives with the arrests.[24]

In addition to Casto and Stanton, Nelson seized James H. Hall, a prominent Maysville businessman. Born on December 24, 1817, in Pittsburgh, Pennsylvania, after James's father died, he went off to work at an early age. By the time Hall was ten years old, he was delivering merchandise to stores by "driving a six-horse team from Pittsburg to Philadelphia." Six years later, he apprenticed with a local blacksmith. In 1836, James hopped on a steamboat and landed at Maysville with $1.25 in his pocket. Hall's life is emblematic of the American Dream, an up-by-your-bootstraps, rags-to-riches, Horatio Alger tale. He worked for two years as a blacksmith, and in 1840 married Mary C. Brooke, with whom he had seven children. That same year, Hall began making plows. As he expanded his business, he personally delivered the implements to farmers along the Ohio and Mississippi Rivers. With cotton booming

Maysville resident James H. Hall was among the pro-Confederate civilians arrested with William T. Casto. Hall was a successful plow maker and businessman. *Kentucky Gateway Museum Center, Maysville.*

in the Deep South, his plows found a ready market. In addition to investing in several businesses, Hall also embraced politics. He was elected a member of the Maysville city council, a post he held for many years. He worked to promote Maysville and became an avid booster for the Maysville–Lexington Railroad. He also served as that railroad's president for one year. By 1860, he owned four enslaved African Americans, including three women and one man. That year, he was a forty-three-year-old plow maker and flour-mill owner with $1,700 in real estate and $11,000 in personal property. Arrested with Casto and Stanton, Hall was also accused of aiding the Confederacy. His business ties to the South and his support of slavery likely bound this Pennsylvania-born entrepreneur to the rebellion.[25]

Hall was not the only businessman snagged in Nelson's dragnet. Another, William Hunt, was a forty-two-year-old tobacconist and cigar maker who owned $20,000 in real estate and $1,500 in personal property. Hunt made "plug tobacco and cigars" and did a booming business. Isaac Nelson, another arrested man who later played a prominent role in the Casto–Metcalfe duel, was a liquor merchant who owned "the largest mercantile enterprise in the city." When Isaac was arrested, one of his employees closed the shop and gave the business's money to Isaac's father for safekeeping. George Forrester, also detained in the sweep, was editor of the *Maysville Express* and was confined for publishing secessionist articles.[26]

Upon the arrest of the Maysville men, several of Stanton's friends contacted a local circuit judge and asked for a writ of habeas corpus. The writ was issued, but Union soldiers prevented the sheriff from executing the order. Moreover, when the arrested men were in Cincinnati, they were placed under the authority of Gen. Ormsby Mitchel, who commanded the federal Department of the Ohio. A US district court judge in Cincinnati also issued a writ of habeas corpus, but Mitchel blocked it from being served. To keep the case out of Cincinnati courts, authorities sped the prisoners off to Camp Chase without explaining the charges that had been leveled against them.[27]

At the time, Camp Chase was a prison that housed captured Confederate soldiers and suspected secessionist civilians. Four miles from Columbus, Ohio, one pro-Confederate newspaper described the camp in October, around the time that Casto and the other Maysville prisoners were there. The correspondent wrote that the site, "a large pen, closely planked up with sentinel towers, was made to serve as a prison. Within this enclosure of plank, which was about sixteen feet high, two long sheds had been erected as places of confinement.—These were divided into mere stalls without one single article of furniture, not even bedding or blanket. Into these mere petitions, resembling stalls for cattle, [the prisoners] were thrust." When Casto arrived, the camp housed about 190 inmates. By the end of the month, that number had grown to 250, and it was reported that "the barracks are full." Dressed in army uniforms supplied by the US government, prisoners shared bunks and sometimes lived on meager rations. While confined there, Stanton and five of the arrested men wrote friends in Maysville asking for help in getting released. Casto, however, just seethed over his treatment.[28]

Andrew Jackson Morey, the editor of the *Cynthiana News,* who had been arrested with the judge and sheriff of Harrison County, Kentucky, was among those confined with Casto at Camp Chase. Morey wrote that living conditions were difficult: "Men of every class and grade are huddled together, and all treated as felons." Morey, at Camp Chase by October 1861, claimed that the inmates were not allowed to build fires, despite frigid temperatures. He also complained that they had no stoves, few blankets, and "inferior" food. Because the roof leaked, prisoners and their beds were constantly soaked. Therefore, illness ran rampant. "This treatment of human beings by those calling themselves Christian is unparalleled," Morey lamented. He did have an axe to grind, and his notes about the camp were published in a pro-Confederate newspaper in Nashville after his release. Like several of the men swept up in the fall 1861 arrests, after the war Morey found himself entangled in a violent street fight that had its roots in the Civil War.[29]

Morey was born in Canada and moved to Lexington, Kentucky, when he was a child. He served in the Mexican-American War and in 1849 established the *Cynthiana News,* forty-five miles from Maysville. Like most Kentuckians, Morey supported John Bell during the 1860 presidential election. During much of the secession crisis, the *News* was "a zealous Union paper." That stance, however, soon changed. After Lincoln called for seventy-five thousand troops to crush the rebellion, the newspaper embraced Kentucky's neutrality before calling for secession. "I am now in favor of a Union of the South," Morey wrote in a June

1861 editorial. "Lincoln has driven us to the wall, and Union men must choose whether they will fight the Northern Abolitionists or their home folks." Shortly thereafter, an Ohio newspaper called Morey "the bitterest secession editor in Kentucky."[30]

Union authorities arrested Morey in September 1861, when they swept up the Harrison County judge, the clerk of the county court, and the county sheriff. Accused of supporting the Confederacy, they were locked in the Newport Barracks across from Cincinnati before being sent to Camp Chase. This arrest, like Casto's confinement, nearly led to an affair of honor. Morey was so angered by his treatment that he challenged the man who had arrested him—the six-foot-two-inch Wilkinson Beatty—to a duel. Beatty, who called Morey a "pompous little fellow," accepted the invitation. Under the formal rules of dueling, Beatty, as the challenged party, had the right to pick the weapons. As the larger man, he chose knives. The more diminutive Morey preferred firearms. Therefore, discretion was the better part of valor and Morey declined to fight.[31]

Morey's politics also changed while he was in prison. By October 3, after a few weeks at Camp Chase, Morey supposedly recanted his Rebel ways. He wrote a letter to an Ohio newspaper explaining that he was not a diehard secessionist: "To tell you the truth, I have never been in my heart for secession, but circumstances carried me down into the vortex, and it was almost next to impossible, while remaining at home, to abandon it." Although he had previously been a Union man, Morey claimed that he went astray and "fell in with this Southern fanaticism." When Kentucky's government embraced neutrality, so did Morey. Then, when Morey expected Kentucky to secede, he, like a weathervane, twisted with the political winds and supported secession. "I made a grand summersault," he said, "and have since been laboring for the advancement of that ruinous, rebellious folly, secession." He was convinced to convert to unionism after the state legislature passed resolutions urging his release. He then took a Union loyalty oath. By mid-October 1861, Morey was out of prison.[32]

Morey's conversion did not last. Upon his release, he returned to Cynthiana and attended the funeral of his wife, who had died immediately before he was freed. She had been ill prior to his arrest, and her condition deteriorated during his confinement. Morey blamed federal authorities and his arrest for her demise. Immediately after the funeral, Morey, who had sworn he would stay out of seceded states, violated his parole and went to Tennessee. There, he began editing a secessionist newspaper. His wife's death, and his inability to care for her while he was in a Union prison, rekindled his anger toward the Federal government. Of course, he had likely feigned his conversion to unionism to get released to care for his dying wife. Regardless, Morey, safe in Confederate lines, spilled his fury with his editorial pen and promised revenge. He wrote, "With my musket in one hand and the black flag of extermination to the foe in the other, I intend to avenge my own and my country's wrongs." Kentucky unionists were disgusted that Morey had violated his parole, and the *Lexington Observer and Reporter* called him "a great scoundrel and coward."[33]

While Morey slipped away to the Volunteer State, Casto and the other Maysville prisoners remained at Camp Chase for more than a month, confined without formal charges or trial. Bull Nelson, planning his military campaign into Eastern Kentucky, told Seward that Richard Stanton needed to be transferred farther away from Kentucky. Therefore, Seward, on October 14, told Nelson to send the Maysville men to Fort Lafayette, in New York Harbor. Transported "for safe custody," Union authorities reported, the men arrived on November 2. Several days later, the *Ohio Statesman* incorrectly reported that the men had been moved because they had "concocted well laid plans for an escape from Camp Chase." While the Maysville men certainly had an uncomfortable experience at Camp Chase, they thanked the captors who had treated them kindly. Upon their transfer, Casto and seven other prisoners, including Stanton, Isaac Nelson, Forrester, Hall, Thomas, Hunt, and W. B. Tolle, published a card in a newspaper recognizing the Union's Lt. Col. A. E. Jones, Capt. Charles Johnson, and their men "for their kind, considerate and gentlemanly treatment of us while prisoners under their charge."[34] While Jones and Johnson may have treated the men well, Stanton was also a wily politician who may have orchestrated the card to engender sympathy for their release. Despite these efforts, the Maysville secessionists found themselves in Fort Lafayette, a stark prison that became known as the "American Bastille."[35]

6

Down with Them

Gen. William "Bull" Nelson's planned military campaign into Eastern Kentucky pushed Nelson to ask Secretary of State William Seward to send Casto, Stanton, and the other Maysville prisoners far away from Kentucky. Seward obliged and sent the men to Fort Lafayette in New York Harbor. When the confined men reached the "American Bastille," they realized that published cards thanking their captors neither eased their burden nor sped their release. Instead, they found themselves locked in a fortress, far from home and any sympathetic friends who could help them.

A detachment from the Forty-second Ohio Infantry Regiment transported Casto and the Maysville prisoners to New York Harbor. They first stopped at Fort Hamilton, near Brooklyn, where soldiers searched and processed them. The Maysville men always tried to maintain a gallant air; upon their arrival in New York, the prisoners gave the Buckeye officer in command of the detachment "a letter of thanks for the courteous and gentlemanly treatment they had experienced during their journey." Soldiers then transported them by boat to Fort Lafayette, where jailers confiscated their money and personal belongings. The prisoners discovered that Fort Lafayette was even more spartan than Camp Chase. The lack of quality food was a daily complaint. While meals could be taken at the mess for a dollar a day, penniless prisoners were given the dregs of a soldier's ration. According to one reporter, this included "pork, beef, potatoes, rice, and coffee twice a day. . . . The facilities for cooking are, however, very bad, and it is not infrequently that the food is only partially cooked when served upon the table."[1]

Because of its location, Fort Lafayette was an ideal place to hold political prisoners. It was difficult to reach, and authorities controlled prisoners' communication with the outside world. Completed in 1818 and initially called Fort Diamond, it was renamed seven years later to honor the Marquis de Lafayette. The octagonal fortress with thirty-foot-high walls was built to protect New York from naval attack. Constructed across from Fort Hamilton and located between Staten Island and Long Island, it was converted into a prison in July 1861. The next month the *New York Times* reported: "Ft. Lafayette is rapidly filling up with prisoners of State." Eighty-one men were initially kept there, guarded by eighty-two soldiers. By late September, prisoners from more than fifteen states filled the cells. On October 7, Lt. Col. Martin Burke, a US officer at the fort, told Secretary of War Simon Cameron that there were 134 prisoners present and that it was "all full." Men were confined for supporting secession and the Confederacy, urging enlistments into the Southern army, and for other political charges. Morehead, Durrett, and Barr were imprisoned there for a time, and in August 1862, Edson B. Olds, a former Ohio congressman, was sent there "for uttering intensely disloyal and seditious language."[2]

From privateers to men of prominence, Fort Lafayette was a great equalizer. The cells, built of brick walls that seethed moisture, contained iron beds covered with bags of straw. Few blankets were available, and, one prisoner complained, it was "an atmosphere rendered pestiferous by the want of the common decencies of life." Inmates were allowed two hours for exercise out in a yard. Lights were extinguished at 9:00 p.m. The men frequently grumbled about bad food, fetid water, poor coffee, and stark conditions. One Canadian inmate wrote that he was "imprisoned in a dark, unventilated room with forty-eight other prisoners. . . . The foulness and filthiness cannot be described."[3]

Inmates were also unable to communicate with their accusers. Prisoner James W. Wall complained, "I cannot learn why I am here as the Departments are sealed books to the poor prisoners here. No communications are answered. No consultations with counsel. You cannot meet your accusers face to face. In fact not a single constitutional right is permitted." The Maysville prisoners—at least those who tried to communicate with the Federal government—also had difficulty getting answers. By the time the Maysville men arrived, Governor Morehead, Barr, and Durrett had been transferred to Fort Warren in Boston Harbor. The Maysville secessionists were then the only Kentuckians confined in the American Bastille.[4]

While Casto paced his cell, arrests continued in the Bluegrass State. Although the number of confinements slowed after September and October 1861, some unionists argued that Kentucky was still not safe and urged the federal government to stay the course. In November 1861, for example, Joseph Holt told Seward, "The arrest of these traitors has done immense good in Kentucky and has given the Government a prestige for determination and power which would be destroyed by the retrograde movement at a time when the invading enemy is still upon the soil of the State." Within weeks, however, the policy softened. Union authorities, worried that additional confinements would push Kentuckians into the Confederacy, slowed the number of detainments. On October 7, authorities announced their "deep regret that arrests are being made in some of the State upon the slightest and most trivial grounds." Brig. Gen. Robert Anderson, the Union commander of the commonwealth, told his subordinates to arrest only citizens who were joining the Rebel army or "giving aid or information" to the enemy. He also directed that there needed to be concrete evidence to convict the suspected men in court. Furthermore, Anderson did not want arrested civilians sent out of state. While Anderson noted that home guard units had made some arbitrary confinements, he hoped a conciliatory policy that avoided "ill-timed and unlawful arrests" would convince secessionists to embrace unionism.[5]

Three weeks later, Anderson's successor, Brig. Gen. William T. Sherman, reinforced the policy. He issued an order confirming that arrested civilians should receive trials and that they needed to remain in Kentucky until their hearings. "We cannot imprison and keep in custody all suspected persons," Sherman wrote, "and the only course is to follow the law of the State of Kentucky which makes arrests only proper when overt acts of treason are established." He told his subordinates to send evidence to "Judge Bullitt, a good Union man," a member of the Kentucky Court of Appeals. Although Sherman believed Judge Joshua F. Bullitt to be loyal, he was later confined for supporting secret secessionist organizations. Sherman also realized that home guard arrests did not follow the rule of law, and this helped the Rebel cause. "So many improper arrests were made by self-constituted authorities that there was a physical impossibility of keeping them," he wrote. "To inflict any cruelty on them would not be tolerated by the laws of war or peace, and the consequence is many dangerous men are set free." While updated policies dictated that arrested men should remain in Kentucky, these changes did little to help Casto, lying on his bed of straw in New York Harbor.[6]

As Union policies in Kentucky eased, most of the Maysville men went to work trying to secure their release. On October 7, all of them—except Casto—wrote two lawyers in Maysville, Harrison Taylor and F. T. Hood, asking for help. "We authorize you for each of us to pledge us to the proper authorities that as good citizens we will give implicit obedience to the laws of the Federal and State governments and in no manner knowingly resist or violate either," they wrote. "We are citizens of Kentucky; our fate and fortunes are identified with her. . . . We trust you know as well enough to believe this pledge will be kept in good faith." Taylor and Hood forwarded the letter to Lincoln on November 18.[7]

Casto did not sign it. His absence points to brewing resentment about his treatment. Casto consistently maintained that he was guilty of no crime. He had done nothing wrong, so he would not sign a letter that begged Union authorities—those who had violated his constitutional rights—for release. Therefore, while his fellow prisoners wrote letters, Casto brooded. In doing so, he affixed his rage on one man who was emblematic for how he had been wronged: Leonidas Metcalfe.

Despite Casto's silence, Richard Stanton continued his efforts to secure their freedom. On November 4, Stanton wrote to Seward on behalf of all of them, insisting that they never "engaged in the rebellion or intended to do so, never contributed money, never advised men to go in the Southern army nor in any other manner committed any act of disloyalty to the Government." Stanton insisted that they had only favored Kentucky's neutrality. They were against the presence of both Federal and Confederate troops in their home state and simply wanted Kentucky to mediate a peace between the warring sides. He wrote that they had never aided the rebellion and were never charged with any crime and thus asked if they could be sent to Cincinnati, closer to home. Stanton also wrote Lincoln that he had only supported neutrality and was against the "Lincoln guns" sent into the state. Union authorities, however, believed Stanton's claim of supporting neutrality—rather than the Federal cause—was "conclusive proof of a disloyal heart." In their eyes, the letter shone further light upon his guilt.[8]

Despite US authorities' insistence that the men were guilty of supporting the Confederacy, loyal Kentuckians urged their release. About forty unionist members of the state legislature signed a petition asking for their freedom. Maysville residents also sent letters proclaiming the prisoners' innocence and asked for their discharge.[9]

Among those writing letters was Mayor William H. Wadsworth of Maysville. In December 1861, Wadsworth wrote Seward, "A number of my constituents and townsmen were arrested by Brigadier-General Nelson in Maysville, Ky., sent to Camp Chase, Ohio, and thence to Fort Lafayette, New York Harbor." Wadsworth, who had served as a volunteer aide on Nelson's staff, reminded the secretary of state that the prisoners had been dragged from their homes without charges or trial: "The public safety may require the arrest and detention in this manner of dangerous and important persons; nonetheless, I do not entertain a doubt but that a number of these citizens should at once be discharged and sent home to their families and friends." While the mayor urged the release of Hunt, Thomas, Isaac Nelson, Forrester, and Hall, he did not mention Stanton or Casto. According to Wadsworth, Bull Nelson had told him that he would soon encourage authorities to release the prisoners. "Their families (my neighbors) are in great distress," the mayor wrote. "They promise obedience to the laws. They are slight, unimportant people." It is unknown why the mayor did not mention Casto or Stanton. Perhaps he was at odds with them. Or the mayor, who could have received additional information from Bull Nelson, may have known that Casto and Stanton were more ardent secessionists than the other Maysville prisoners. Regardless, this plea, like others, fell on deaf ears. Union military successes, however, ultimately helped the prisoners. Ironically, Col. Leonidas Metcalfe contributed to their release by helping secure these Northern victories.[10]

Metcalfe played an important role in Bull Nelson's successful campaign to remove Confederate troops from the Big Sandy Valley of Eastern Kentucky. Sherman had ordered Nelson to move on Rebels led by Col. John Stuart Williams who were recruiting men at Prestonsburg. So Nelson, with several Ohio regiments and scattered Kentucky units—including the Sixteenth Kentucky Infantry Regiment, which had been organized at Camp Kenton in Mason County—left Maysville to drive off the Southerners. After pushing the enemy away from Hazel Green and West Liberty, Nelson's command neared Prestonsburg. The out-numbered, badly supplied, and poorly armed Confederates withdrew toward Piketon. Metcalfe, at the head of twenty-nine men, was among the first to secure Prestonsburg. According to Union soldier James P. Hendrick, the Confederates had left a Rebel flag flying over the court-house. "Metcalfe and his men advanced into the town," Hendrick wrote, "tore down the secession flag, ordered their suppers, obtained all the information possible, and returned to [the Union army] about twelve o'clock last night in triumph." Capt. William Oden, who later served as Metcalfe's second in his duel with Casto, tore down the Rebel flag and kept the banner as a souvenir. With Prestonsburg secure, Nelson pursued the Confederates. The Union commander sent a portion of his command, which included an Ohio regiment, several companies of Kentuckians, and 142 mounted men commanded by Metcalfe, in one direction toward Piketon while he advanced from another way.[11]

On November 8, Nelson's men reached Ivy Mountain in Floyd County. There, part of Williams's army made a stand. "The skirmish was very sharp," Nelson reported. "The mountainside was blue with puffs of smoke, and not an enemy to be seen." The Federals attacked, and, after fighting for nearly one and a half hours, the Confederates withdrew. The Union army suffered six killed and twenty-four wounded, while the Southerners lost ten killed, fifteen wounded, and forty missing. Nelson continued toward Piketon, which, after another intense skirmish, Metcalfe secured the next day. With supplies dwindling, the Confederates withdrew into Virginia via Pound Gap. For the time being, Eastern Kentucky had been cleared of Southern soldiers. Nelson congratulated his men: "In a campaign of twenty days you have driven the rebels from Eastern Kentucky, and given repose to that portion of the State." Nelson's army then returned to central Kentucky. Sherman gleefully reported, "Nelson has succeeded in breaking up Williams' party."[12]

On November 29, 1861, Nelson told Seward that his campaign in the Big Sandy Valley had "quieted" the region. Therefore, he asked that the Maysville prisoners—except for Stanton—be released if they took the oath of allegiance. Nelson still viewed Stanton as the head of secessionists in northeastern Kentucky. "This man's industry and being wholly unscrupulous renders him too dangerous to be turned loose," he contended.[13]

Despite Nelson's concerns, the conclusion of the Big Sandy Campaign led to most of the prisoners' release. Nelson told Seward, "My object is to show these rascals that we believe ourselves strong enough to afford to be generous." On December 4, Seward agreed. The Maysville men had to swear a Union loyalty oath that said they would not travel to seceded states, correspond with secessionists, or aid the rebellion. On December 7, Isaac Nelson, William Hunt, George Forrester, James Hall, and B. F. Thomas signed the oath and were released. Casto, however, refused. As five of the Maysville men were rowed to freedom across New York Harbor, Casto and Stanton remained incarcerated.[14]

While most of the freed men went home, George Forrester did not return to Maysville. Instead, Forrester violated his parole, headed south, and joined John Hunt Morgan's Confederate cavalry. Forrester became a captain under Morgan's raiders, was severely wounded at Woodburn Station, Kentucky, and was eventually brevetted colonel. While riding with Morgan, Forrester extracted some revenge against the federal government that had confined him.[15]

Casto was uncooperative, and, it would appear, Stanton was to be incarcerated for the long term. There were, however, continued attempts to secure their release. On December 19, a delegation of unionist legislators wrote Seward, asking for Stanton's freedom. They did not mention Casto. Perhaps they knew Casto could secure his own liberty by taking the oath of allegiance. Or they may have realized that Stanton's case, with Bull Nelson advocating for the man's extended imprisonment, was a more delicate issue. Stanton, however, did not wait for others to help him. He pushed for his own liberation, writing Lincoln, "I never did advocate the secession of Kentucky and no man lives who can truthfully say I did." Despite Nelson's entreaties to keep Stanton locked away, Seward ordered Stanton's release on December 24. Stanton signed the oath of allegiance and left prison two days later. The stubborn Casto remained behind bars.[16]

When the new year arrived, Casto was the only Maysville resident still confined at Fort Lafayette. On January 10, 1862, he finally asked politicians to intervene on his behalf. Casto wrote Illinois congressman William A. Richardson and reminded Richardson that they had once met. Casto said that he had never been formally charged. Furthermore, he claimed "there was no excitement whatever" in Maysville during the time he was arrested. Casto insisted that he had done nothing wrong. He had not been involved in secession crisis politics; he simply wanted Kentucky to remain neutral. Proclaiming his innocence, Casto asked for a parole without having to take the oath. A week later, Seward reiterated that Casto would be released if he took it. Casto again refused. According to Maysville residents who petitioned for the prisoners' freedom, Casto "protests his innocence of any offense and demands a trial." He would not sign an oath, he argued, because he was not guilty. Since he had been unjustly arrested, he wanted a trial to clear his name. Casto told Seward that signing the oath was tantamount to proclaiming guilt. He had done nothing wrong, and he believed this act would embolden unnamed enemies, who had secured his arrest in the first place. "I am confident as are all my friends at home that my arrest was made to gratify the private malice of secret enemies and not on account of any disloyal acts or intentions," he told the secretary of state. Four months in prison, he contended, should be enough to satisfy anyone who hated him. He also argued that his extended confinement had hurt his business pursuits and prevented him from visiting a dying relative.[17]

Casto's incarceration continued. On February 21, Seward sent another letter to Fort Lafayette, telling authorities to release Casto if he agreed to give no aid or assistance to the Confederacy. While it was not the more stringent loyalty oath signed by the other Maysville men, it was a compromise that would get Casto out of prison and out of Seward's hair. Casto agreed and was released the next day, after pledging to "render no aid or comfort to the enemies in hostility to the Government of the United States." He returned to Maysville, having spent months ruminating about his arrest, confinement, and the men who had thrust him into a faraway prison. Upon his return home, he began practicing with firearms, biding his time until he could extract revenge.[18]

By the time Casto was released, much had changed in the Bluegrass State. From a political standpoint, Kentucky's status as a loyal state was secure. The legislature was in Union hands, and Federal authorities— aided by arrests, the suspension of newspapers, laws passed by the General Assembly, military victories, and the presence of Union soldiers—had consolidated their control over the commonwealth. Moreover, municipal elections also put political power in unionists' hands. In January 1862, when Casto began to ask for his release, unionist candidates were overwhelmingly elected in a local election in Maysville. For Casto, that surely stung.[19]

Securing Kentucky for the Union had not been easy. Wresting the state from active Rebel influence took a multitude of small steps and larger Federal victories. In early October 1861, the Kentucky legislature passed a law penalizing Kentuckians who had either enlisted in the Confederate army or invaded the state. That same month, skirmishes broke out across the commonwealth, including a sharp fight near London at Camp Wildcat on October 21. As gunfire sputtered across multiple counties, Joshua Speed urged Lincoln to send more troops to Kentucky. Speed hoped to push the Rebels out of the state and to "carry the war into Tennessee." He added, "Public sentiment is with us & I think improving." A few days later, however, Judge John Catron, who had called for writs of habeas corpus to be issued when Kentucky citizens were arrested, noted that "indictments for Treason [were] rife" in Kentucky courts. Speed may have thought public sentiment was improving, but fear had quieted many. Kentucky citizens were still under the watchful gaze of Federal authorities. Union troops seemed to be everywhere; by October 20, 1861, at least fifteen thousand Kentuckians had joined the Union army. In addition, seventeen Indiana regiments, thirteen Ohio, three Pennsylvania, and multiple regiments from several other states were posted across the commonwealth. When Casto returned home, his native state was awash in blue uniforms.[20]

Despite the strong Federal presence, Confederate soldiers still held a defensive line across southern Kentucky, extending from Cumberland Gap, through Bowling Green, and on to Columbus on the Mississippi River. With this position secure, Southern sympathizers hosted a convention in Russellville to create a provisional Confederate government of Kentucky. George W. Johnson, a Scott County planter, became the provisional Rebel governor. His executive tenure was cut short, however, when he was killed in April 1862 at the Battle of Shiloh.[21]

When Casto returned to Maysville, Kentuckians were still complaining about heavy-handed federal policies. On New Year's Day in 1862, for example, an anonymous writer grumbled to the *Lexington Observer and Reporter* about the continued arrests: "Their imprisonment in defiance of law, justice and the constitution is a hideous satire upon our boasted freedom, and its longer continuance is a shame and a reproach to every American—more especially to every Kentuckian—who is content to witness such an outrage without at least the utterance of his indignant protest."[22]

Later that month, however, unionists gained full strategic control of Kentucky when the Confederate defensive line across the southern part of the state collapsed. After the Battle of Mill Springs, fought in the fog and rain near Somerset, on January 19, the victorious Union troops drove Maj. Gen. George Crittenden's Confederate army into Tennessee. This turned the Rebels' eastern flank and fractured their defensive line from the Cumberland Gap to the Mississippi River. Mill Springs also led to other Federal victories. Shortly before Casto was released from Fort Lafayette, Confederate troops lost Forts Henry and Donelson in Tennessee. Days later, the Rebels evacuated Bowling Green. Union forces then took Nashville. Upon Casto's return to Maysville, there were few Southern soldiers in Kentucky.[23]

Casto was not deterred by the lack of Confederate troops. Having spent his time in prison thinking about revenge, the Maysville resident placed a target in his sights: Col. Leonidas Metcalfe. After helping Nelson secure Eastern Kentucky, Metcalfe remained active in the state, raising troops and promoting unionism. On April 14, 1862, he gave a speech in Carlisle that sparked the ire of proslavery secessionists. It is also likely that Metcalfe's speech, in which he condemned men like Casto, was the flint to Casto's steel that sparked the duel that altered both men's lives.

When Metcalfe spoke at Carlisle, he vented his anger against local secessionists. Kentuckians, Metcalfe said, had voted to stay loyal when they elected a unionist legislature. Therefore, residents had exercised their own "state rights" at the polls. Despite this, Confederate soldiers, unwelcome to most Kentuckians, and "regardless of all their professions about State Rights," had invaded the commonwealth. If the Rebels truly respected states' rights, Metcalfe contended, they should have left Kentucky alone. Their presence ran against Kentuckians' wishes and prevented residents from acting upon their own right of self-determination. Although Metcalfe condemned Southern soldiers, he pointed most of his wrath at his secessionist neighbors. Metcalfe suggested that those who had gone south to join the Confederacy should be permanently banned from Kentucky. Unionists should, he spat with fury, "rid the country or the world of such vipers." He added that local secessionists should stop their support for the Confederacy or accept the consequences. The Rebels "must behave, or share the fate of other traitors. Sympathizing with the enemy will no longer be tolerated."[24]

Rebel snakes, Metcalfe said, were living among them, and some even held political office. Therefore, in words that would have resonated with his father's generation, he recalled the state's white settlement history and reminded listeners about Manifest Destiny: "Who of you would have put up with a man that sympathized with Black Hawk or Santa Anna?" Waving the bloody shirt of past conflicts with Native Americans and Texas Independence, Metcalfe exclaimed that local secessionists returning from the South should be met by grim-faced patriots. "In plain English," he said, "shoot the traitors upon sight. It is a right they are justly entitled to." Casto, having recently returned to Maysville, surely chafed at this remark from the man who sent him to prison.[25]

Metcalfe complained that pro-Confederate legislators who lived under unionists' protection were "permitted to remain there undisturbed." He warned the audience that Tennessee—a state that held a significant unionist population—had fallen to the Confederacy. Therefore, Kentuckians should be alert for enemies in their midst. Moreover, with vigilance came responsibility. If loyalists saw a problem, he admonished, "Correct it yourselves, and remember that our laws are for the protection of loyal citizens AND NOT FOR THE PROTECTION OF THE ENEMIES OF OUR COUNTRY." For Casto, who had sat in a dank cell for months without a hearing or a trial, that sentence from the officer who had arrested him must have stung particularly hard.[26]

Metcalfe then pushed the knife to the hilt. Local Confederates, he remarked, had threatened to drive out unionists. He then said wryly— surely referring to Casto and those arrested in Maysville—"Some of them have invaded Camp Chase, Camp Morton, Fort Lafayette, etc., and some are trying to slip back among us." He added, "A class of men who have returned from the South lately, say . . . that they have not aided the enemy. But look at their course here amongst us. They are advocating the cause of the enemy—adhering to the enemy in time of war." Because of their presence, he remarked, "all of you will catch hell before long."[27]

For Metcalfe, there were no shades of gray. One either supported secession or was a unionist who should condemn, expel, or shoot the enemy. "If these men expect to stay here they must stop their treasonable talk," he exclaimed, "or they are no better than the traitors who have gone from here and joined the army, and should be dealt with in the same manner." Metcalfe asked his audience, "Will you be mealy-mouthed any longer with vipers in your midst, who consider it one of the Southern rights to invade your State, cut your throats, and make you feel all the horrors of war at your own fireside?"[28]

Metcalfe's fury was not aimed solely at secessionists. In this speech, delivered five months before Lincoln issued a preliminary version of the Emancipation Proclamation, the unionist Kentucky slave owner placed the blame for the war on the doorsteps of his neighbors' plantations. The conflict, he said, was caused by enslavers. Therefore, slave owners should be forced to pay for it.

For decades, Metcalfe said, Southerners had pinned the word *abolitionist* on political enemies and had ruined their reputations across the South. Metcalfe called out the backwardness and hypocrisy of this label and lashed the nation's ills to the backs of slave owners. Although he was in Kentucky—a state that had excoriated antislavery men; destroyed the printing presses of emancipationist newspapers; driven abolitionist editors from the state; and attacked men like Cassius Marcellus Clay, who had advocated for gradual emancipation—Metcalfe said that it was time to end slavery. Kentuckians also needed to realize that slave owners had started the Civil War, and therefore, enslavers should pay. "N——— and cotton has produced this rebellion," Metcalfe said, "and should be made to foot the bill. . . . It is not just that loyal men should fight out the battles to save the country from the iniquity of traitors, and then pay the damages they caused." With 1,600 enslaved African Americans and 365 slave owners living in the county in which he was speaking, multiple enslavers would have been in the audience. Therefore, this was dangerous talk. Metcalfe concluded that slaves—part of an exhausting, cyclical institution—did more than drive the Southern economic engine. They were, in modern parlance, a political football. Slaves were "the scarecrow, that is continually held up to your view, never-ceasing agitation. You must stand sentinel all night, you must stand sentinel all day, with your musket, over your darling black angels, while they work in the field, to keep somebody from stealing them. And you must stand watch to keep down insurrection———ETERNAL VIGILANCE IS THE PRICE OF THE N———. All of this hue-and-cry is kept up when there is not the slightest danger."[29]

Slavery, Metcalfe contended, had caused the nation's ills. The South had used the institution and fear-mongering to hold the country captive. Southern politicians painted opponents as abolitionists and said that "the North favors amalgamation." Hypocritical slave owners, however, needed to check their own fields. "Now, to tell the truth," Metcalfe said, "it is practiced to a fearful extent throughout the South and Kentucky. Go into any of our towns and see the different shades and colors." These slave owners said the institution was ordained by God because they were making their slaves Christian. Yet, Metcalfe said, "some of these traitors are helping to populate heaven with angels only half black."[30]

For Metcalfe, soft conciliatory policies had no place in divided Kentucky. He said that traitors do not "hide behind constitutional arguments that are abstractions," so unionists should not be merciful toward Rebel neighbors. "Mad, demented fiends are amongst you," he warned, "doing and prompting every possible injury to you and your country . . . and you are protecting them." If these men were killing Union soldiers elsewhere, would it be "unconstitutional for you to kill his murderer or accessory here? Down with them."[31]

As the speech was reprinted widely in regional newspapers, Casto likely took Metcalfe's threats seriously. He was one of those secessionists who had crept back into Maysville. He was one who should, in Metcalfe's words, be banished from the state or shot on sight. He was one to whom the laws should not apply. In Casto's mind, Metcalfe had thrown down the gauntlet with this speech. The colonel—the man who had arrested him—had condemned him and his institutions. He had committed the ultimate sin by excoriating slavery and slave owners. Furthermore, Metcalfe called for slave owners to pay for the war, which, Casto surely believed, Lincoln had started. He and several others whom Metcalfe had arrested at Bull Nelson's order became determined to end the influence of this impertinent unionist who faulted enslavers and advocated banishing or executing them. They would not condemn themselves by murdering him in cold blood. Instead, they would convert the field of honor into their own battlefield. Casto had been practicing with rifles and pistols. He was now determined to kill Metcalfe. The Union colonel was attempting to make them bend, yet Casto, like the Kentuckian in Maysville native Mary E. Wilson Betts's poem, would kneel to none but God.

7

A Matter of Honor

On May 6, 1862, the forty-three-year-old Leonidas Metcalfe walked out of the Lee House, a hotel in Maysville on the corner of Front and Sutton Streets. The building was among those damaged in the 1854 powder magazine explosion, and the colonel was leaving a Union Party meeting that had nominated candidates for an upcoming judicial election. Nearly a month had passed since Metcalfe gave his speech in Carlisle condemning secessionists and slave owners, and he was likely still pleased with having made a principled, yet unpopular, stand. As he left the Lee House, Isaac Nelson appeared and handed the officer a note.[1]

Metcalfe may have recognized Nelson, whom he had arrested with Casto, Stanton, and the other Maysville secessionists. It is also likely he knew Nelson by reputation. In addition to having been confined at Camp Chase and Fort Lafayette, Nelson "belonged to one of the oldest families in the city." The thirty-six-year-old Maysville native ran a successful wholesale grocery and liquor business. Indeed, his store on Market Street reflected how the Ohio River enabled Maysville businesses to offer a broad palette of foods and goods. In 1862, Nelson's shop carried a variety of spirits, groceries, and other delicacies.[2]

"While he was a man of strong prejudice," it was once said of Nelson, "a more generous soul never existed." Immediately before the Civil War, Nelson was a captain in the Kentucky State Guard, the commonwealth's Southern-leaning state militia. While some local Rebels were muted in their sentiment during the secession crisis, Nelson was a vocal advocate for the Confederacy. His boisterous opinions led to his arrest in October 1861. Unlike Casto, Nelson took the Union loyalty oath at the first opportunity and was released. He likely relished the chance to spur a fight between Metcalfe and Casto.[3]

Metcalfe unfolded the paper and scanned Casto's message. It had only been three months since Casto was freed from Fort Lafayette. "Sir: Having done me great wrong, under circumstances accompanying indignity with outrage, you can not refuse that which is the object of this note to demand—the satisfaction due from one gentleman to another. My friend, Mr. Isaac Nelson, is authorized to arrange the terms of our meeting. Very respectfully, W. T. CASTO."[4]

This challenge to duel was born from Casto's confinement, the result of his spending weeks in prison ruminating over his arrest. He believed that his detention—where he had been treated like a common criminal—had tarnished his reputation. Kenneth S. Greenberg writes that "dueling was an elite response to insult," and that those "who dueled did so to avoid shame before a public audience." Christopher G. Kingston and Robert E. Wright, who analyze dueling through an economic lens, write, "Honor—a trustworthy reputation—is therefore a valuable asset, and well worth defending if necessary." In examining the challenge through these historians' lenses, it is evident that Casto wanted to duel because he felt disgraced and needed to defend his reputation, which the arrest had called into question. He blamed Metcalfe for his imprisonment. Union troops under Metcalfe's direct command had awakened Casto in the night, surrounded him with armed guards, and sent him in chains across the Ohio River. Metcalfe had done Casto a "great wrong" by arresting him unjustly. This unwarranted arrest and imprisonment was a public humiliation; while Casto could not attack the men who had dragged him away in irons, he could strike their commander. Freed from prison, at the first chance Metcalfe was in Maysville, Casto sent the challenge. Casto was neither of age nor temperament to join the Rebel army and haul a musket across a battlefield. Instead, he would face the Union officer who had wronged him, and, by extension, the Federal government that had trampled his rights.[5]

Metcalfe, however, did not recognize the challenge to be based on Casto's ideals. Instead, the colonel believed Casto's "rebel friends" had cajoled him into dueling because they wanted Metcalfe, one of the region's most prominent unionists, dead. Metcalfe's star was ascending, albeit with controversy, after his speech in Carlisle. The Rebels, however, knew that such a vocal unionist—one who had advocated banishing them, shooting them, and making them pay for the war—was a dangerous enemy. They could not target him on the battlefield, so they would try to kill him through the formality of a duel.[6]

Metcalfe read the note and the name of the man who signed it. He did not know Casto and did not recognize his name. For clarification, he walked down the street to the office of the *Maysville Eagle,* one of the town's newspapers. His trusted friend Thomas Marshall Green, the *Eagle*'s editor, was familiar with the code duello, the formal rules of fighting. If anyone knew the proper course, it would be Green.[7]

Green proved to be a solid negotiator on Metcalfe's behalf. Born on November 23, 1836, at Waveland, his father's farm just south of Danville, Kentucky, Green attended Centre College in his hometown. He graduated with the noted class of 1855, which included future US congressman W. C. P. Breckinridge, Kentucky governor John Young Brown, Missouri governor Thomas T. Crittenden, politician Thomas Z. Morrow (a Union officer and one of the founders of the Republican Party in Kentucky), and other future leaders. Even at an early age, Green was recognized for his eloquence. When he was in college, a man who heard him address a literary society said Green would have "a brilliant and almost unclouded future." Although Green had studied to become a lawyer, a year after graduation he began writing for the *Frankfort Commonwealth.* In 1857, he became editor, a post he held for three years before taking over the *Maysville Eagle.* Later, he wrote the books *Historic Families of Kentucky* (1889) and *The Spanish Conspiracy* (1891).[8]

Metcalfe visited Green because the editor was acquainted with affairs of honor, having had his share of such encounters. Five years before Metcalfe dueled Casto, when Green edited the *Frankfort Commonwealth,* Green had lost his law license for sending a challenge to S. I. M. Major, the editor of the rival *Frankfort Yeoman.* The men had insulted one another in their respective newspapers, and their arguments soon spilled off the page. Green challenged Major, who accepted. As the challenged party, Major chose the weapons: Kentucky rifles (long-barreled flintlock muskets) at ninety yards. Green refused the terms and the negotiations stalled. Although they never fought the duel, all points surrounding the practice, including the issuing of challenges, were against the law. Therefore, authorities revoked Green's law license. Green eventually asked attorney James Harlan to secure a him pardon so he could have his license restored. Later, Green would have another

In 1857, S. I. M. Major, editor of the *Frankfort Yeoman*, nearly dueled Thomas Marshall Green, who was Metcalfe's primary negotiator in Metcalfe's duel with Casto. *Kentucky Historical Society, Frankfort, 1953.1.*

The most famous duel in US history was Alexander Hamilton's fight against Aaron Burr in Weehawken, New Jersey. Burr mortally wounded Hamilton. *Library of Congress.*

violent affair, a deadly fight on the streets of Lexington that ignored the code duello and any pretense of honor.[9]

Green, Metcalfe, Casto, and other Kentuckians who considered themselves gentlemen sometimes followed the rules of the code duello to settle arguments, insults, and slights. Although duels were illegal, the Bluegrass State was steeped in Southern honor culture. So, among some elite white Kentucky men, the practice was socially acceptable.[10]

For these upper-class Kentuckians, the concept of honor framed society's perception of the individual. It also guided that individual's perception of himself. Societal guidelines rooted in honor directed some white Southern men's interactions with each other and influenced their social standing. In his book *Kentucky Justice, Southern Honor, and*

American Manhood, historian James C. Klotter writes, "Honor represents a set of external, ethical rules supported by a collective community consciousness, a group of principles of socially expected conduct that establish what actions should be taken under what conditions." Edward L. Ayers explains that, in addition to serving as a community playbook, honor was also "a system of values within which you have exactly as much worth as others confer upon you." When honor was maligned—from insults, social slights, political squabbles, failed business deals, arguments, and more—blueblooded Kentuckians sometimes sought to solve the affront by fighting each other in a structured way outlined by the code duello. However, when dealing with one from a lower class, they rejected formality. The response was instead immediate and often involved caning, horsewhipping, or a street fight. Any disgrace had to be confronted, historian Bertram Wyatt-Brown writes in *Southern Honor: Ethics and Behavior in the Old South,* or else the brand of being a coward would "haunt the bearer forever." Failing to defend one's honor, he writes, "was inseparable from community evaluation of the individual" and led to "the stigma of shame." Avoiding shame was paramount, and if a man did not defend his honor by confronting an insult, the result was public humiliation and a downward spiral off the social ladder.[11]

Historians including Richard Hamm and John Mayfield also emphasize the public side of honor. Mayfield contends that it "also meant personal attributes—character, self-worth, reliability, graciousness, valor, style. . . . As a behavior, however, it meant something more Homeric: to affirm one's worth publicly and to resist, at any cost, threats to that reputation." Because honor represented public, societal guidelines, honorable behavior had to be recognized within the larger community. It was, Mayfield attests, "identity on display, monitored by public opinion." The same held true for shame—honor's nemesis—which was also granted by the larger community and coexisted within the public sphere. So Casto challenged Metcalfe to defend his character. As historian Lorien Foote explains, reputation and social standing were tied to the code, as "honor continued to function in a socially mobile society because men who sought advancement in the world believed that their reputation mattered."[12]

William Faux, who visited Kentucky during the early nineteenth century, noticed how public shame pushed men onto the field of honor. Upon learning of a recently cancelled duel—one that would have involved "muskets charged with grapeshot and two balls" with the participants firing fifteen feet from one another—Faux wrote, "The barbarous baseness and cruelty of public opinion, dooms young men, when challenged, to fight. They must fight, kill or be killed, and that for some petty offence beneath the notice of the law. Established names only [a Kentuckian told him] may refuse to fight, but that is rarely done; to refuse is a stain and high dishonour."[13]

While the honor code was public, it also had a personal side, which included mastery over the self and the need "to have good character" based on self-control. If honor was maligned and a duel occurred, control and dispassion were to rule the duelists' behavior. The code also dictated mastery over others, whether sustaining an elite status over those from a lesser class or maintaining control over enslaved African Americans.[14]

It made sense that Kentucky—a border state between the North and South—developed its own honor culture that evolved before and after the Civil War. Mayfield contends that "there was no unified South to act out one version of honor"; therefore, honor culture in each state, influenced by both internal and external circumstances, norms, state history, and identity, evolved in different ways. Ayers notes an "old saying" that shows the regional distinctiveness of honor culture: "Call a man a liar in Mississippi, and he will knock you down; in Kentucky he will shoot you; in Indiana, he will say 'you are another.'"[15]

Differences in honor culture also held true between Northerners and Southerners. As historian Joanne B. Freeman writes in *Affairs of Honor: National Politics in the New Republic,* during the early nineteenth century, "Northerners were as well versed in this code as southerners; it was in their utilization of violence that they differed most noticeably." Northerners were less likely to duel than their Southern counterparts. Furthermore, Freeman argues, "northerners and southerners spoke different dialects of the language of honor, balancing the conflicting value systems of honor, religion, and the law in regionally distinct ways."[16]

In Kentucky, where violence had permeated society since the Anglo settlement period, it is unsurprising that the commonwealth's own "dialect" of honor led to duels. Authorities frequently ignored affairs of honor, which meant that society, from a legal standpoint, sanctioned the practice. In fact, in 1850, the *Christian Register* recognized that Kentuckians were quick to duel. "There is no community which will better illustrate the practice and extreme folly of duelling than the State of Kentucky," the newspaper wrote. This reliance on violence to settle disputes remained even after the Civil War, when Kentucky's brand of the honor code among the upper classes shifted from formality to spontaneity. After the conflict, upper-class Kentuckians sparred brutally on the street with concealed pistols and knives, rather than on the dueling ground with formality, dispassion, and chosen weapons.[17]

While Kentucky had its own brand of honor culture, Bluegrass State gentlemen and other Southerners also exported their own hot-headedness to Missouri, the commonwealth's western neighbor. Dick Steward writes in *Duels and the Roots of Violence in Missouri*, "No deterministic pattern, whether it be geographical, cultural, economic, class, or demographic, can explain the quantum leap in violence that occurred with Missouri's absorption into the Union." While the import of pro-slavery and abolitionist factions into Missouri during the 1850s played a major role, the emigration of Kentuckians (and other Southerners) into what became the Show-Me State undoubtedly bolstered local violence.[18]

A fight between Thomas T. Crittenden and physician Walter Fenwick, both former residents of the Bluegrass State, provides an example of Kentuckians who took their dueling culture to Missouri. Crittenden, the brother of Kentucky politician John J. Crittenden, had been the attorney general for the Louisiana Territory. After moving to Missouri, Crittenden was an attorney in a larceny case involving Fenwick's brother, whom Crittenden castigated during the trial. Insulted, the brother challenged Crittenden to a duel. Crittenden refused because, he said, the brother was no gentleman. With this additional barb thrust into the family's reputation, Fenwick challenged Crittenden to fight. Because Fenwick had an unblemished reputation and was a professional and social equal, Crittenden accepted. On October 1, 1811, on an island in the Mississippi River near St. Genevieve, Missouri, Crittenden and Fenwick fought with large-caliber pistols with twelve-inch barrels. Crittenden mortally wounded Fenwick, leaving his widow to raise seven children. This did little to deter Crittenden's political aspirations. In fact, participating in the duel may have helped. Crittenden returned to Kentucky, where he became a legislator and Kentucky's secretary of state under Governor Thomas "Stonehammer" Metcalfe.[19]

In 1856, Frankfort, Kentucky, native Benjamin Gratz Brown was shot while dueling Thomas C. Reynolds in Missouri. Brown became a US senator and governor of Missouri. *Library of Congress*.

Another instance of a Kentuckian dueling in Missouri involved Benjamin Gratz Brown, grandson of Kentucky's first US senator, John Brown. As a child, Benjamin lived in Liberty Hall, the senator's Frankfort home. After moving to Missouri, the younger Brown became a newspaper editor and a vocal antislavery advocate. His stance against the institution caught the ire of Thomas C. Reynolds, a South Carolina native, attorney, and politician. Soon, Brown and Thomas rebuked one another in the pages of Missouri newspapers. Once the insults mounted, Reynolds challenged Brown to duel. On August 26, 1856, they fought with English-made dueling pistols. The men fired simultaneously. Brown's shot missed, but Reynolds's found its mark, striking Brown above the knee. Brown, who became a US senator and governor of Missouri in 1871, limped for the remainder of his life. Reynolds became Missouri's lieutenant governor and served as one of the state's provisional Confederate governors. Reynolds met a sad end in 1887 when he committed suicide by jumping down an open elevator shaft. Again, in Missouri as in Kentucky, dueling did little to diminish one's hope for political office. In fact, these encounters were so prevalent that George Graham Vest, a Kentucky native, Centre College graduate, and Missouri politician, called dueling an institution in Missouri. It was one that Kentuckians helped bring to the Show-Me State.[20]

These men were driven to the dueling ground to protect their reputations within communities that put high prices on personal honor. Fenwick and Reynolds, both feeling the sting of insults, issued challenges. In doing so, Fenwick paid the ultimate price. John Lyde Wilson, a governor of South Carolina who wrote a book outlining the rules of dueling, described how insult-driven community shame motivated men—like these Kentucky natives—to pick up pistols despite the risk of death. "When one finds himself avoided in society," Wilson wrote, "his friends shunning his approach, his substance wasting, his wife and children in want around him, and traces all his misfortunes and miseries to the slanderous tongue of the calumniator, who, by secret whisper or artful innuendo, had sapped and undermined his reputation, he must be more or less than man to submit in silence."[21]

As a politician, Wilson drew a commonality between the defense of home and the defense of the individual. If a nation could be wronged and embrace violence, Wilson argued, then insulted individuals should also be allowed to defend their reputations on the dueling ground. White Southerners—who lived in a society that supported an abundance of military academies and the organization, support, and drilling of local militia that existed for the defense of their communities— certainly would have understood this comparison. This was true in Kentucky towns that supported militia units like the Lexington Rifles, the Lexington Chasseurs, the Nelson Grays, the Bitter Water Blues, the Governor's Red Artillery, the Warren Voltigeurs, and the Flat Rock Grays, to name a few. While there was certainly a social aspect to these organizations, historian Dickson Bruce contends that dueling and the proliferation of military units "was understood to be a symptom of a violent people." Some, thus, believed that dueling and the South's perceived militarism harmed the region's reputation.[22]

In Wilson's world, and in the eyes of many Southerners, when a man of elite status was insulted, a formal challenge could be issued under the code duello. The aggrieved party would ask for "satisfaction" in writing, as Casto did of Metcalfe. Then, their seconds—friends who stepped in to mediate the affair, like Isaac Nelson and Thomas M. Green—tried to settle the matter amicably. If no arbitration could be reached, the challenged party picked a date, time, and weapons for the fight. A formal duel then took place, ending with missed shots (and honor satisfied), drawn blood (with one or both duelists wounded), or the death of one of the antagonists.

This dangerous process was followed, Klotter writes, because "honorable individuals most feared not death but public humiliation, as a betrayal of manhood and honor. Honor required courage; cowardice meant shame; insults could not be tolerated. Action must follow, for only blood could cleanse the stains of honor." Therefore, a Southern gentleman could not simply ignore a challenge from a man of equal social status. Doing so would lead to charges of cowardice, shame, a loss of honor, and deep social stigma. As Wyatt-Brown writes, dueling was "inseparable from community evaluation of the individual," so a refusal to duel could make one a social outcast. Moreover, as the editors of *The Field of Honor: Essays on Southern Character and American Identity* explain, dueling was "a means of establishing rank" and "asserting, maintaining, or even creating a reputation as a gentleman of honor and standing." Dick Steward adds that dueling "connoted upper-class status" and was "a symbol of upper-class respectability and gentility." However, one could not achieve higher status through dueling alone. Steward adds, "A duel could not confer honor, it could only restore it." To give a further layer of complexity to dueling, Joanne Freeman explains that "political duels" differed from those caused by insult. "The point of a political duel was to prove a man willing to die for his honor, not to shed blood." In his duel with Metcalfe, however, Casto was looking for gore.[23]

Of course, duels were only conducted between social equals and were typically fought by those from the upper classes. As one Southerner wrote, dueling "towers above the cloud of laws that blanket and hold in place the lower orders." If a gentleman was wronged by a man of lesser social standing, he would publicly cane or horsewhip the lesser man in retribution. Horsewhipping, a reflection of the way an enslaver could punish his slave, demonstrated another layer of social dominance. No white man in the antebellum South wanted to be treated as an enslaved African American.[24]

While, Freeman writes, the "culture of honor was a crucial proving ground for the elite," historians have also explained that all classes followed their own version of the code of honor. Lorien Foote notes that all Southern men adhered to a code, but "men from different social classes in the south manifested honor through different rituals." Among bluebloods, Foote adds, only gentlemen were meant to duel "because supposedly only men of high social status had carefully cultivated the ability to channel and control passion." Therefore, lower classes, which "also had honor," engaged in "brutally violent rituals such as rough and tumble fighting." Kenneth S. Greenberg agrees, writing that honor "was not confined to a single class of white males (although there were significant variations in expression among men of different classes), nor was it confined to a single region of the South."[25]

The application of honor also had few age limits. During the antebellum period, for example, students at the University of Virginia fought over honor and their reputations. Closer to Casto and Metcalfe, young men at Centre College in Danville, Kentucky, also met on the field of honor. When Nicholas Perkins attended school there, a fellow student shot him in the hand during a duel. The appendage was mangled for the rest of his life.[26]

Although dueling was often driven by Southerners' touchiness, the formalized structure of the code duello was created to control participants' emotions. When honor was on the line, a fight needed to be dispassionate and fair. One witness to a 1798 duel wrote, "In well-bred Society, when a man receives an affront, does he knock down the person giving it? No. He represses his feelings; and takes another time and place to obtain justice." As Wyatt-Brown notes, "Rules governing the classical fight served to check passion and transform it under the rubric of honor." Duels also "provided structure and ritual" with "Referees" (the seconds) who created "impartiality" during the fight. The seconds, who negotiated the terms of the duel, were also supposed to remain dispassionate, and, under the code duello, these negotiations could stretch out over a long period. In 1806, for example, when future president Andrew Jackson and Charles Dickinson dueled, the terms were only finalized after six months. While Jackson and Dickinson were supposedly reluctant to clash, which likely led to the plodding negotiations, others pushed the fight. This episode reveals how external pressures could also lead one to defend his honor. Society wanted the men to uphold their social standing, so it would see blood drawn. The two men eventually fought their duel in Kentucky with pistols at eight paces, approximately twenty-five feet. Dickinson shot Jackson, breaking the future president's ribs, while Jackson's bullet killed Dickinson.[27]

Many men associated with duels, including Green, Metcalfe's primary negotiator in his duel with Casto, were likely familiar with John Lyde Wilson's *The Code of Honor; Or, Rules for Principals and Seconds in Dueling*. Wilson wrote it in 1838, and multiple variations were later reprinted. He said he wrote the book to save lives by establishing formal rules for honor-bound conflicts, and it became a benchmark for how affairs of honor were carried out across the South.[28]

Wilson's words offered guidance for how to take an insult and how to issue challenges. "Let your note be in the language of the gentleman," he wrote. To keep one's honor intact, challenge notes, like Casto's to Metcalfe, should be dispassionate and businesslike. Wilson sought to keep every aspect of the duel high-toned; he wrote that one should, if he received a note "not written in the style of a gentleman, refuse to receive it, and assign your reason for such refusal."[29]

Although many duels were kept private, historian Todd Hagstette recognizes the public nature of challenges, writing that there was "an unacknowledged public-mindedness in their context and tone." Furthermore, "Reputations hung on nearly every word of a duel communication." If challenges were not kept dispassionate, it was a mark of dishonor: "Free indulgence in emotion—especially anger, hatred, and aggression, became the mark of ungentlemanly behavior."[30]

For Wilson, the role of the second was paramount: "I believe that nine duels out of ten, if not ninety-nine out of a hundred, originate in the want of experience in the seconds." He argued that seconds who were unfamiliar with the code were to blame for many duels that should not have been fought. To prevent bloodshed, he wanted to educate men about this role. A second needed to be chosen wisely, as "he has the custody of your honor." The second should be carefully consulted, his opinion heeded (again stressing the lack of passion in the affair), and his authority respected. "You are supposed to be cool and collected," he directed, "and your friend's feelings are more or less irritated." A second should "use every effort to soothe and tranquilize your principal [the duelist]." Calm your friend if he is angered over an insult. Cool his passion. Ensure that he acts as a gentleman. "Check him if he uses opprobrious epithet towards his adversary," Wilson wrote. Thus, in negotiating the Casto–Metcalfe duel, Nelson and Green were to keep their duelists calm and protect their honor by ensuring a detached, honorable demeanor.[31]

While duelists needed to be composed, they also had to be social equals. "Equality" on the dueling ground was important to Wilson, who wanted to ensure that all phases of a duel were carried out between gentlemen. Because duels should only be fought between equals, a gentleman could refuse a challenge note "from a minor . . . one that has been posted [as a coward]; one that has been publicly disgraced without resenting it; one whose occupation is unlawful; a man in his dotage and a lunatic." A man should not fight a child, and a gentleman should not fight a coward because that disgraced man may be trying to shoot his way back into society's good graces. One should not duel someone who did not care if he was disgraced in the eyes of society, because recklessness was not dispassionate and a true equal would recoil at the idea of lost shame. Lawbreakers were dishonorable and, therefore, were not gentlemen. Fighting an old man or a mentally ill person was also not fair.[32]

Wilson also believed most difficulties were caused by misunderstandings. Hence, seconds should root out the problem and find a

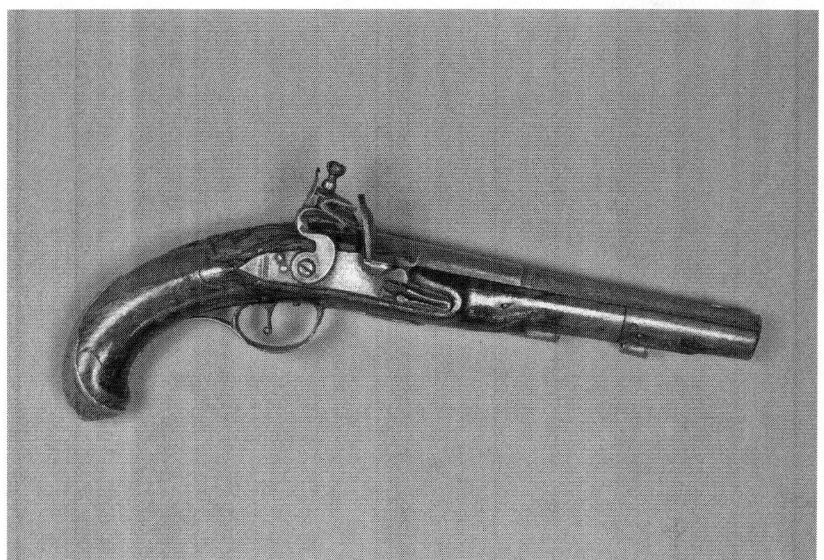

While pistols were typically used in Kentucky duels, Casto and Metcalfe fought with rifles. This flintlock dueling pistol—one of a pair once housed in a carved wooden box—is now part of the Kentucky Historical Society's collection. *Kentucky Historical Society, Frankfort, 1962.137b.*

solution; no true gentleman would intentionally insult someone, so real gentlemen should be able to untangle any error that led to an insult. In Casto's case, however, there was no misunderstanding. The two men were equals; Metcalfe was the son of a governor, and Casto was a prominent figure in Maysville. Metcalfe had arrested Casto, and, Casto believed, had sullied his reputation, dishonoring him in a way that could not be settled between the seconds.[33]

Casto initiated the duel by following the code duello. His second, Nelson, delivered Metcalfe a dispassionate, formal challenge. Under the code, when the challenged man accepted, the seconds set up the details of the duel. Wilson contended that the "old notion" that the challenged man should "name the time, place, distance and weapon, has been long since exploded; nor would a man of chivalric honor use such a right, if he possessed it." In nineteenth-century Kentucky, however, the challenged party most often chose the weapons and other details. While pistols at ten paces (thirty feet) were a common choice, antagonists sometimes picked rifles, swords, and knives. Wilson remarked that the weapon that should be "most generally used" was the pistol and that "twenty paces" was recommended. Wilson, who first published his tract in the 1830s, also suggested that the men face off with smooth-bore dueling pistols with barrels shorter than nine inches long. They should be fired by flint and steel, although percussion cap guns were acceptable if all parties agreed. In Kentucky, pistols at ten paces were the traditional choice, and the suggestion of other weapons could end negotiations. In 1828, for example, one duelist suggested short swords. An indignant second said that this choice "put an end to the correspondence; it being properly regarded by my friend as alike indefensible and unprecedented with the *Dirk,* in the adjustment of affairs of Honor."[34]

Once the weapons were chosen and the details of the duel negotiated, the contending parties met at the dueling ground to fight. Each duelist's party typically consisted of the duelist, his second, a surgeon, possibly an assistant surgeon, and any number of friends whom the duelists had agreed could attend. These allies provided moral support and acted as witnesses. Immediately before the duel commenced, the seconds determined which one would give the "word," or the call to fire. They also picked the position where each duelist would stand. This was typically done by drawing lots or flipping a coin. While on the dueling ground, Wilson wrote, the duelists had to be "respectful" and "passive" and should not "irritate each other." Again, in the moments before the duelists were to shoot or stab one another, honor called for dispassion. The seconds, usually the only armed men on the dueling ground (weapons were presented to the duelists immediately before the fight), remained in charge and enforced fairness. If one duelist disregarded the rules and fired early, the offended party's second "is at liberty to fire at him." If a principal was wounded at the first fire, the duel automatically stopped, since continuing to duel against an injured man was not a fair fight. Again, fairness dictated that neither principal should have an advantage over the other. Equity was one rule of the code duello that Metcalfe recognized and enforced, nearly to his own peril.[35]

If neither duelist was injured at the first fire, the rules called for the challenged man's second to ask if honor had been satisfied or if the duel should continue. If honor was satisfied, the duelists agreed that their differences were reconciled. They should then shake hands. If, however, "the insult be of a serious character," Wilson wrote, and one duelist wanted retribution through drawn blood, the duel could continue. If one duelist refused to proceed after the first fire, then that man's second should say to the other party, "I have come upon this ground with a coward, and do tender you my apology for an ignorance of his character; you are at liberty to post him," thus publicly declaring his cowardice. Postings could take on multiple forms, including newspaper notices and printed public announcements. In October 1819, for example, Burr Harrison published a broadside that announced, "I publicly proclaim Martin Hardin Wickliffe, a gasconading cowardly poltroon and lying scoundrel, unworthy of the notice or credit of any but persons as base and contemptible as himself." Harrison, a doctor, was a member of the Kentucky legislature from Nelson County. Wickliffe, a War of 1812 veteran and businessman who also lived in Bardstown, had evidently ignored Harrison's challenge. In 1815, Wickliffe had succeeded Harrison in the state senate. One wonders if politics was at the root of their disagreement.[36]

Casto believed his honor had been impugned when Metcalfe's soldiers sent Casto to an out-of-state prison, so he felt the sting of public shame and fallen reputation and needed to wash Metcalfe's sins away with his blood. The honor-bound Casto would not murder Metcalfe on the street when he walked out of the Lee House in Maysville. Instead, as a gentleman, he followed the code duello, issued a challenge via his second Isaac Nelson, and kept the affair dispassionate. Metcalfe was also a member of the Kentucky elite, well-heeled in the code of honor. His response would bring the two men together alongside the Ohio River.

8

Kentucky and the Code Duello

For nineteenth-century Southern bluebloods, the code duello provided a formal structure that determined how a man handled insults or other infractions of honor. Although duels were meant to be dispassionate, when stripped of their pretense, they were, at their core, two men trying to harm each other over an affront, social slight, or other infraction. As Bertram Wyatt-Brown notes, "dueling served essentially the same purpose as the lowliest eye-gouging battle among Tennessee hog-drivers." These formalized fights were, however, accepted by higher society, which the elite believed separated them from the lower classes. As historian John Hope Franklin writes, "dueling was a means of displaying manhood and reflecting gentility."[1]

Many Americans, however, recognized that one could not reflect elite status while trying to kill another person. Anti-dueling societies formed in multiple states, and numerous churches condemned the practice. Some politicians and newspapers also joined the call to end the code duello. In October 1852, for example, the *Sunbury American* in Pennsylvania judged dueling to be an "historic barbarity, a custom as venal as cowardly." The newspaper added, "The *duello* is the braggart's argument—the coward's refuge. No true man, unless forced by overwhelming public sentiment, would dare lift his hand against a fellow mortal, and for a trifling insult, or words uttered in the heat of altercation, deprive him of that which he cannot return." In the Bluegrass State, arguments against dueling appeared shortly after statehood. In December 1795, for example, a Kentuckian published a notice imploring "the citizens of the North-Western Territory to desist from the horrid practice of staining the Kentucky bank of the Ohio river with human gore, by duelling—as it is an open violation of the commonwealth." Sixty-seven years later, Casto and Metcalfe played their own part by staining that same riverbank. Laws did little to deter men like this when honor was at stake.[2]

A quarter of a century after that Kentuckian issued his card, George Trotter and eighty-four Lexington residents signed a pledge that they would not duel. They stated, "No circumstances can arise between our citizens where their honour might be better sustained by a reference to the deliberate opinion of a few judicious and pacific men, than by an appeal to deadly combat." They would not fight and would intervene to stop any duels. Like John Lyde Wilson, they recognized that misunderstandings typically caused affairs of honor and that "explanations would reconcile" the warring parties. There were, however, caveats. One signer, S. H. Woodson, signed the pledge but added, "S. H. Woodson concurs, except in very extreme cases." Trotter also was a fair-weather signatory. In 1829, eight years after signing the promise, he killed Charles Wickliffe in a duel. Ultimately, those who chose to duel believed "that laws and authority cannot replace" honor as the guiding hand of society. They ignored anti-dueling legislation, or, in the case of Trotter, violated their own pledges, which seems an infraction of honor in its own right.[3]

Anti-dueling sentiment in Kentucky was also aimed at out-of-state residents who traveled into the commonwealth to duel. In 1827, two Tennessee lawyers, C. M. Smith and a man named Brank, went to Simpson County, Kentucky, to settle their differences. Simpson County was the site of several affairs of honor, including one where the Virginia-born Sam Houston, the future Texas soldier and politician, shot his opponent, Gen. William White. After Smith killed Brank, the Simpson County grand jury indicted him for murder. Kentucky governor Joseph Desha asked the governor of Tennessee to send Smith to the commonwealth for trial. Newspapers also condemned the incident. The *Kentucky Argus* complained,

> Brank has left a wife and children. This is *honor!* What good will such honor do him when approaching the bar of his Maker? What good does it do his wife and children? How lofty and honorable must be the feelings of Smith, when he sees the widow and orphans whose husband and father he has murdered? Is it not a brave man, yea, and an honorable man too, who can bear all this? But he had no malice. So much the worse;

the murder was the more causeless and cool; it finds no extenuation in deadly wrongs or irresistible passions.

Smith was neither extradited nor prosecuted, leaving the *Western Recorder* to complain, "The arm of the law is impotent, since lawyers and legislators themselves are sometimes duelists." Smith was initially disbarred from practicing law in Tennessee, but the state supreme court reinstated him since the duel did "not relate to any act done in the course of his professional duty." Even when Kentucky authorities attempted to prosecute duelists, honorific killers went free.[4]

Despite duelists dodging prosecution, lawmakers who opposed dueling did wrestle with ending the practice. Kentucky laws against formalized affairs were proposed as early as 1799, and attempts continued into the nineteenth century. In 1840, for example, the General Assembly created economic disincentives for dueling when it passed a law stating that if a man was killed in an affair of honor, his surviving wife and children could "have an action of trespass" against anyone involved. This allowed a jury "to give vindictive damages" against killers. Kentucky laws also stated that anyone convicted of giving a challenge, accepting a challenge, or fighting a duel was banned from holding any state office for seven years. To deter public servants, all public officials—including lawyers, legislators, the governor, and others—had to swear an oath that they had not challenged, dueled, or acted as seconds. This oath became part of the Kentucky constitution in 1850, and it remains in use today. Lawyers could lose their licenses, and guilty parties could be fined or imprisoned. One who sent a challenge could face up to a year in jail and a $500 fine, while accepting a challenge could garner a $250 fine and six months in jail. If a second delivered a challenge note, he faced three months incarceration and a $150 fine, while acting as seconds or participating as surgeons—even to help an injured duelist—could result in the same punishment.[5]

Therefore, while the code duello formalized violence among Kentucky gentlemen, some worked to make it illegal. However, prominent Kentuckians' participation in duels sanctioned the fights among some members of the public. Having men like Henry Clay fight duels placed a cultural stamp of approval on the practice, despite any laws against it. Duels thus became by default a form of regulated, community-sanctioned violence and a socially acceptable way for upper-class white men to resolve personal difficulties. In some instances, historian Edward Ayers contends, duelists fought because they did not believe the court system could provide justice. Because those same courts rarely prosecuted duelists, Kentucky had an impotent and inconsequential justice system as it pertained to the causes and consequences of affairs of honor.[6]

In 1850, when Kentucky legislators considered a new constitution, they debated dueling. Ben Hardin, a prominent lawmaker from the Bardstown area, condemned the code. He said, "There is a notion, a ridiculous kind of opinion going abroad, invisible, intangible, and which no man can touch, called the code of honor, which compels a man to fight in certain cases. . . . There is some imaginary insult—some supposed injury, and some sickly sensibility feels itself insulted, and asks for an explanation. The man who is asked feels a little too proud to give it and the parties correspond a little, and finally fight—and all about nothing." Hardin hoped laws would end dueling and believed "nothing will stop it but a sense of certain, positive, and speedy punishment." Yet, he explained with only slight hyperbole, "Kentucky is the only country where no man has ever been punished for giving, accepting, carrying a challenge, or killing his antagonist in a duel." Kentucky's 1850 constitution made dueling illegal and allowed the legislature to determine punishment. It also gave the chance for a reprieve. The governor was given the authority to pardon a duelist after five years. Regardless of these laws, however, prosecutions were rare. Matthew A. Byron estimates that there were at least 450 fatal duels in the United States, yet "only eleven resulted in convictions—two for murder and nine for manslaughter." Because duels were seen as an impartial, "fair fight," authorities turned a blind eye.[7]

Laws forbidding dueling may have even made the practice more popular. Kentucky jurist John Rowan, who once killed an opponent in a duel, remarked that while the code duello was meant to "prevent the effusion of blood" through extended negotiations, "the effect [of anti-dueling legislation] was to increase it tenfold." Historians Todd Hagstette and Dickson Bruce also argue that duels became popular in the South because they were associated with the region. The "Southernness" of the duel made it more "distinct" for regional residents and led to more affairs of honor. Moreover, this behavior likely trickled down to other classes. With elites engaging in duels, Dick Steward writes, "the notoriety and glamour associated with dueling influenced and encouraged other and more rowdy elements of society to engage also in acts of violence." Formalized violence begat informal bloodshed.[8]

The popularity of dueling and authorities' refusal to prosecute participants led to complaints. In August 1824, two Louisville residents fought a duel in Indiana and exchanged three shots. One journal lamented, "The civil authority of Indiana being too weak to arrest, or dislodge, them, and the civil authority of Kentucky being supine, inert, insane, drunk, crazy, or in the hands of pusillanimous men whose heads or hearts are so *disordered* that no attempt or effort was made to suppress this public outrage of the laws." Kentucky's lax attitude toward violence and honor-bound killings was well-known, prompting one out-of-state duelist to say about his future opponent, "I wish I had him in Kentucky, that I might kill the dog without the trouble of fighting him."[9]

Kentucky's adherence to the code of honor, coupled with an individual's need for self-respect and the esteem of the larger community, meant that keeping one's honor intact outweighed the risk of breaking the law by dueling. Honor must be upheld, despite the consequences. Therefore, historian Robert Ireland notes, in forty-one duels fought under the code duello in Kentucky from 1790 to 1867, at least sixteen men were killed or mortally wounded. Few participants were convicted. According to historian Matthew A. Byron, at least 1,095 duels took place in the United States, with 450 of them, or 41 percent, leading to the death of one of the duelists. James C. Klotter argues that in Kentucky, these affairs of honor arose because of a "warrior mentality" that had pervaded the state prior to its founding. Klotter writes that Kentuckians had an "aptitude for violence" that showed itself in street fights, duels, violence against slaves, and sport, including cockfighting. A judge, he explains, once summarized residents' attitudes, writing that "human life in Kentucky is not worth the snapping of a man's fingers." Visitors to Kentucky also recognized this penchant for violence. In July 1814, one wrote, "The character of the people here is too chivalric—a mixture of generosity and barbarity. I admire it, and still I hate it. Duels, stabbings, and [other forms of violence] happen every few days, but are seldom fatal."[10]

While the Anglo settlement period was a violent one in Kentucky history, formalized dueling did not arrive in the state until a new

Kentucky politician Henry Clay fought multiple duels during his lifetime. *Library of Congress.*

generation of easterners moved into the commonwealth. These "gentle-men" avoided unsavory street fights and instead embraced the code duello as the structured way to manage insults and social difficulties.[11]

These gentlemen included some of Kentucky's most prominent citizens. In 1807, state legislators Henry Clay and Humphrey Marshall argued in the Kentucky House of Representatives. Tensions were high with Great Britain, and Clay proposed that Kentuckians should only purchase American-made clothing. Marshall, a former US congressman, called Clay's idea the "clap-trap of a demagogue." Insulted, Clay challenged Marshall, who accepted. They dueled near Louisville, with pistols. Although each man missed twice, on the third fire Marshall shot Clay in the leg, giving the man who would become known as the "Great Compromiser" a minor wound. Despite the fight, Clay and Marshall retained their General Assembly seats.[12]

This was not Clay's only duel. In 1826, when Clay was a US senator, his colleague John Randolph called him a "cross between the Puritan and the Black-Leg." Insulted, Clay challenged Randolph. According to Thomas Jessup, who negotiated the terms of the duel, Clay told him "that Mr. Randolph had thrown down the gauntlet, and had left him no alternative but to take it up." Jessup tried to dissuade Clay from dueling, but the politician told him, "No public station, no, not even life, is worth holding if coupled with dishonor." The two men fought with pistols outside of Washington, DC. Each man missed on the first volley. On the second shot, Clay fired first and missed. Randolph could have aimed and shot Clay, but he instead fired into the air. This gesture impressed Clay, and the two men reconciled. Less than a year later, Clay called dueling a "pernicious practice,—condemned by the judgment and philosophy of every thinking man." Although Clay would have considered himself a "thinking man," he was primed to use pistols when his honor was maligned.[13]

A willingness to duel ran in the Clay family. Henry Clay's cousin, Cassius Marcellus Clay, was a noted politician, newspaper editor, and leading Kentucky emancipationist who found himself entangled in duels and knife fights because of his antislavery views. In May 1841, he fought a duel with Robert Wickliffe Jr. near Louisville with pistols at ten paces. Clay was a crack shot, and it was said that he could shoot a silver chain at ten paces. When Clay and Wickliffe dueled, however,

Cassius M. Clay fought a duel against Robert Wickliffe in 1841. *Library of Congress.*

each man missed three times. Honor satisfied, the affair was settled without bloodshed. After the duel, a friend asked Clay how he could sever a chain with a pistol shot and yet not hit Wickliffe. "Oh, the d——d string had no pistol in its hand," Clay responded. Albert Sidney Johnston, the Mason County native who became a Confederate general, acted as Wickliffe's second in the duel.[14]

As Cassius Clay learned, fear was common on the dueling ground, but it was rarely discussed within the confines of the masculine-bound

Southern code of honor. One witness to a duel, at least, made a joke about two duelists' worry. In 1826, the principals missed each other at the first fire. One of the seconds then suggested that the duelists should shake hands. The other second commented that this was not needed: "Their hands have been shaking this half hour."[15]

Even those who saved lives were not immune to the call of the code duello. Although the Hippocratic Oath calls for physicians to avoid causing harm, in 1818, a public feud over a postmortem examination threw two Lexington doctors onto the field of honor. After Benjamin Dudley argued with another doctor about the autopsy, Dudley challenged the other man to a duel. When that doctor refused, the challenged man's friend William H. Richardson, also a physician, agreed to fight. They fought with pistols, and Dudley shot Richardson in the groin. As Richardson lay on the ground bleeding to death from a severed artery, Dudley stepped in, staunched the flow of blood, and saved his opponent's life. Honor had been satisfied by the act of dueling, so Dudley saved his opponent's life instead of taking it.[16]

Doctors and lawyers were not the only professionals who dueled. As the street fight between George Prentice and Reuben Durrett attests, Kentucky newspaper editors frequently found themselves at odds with readers or each other, and those arguments sometimes led to affairs of honor. Charles Wickliffe was the son of a prominent Lexington family whose siblings were friends with Mary Todd Lincoln. In 1829, he became angry over correspondence that was published in the *Kentucky Gazette* that disparaged his father. The *Gazette* editor, Thomas R. Benning, refused to divulge the author's name, so Wickliffe killed him with a pistol. George Trotter became the new *Gazette* editor, and Trotter and Wickliffe soon argued about the shooting. Wickliffe challenged Trotter, and despite Trotter's previous pledge to avoid affairs of honor, they fought with pistols at eight feet. Trotter mortally wounded Wickliffe. A few years later, Trotter had another violent altercation with Prentice, the *Louisville Journal* editor. Scraps among the ink-stained continued. Two Frankfort editors nearly dueled in 1856, and, a year later, editors Andrew Jackson Morey of the *Kentucky News* and F. L. McChesney of the *Age* battled with cudgels after arguing in the pages of their respective newspapers.[17]

Prominent Kentuckians' participation in duels placed a societal stamp of approval on the practice. However, affairs of honor were illegal

Roger Hanson dueled William Duke in 1848. Duke shot Hanson in the leg. Hanson, who limped for the remainder of his life, was killed at the Battle of Stones River while serving as a Confederate general. *Library of Congress.*

in the commonwealth, so honor-bound residents sometimes traveled to other states to fight. In 1848, William Duke shot Roger Hanson, who survived to become a noted Confederate general. Hanson had become jealous when Duke became betrothed to Caroline Hickman, Hanson's cousin. Therefore, Hanson disparaged Duke to Caroline. When Duke learned of the insult, Duke challenged Hanson to a duel. The twenty-one-year-old Duke fought the twenty-three-year-old Hanson on the shore of the Ohio River near Vevay, Indiana, with pistols at ten paces. Hanson reputedly used one of Andrew Jackson's dueling pistols, while Duke had one of Henry Clay's guns, which Clay had used when he fought John Randolph. Each man missed the first three times. On the fourth shot, Duke hit Hanson in the leg, leaving him "horribly mangled and in great agony." Hanson limped for the remainder of his life, earning him the nickname "Old Bench Leg." Eleven days later, Duke married Caroline Hickman. During the Civil War, Hanson was killed in action at the Battle of Stones River while leading Kentucky's famed Orphan Brigade.[18]

While elites like Hanson and Duke fought in other states, a few Kentuckians even dueled outside of the nation. An illness and the malfunction of weaponry subverted the proceedings in one international duel. During the Mexican-American War, Frankfort native Thomas F. Marshall, a lawyer and former congressman, fought another Kentuckian, James S. Jackson. That duel—Marshall's fourth—was the result of "an old grudge" (John Rowan of Nelson County had once used a quick "hip shot" to shoot Marshall in a previous duel). Marshall rode to the duel, held thirty miles from where he was encamped, on horseback. He was ill with "the flux [diarrhea] and had frequently to dismount. When he reached the ground he could scarcely stand." However, he was determined to kill Jackson, an attorney from Hopkinsville. At the call to fire, Jackson shot and missed. Marshall then took his time, aimed, and pulled the trigger. While the percussion cap popped off, the gun did not fire. Marshall asked his lieutenant, who was also serving as his second, why the gun had not fired. The officer responded "that the ramrod was too short, and he had not rammed the ball home. 'Oh yes,' said Marshall sarcastically, 'I understand; you are my lieutenant, and had I been killed, you would have succeeded me.'" Jackson's second then grabbed the pistol, "rammed the ball home," and gave it back to Marshall, telling him

In 1837, Kentucky native Albert Sidney Johnston was wounded in a duel with another Kentuckian, Felix Houston. Johnston was killed during the Civil War. *Library of Congress*.

After killing James Chambers in a duel in 1801, John Rowan reputedly had this ring fashioned, containing a lock of Chambers's hair. *Kentucky Historical Society, Frankfort, 2016.65.*

to fire again. Marshall, however, was "too weak to stand any longer," and the duel ended. In 1846, Jackson fought another duel, with a man named Samuel Patterson, but the affair ended without bloodshed. In October 1862, Jackson was killed while leading a Union division at the Battle of Perryville.[19]

As the duel between Marshall and Jackson illustrates, men serving in the military dueled despite regulations forbidding the practice. In February 1837, Mason County native Albert Sidney Johnston, who became a Confederate general and was killed at the Battle of Shiloh, fought a duel "using horse pistols" with fellow Kentuckian Gen. Felix Houston when the two men were officers in the army of the Republic of Texas. The men fired six times, and the affair ended when Johnston was struck in the thigh.[20]

Among Kentucky natives who became embroiled in affairs of honor, few became as well-known as Abraham Lincoln. Henry Clay was Lincoln's "beau ideal of a statesman," and, in one episode, Lincoln nearly followed Clay's path to the dueling ground. In 1842, the Illinois state auditor challenged Lincoln over the authorship of several insulting letters written to a newspaper. Lincoln chose broadswords as the weapon, knowing that he had a size advantage over the more diminutive auditor. Lincoln, who had honed his physical strength swinging an axe, knew he "could have split him in two." The auditor wisely avoided the fight. One wonders whether Lincoln would have been elected president had he hacked the man to death with a broadsword.[21]

Duels were typically caused by insults or political controversies, but a few were sparked by stranger occurrences. In 1819, two Kentuckians dueled in Frankfort because one killed the other man's dog. One participant was seriously wounded, and the other was killed. In an 1801 incident, John Rowan, who lived in the house now known as "My Old Kentucky Home," met James Chambers on the field of honor. After drinking and playing cards, the two men supposedly argued about which had a better mastery over ancient languages. Rowan killed Chambers in the fight. He eventually became a US congressman and senator, state legislator, and judge on the Kentucky Court of Appeals. Rowan also had a ring made, which is now in the collection of the Kentucky Historical Society, that reputedly contains a lock of Chambers's hair.[22]

While the code duello dictated the way Southern gentlemen settled disputes, the practice for the most part ebbed away during the Civil War. Although the formal code grew out of fashion during the conflict, there were still some brutal honor-bound killings, from duels to murder. For example, a cuckolded doctor killed the Confederacy's Maj. Gen. Earl Van Dorn after the doctor learned that his wife allegedly had a liaison with the officer. In another instance, William Nichol, a Confederate surgeon, questioned Brig. Gen. George Earl Maney's leadership at the Battle of Perryville. Maney, his bravery impugned, challenged the physician to a duel. Several of Maney's regiments had suffered 50 percent casualties at Perryville, and the brigade commander was not going to allow his honor—or that of his brigade—to be insulted. Maney wounded Nichol in the encounter. The South's Brig. Gen. John S. Marmaduke also fought a duel with Brig. Gen. Lucius M. Walker, a fellow Confederate, in

A doctor killed the Confederacy's Major General Earl Van Dorn after Van Dorn had an affair with the doctor's wife. *Library of Congress.*

In September 1863, the Confederacy's brigadier generals John S. Marmaduke and Lucius M. Walker fought a duel in Arkansas. Marmaduke killed Walker. *Library of Congress.*

Arkansas in September 1863 because Marmaduke had accused Walker of displaying cowardice in battle. Marmaduke, who killed Walker, later became governor of Missouri. During the war, Rives Pollard fought at least two duels, including one with a rebel officer, and served as a second in another. After the war, while working as a journalist, Pollard was ambushed and killed by someone who had been insulted in the pages of his newspaper.[23]

These rebels were not the only military men who engaged in affairs of honor during the Civil War. Lorien Foote examines duels that took place in the Union army and writes that "northern men engaged in a bare minimum of thirty-four incidents that included some element of the dueling ritual—whether it was a written or verbal challenge to a duel or an offer to fight that borrowed language from the code duello." But, Foote argues, "this statistic vastly underrepresents the actual number of affairs of honor that occurred in the Union Army, since it only includes men who were charged in general courts-martial for violating the Articles of War that prohibited challenges and dueling." Metcalfe, never court-martialed for dueling Casto, would be among the underrepresented duelists in Foote's study.[24]

Many of those involved with the Casto–Metcalfe duel—including those on the periphery—also contended with violence. This included the man who had precipitated the fight by ordering Casto's arrest. The Union's blustery, profane Maj. Gen. William "Bull" Nelson met his demise when his insults became too much for one man to bear. Because of Nelson's rough manner, it is, perhaps, unsurprising that he met a violent end. Throughout Nelson's military career, his behavior led to complaints. Several prominent politicians, for example, urged President Lincoln to send Nelson back to the US Navy, where his harsh shipboard discipline would be more palatable. In September 1861, for example, Kentuckian Leslie Combs told the president, "My friend Nelson is excessively unpopular—with his command. Officers and men—have been urging me to ask his withdrawal, but I was reluctant to do or say anything, that might wound his feelings—His whole education and all his habits, fit him for the sea; and I hope you will soon give him a *lift* in his profession and transfer him to a ship." Brig. Gen. William T. Sherman, the Union commander of much of Kentucky for a time, recognized Nelson's strained relationship with citizen-soldiers, telling

In August 1862, Brigadier General Jefferson C. Davis of Indiana shot and killed Major General William "Bull" Nelson, fellow Union officer, at the Galt House Hotel in Louisville. *Library of Congress.*

Brig. Gen. George Thomas, "Nelson has got into difficulty with the militia." Many officers were aware of Nelson's reputation. In late November, another Union general, Don Carlos Buell, reported, "Nelson has been in camp a day, and, I am informed, has already got into difficulty with [another officer]; and, if I am rightly informed, has behaved rather absurdly. As he is a veteran, some allowance must be made for him." Senator Garrett Davis of Kentucky simply told Lincoln, "I think he is the most odious man I have ever known."[25]

Calls to remove Nelson went unheeded. He fought at the Battle of Shiloh, where he threatened to shoot demoralized Union soldiers, and led troops during the siege of Corinth, Mississippi. Authorities eventually promoted Nelson to major general. In August 1862, his superiors ordered him to Kentucky to defend the state from Confederate invasion. Wounded that month at the Battle of Richmond, Kentucky, Nelson went to Louisville to prepare the city for advancing rebels. He established his headquarters at the Galt House Hotel, and to bolster the city's defenses, he appointed Brig. Gen. Jefferson C. Davis (no relation to the Confederate president) to organize local militia. The work of Davis, a regular army officer who had fought at Wilson's Creek, Pea Ridge, and Corinth, soon disappointed Nelson.

Nelson called the man, who had been ill, to the Galt House to learn more about his work with the militia. Davis answered each question from Nelson, "I don't know." This infuriated Nelson, who told Davis he was "disappointed" in him and that he had "made a mistake" in putting him in charge. After the men argued, Nelson stripped Davis of his command and ordered him to leave the state or face arrest. Davis, however, soon returned.[26]

On the morning of September 29, Nelson ate his breakfast at the Galt House. Afterward, he stood near the hotel office when Davis, Governor Oliver Morton of Indiana, and several acquaintances arrived. A major named James H. Cole said Davis "looked pale and was evidently laboring under unusual excitement." Cole, expecting trouble, told Nelson that Davis was at the hotel. True to form, Nelson "boldly walked in front of them," Cole wrote. As he passed the Hoosiers, Davis stepped forward. In "haughty tones," Davis asked, "General Nelson, I want to know why you disgraced me by placing me in arrest?" Nelson said, "Do you know who you are talking to, sir?" Davis said, "Yes! Bill Nelson!"

After an argument, Brigadier General Jefferson C. Davis shot and killed Major General William "Bull" Nelson. *Kentucky Historical Society, Frankfort 2004.41.263.*

Nelson then "slapped Davis with the palm and back of his hand on either side of his face, and at the same time applying to him an opprobrious epithet." Other sources contend that before Nelson struck Davis, Davis had told him that he had been insulted and wanted an apology. When Nelson demanded he leave, Davis kept talking. "Go away, you —— puppy," Nelson said. "I don't want anything to do with you." Davis, who had been playing with a crumpled hotel card, threw the ball of paper in Nelson's face. Then Nelson struck him. Afterward, Nelson turned his rage on Morton, yelling at the governor before leaving for his room.[27]

As Nelson walked away, Davis told him, "I will see you again." Davis then borrowed a pistol from a friend and followed Nelson. Catching his quarry at the foot of a staircase, Davis walked to within three feet of Nelson and fired. The bullet struck him near the heart. Despite the severity of the wound, Nelson walked up the stairs before collapsing. He died within thirty minutes. Davis was never prosecuted for his death. As historian Lorien Foote writes, "Commonly held beliefs about manhood and honor sanctioned Davis's act."[28]

Because the code duello began to wither during the Civil War, the duel between Casto and Metcalfe and a handful of others were exceptional. Wide-scale violence during the Civil War, from battles to irregular warfare, led to a cultural change regarding the way Southern elites settled insults. Most aggrieved gentlemen recognized that there was simply no longer a point to the code duello. While honor and the threat of community shame still hung over these men after the war, violence among the upper classes in Kentucky became unregulated. Formal duels were gone, so white male Kentuckians, laden with concealed weapons—widely available, as surplus military arms were sold to the civilian market after the Civil War—instead handled insults with impromptu street fights. As the *Louisville Commercial* recognized, "it is among the better classes of white people in the State that the habit of carrying concealed weapons is abused." The newspaper added that this habit was reinforced because juries typically failed to convict upper-class Kentuckians charged with carrying weapons. These gentlemen continued to fight, using concealed weapons, because precepts of honor still existed. Those who ignored postwar street confrontations after being insulted or threatened were declared cowards and still suffered public shame. As historian Robert Ireland relates, "The habit of carrying concealed deadly weapons, combined with a hypersensitive notion of personal honor and a penchant for alcoholic beverages, formed a deadly social mix that resulted in many a fatal confrontation." Essentially, Ireland adds, "the outlawing of duelling amounted to a license for men, gentlemen and cowards, to arm themselves with concealed deadly weapons and to use these weapons unfairly in tavern and street fights, which often constituted simply acts of assassination." The Civil War killed the code duello in Kentucky, and the Casto–Metcalfe affair was a last gasp of the dying practice.[29]

9

His Blood Is on His Own Head

Leonidas Metcalfe sat in Thomas Green's newspaper office, confounded that Isaac Nelson had handed him William T. Casto's challenge. Metcalfe told Green that he did not know Casto personally. He did, at least, recall that William "Bull" Nelson had ordered him to arrest the Maysville attorney. Green later said that when Metcalfe arrested Casto, he had done so with the utmost professionalism and had not "offered the slightest indignity to Mr. Casto by word or deed."[1]

Green read Casto's note and assured Metcalfe that he was under no obligation to duel. Since Metcalfe had been following orders when he arrested Casto, and since the colonel did not know the secessionist, no point of honor dictated that he had to fight. Green told Metcalfe "that ninety-nine men out of a hundred would not do it." The colonel agreed but said that "he did not like to be browbeaten"; therefore, he was inclined to accept Casto's challenge. Metcalfe would not hide behind the fact that he had been following orders in arresting Casto. His honor would not allow him to back down. In addition, because he was a unionist who had condemned both secessionists and slave owners in the region, he needed to show that he was willing to defend himself. According to Green, "his life was threatened almost daily at home." A target was on his back; Metcalfe knew that if he refused Casto, he would be met by myriad challenges from men who wanted to prove themselves, ruin his reputation, or kill him. Green added "that men who hated him because of his endeavors to serve his country would be encouraged by such a refusal to provoke collisions with him until he should be obliged to kill some of them or lose his own life." If he refused this challenge, others would follow. Metcalfe also believed "it would release many

Union men from the pressure of similar demands." He saw dueling Casto as a service to other unionists. For those reasons, and to prevent future challenges from those who wanted him dead or wanted to prove their manliness, Metcalfe decided to duel Casto. He was convinced it was a conspiracy to either kill him or ruin him, so he would meet the challenge head-on. As a colonel in the Union army, Metcalfe knew he faced possible civilian charges and a court martial for dueling. Honor, however, outweighed any threat of prosecution.[2]

Only two hours after receiving the note, Metcalfe sent Isaac Nelson his response through Thomas Green, who agreed to act as an intermediary. Following the code duello, the note was formal, dispassionate, and sent through a second. "Sir:" Metcalfe wrote,

> Your note of this date is received. I do not know you by sight, and I have never spoken to you in my life. I have not done you any great wrong, under circumstances accompanying indignity with outrage, or under any other circumstances. I do not, therefore, owe you the satisfaction due from one gentleman to another, or any other satisfaction. I make this statement lest in unconditionally accepting your challenge, which I do, I should be understood as admitting your right to challenge, which I deny. But understanding your purpose to be either to degrade me in public estimation or to wantonly seek my life, and not choosing that any one shall win a cheap reputation for courage at my expense in that way, I will grant you the meeting you desire. My friend, the bearer of this, is authorized to arrange all the preliminaries. Very respectfully, your obedient servant, Leonidas Metcalfe.[3]

With Metcalfe having named Green as his negotiator, Isaac Nelson, one of Casto's two seconds, asked to meet Green at the Lee House in Maysville. There, he hoped to arrange "the preliminaries of the contemplated meeting between Col. Metcalfe and Mr. W. T. Casto." Soon, however, Thomas A. Respess, Casto's other second, brought Green another note. Because of "publicity" surrounding the challenge and to avoid the watchful eye of authorities, Nelson said that they should arrange the terms of the duel through correspondence. Green replied that he would rather meet face to face, but he would soon send him terms in another note.[4]

While Nelson had served time at Camp Chase and Fort Lafayette with Casto, Respess, a lawyer and newspaper editor, had stayed out of unionists' clutches. Born in Bourbon County in March 1826, Respess was called "a remarkable man and . . . one of the foremost scholars of Kentucky." His family had moved to Maysville when he was ten years old. He attended Miami University in Ohio and was a respected attorney in Mason County. Like his counterpart Thomas Marshall Green, Respess was a lawyer with a scholarly bent.[5]

Since Casto had challenged Metcalfe, the code duello as practiced in Kentucky gave the Union colonel the right to choose the duel's weapons and location. On May 7, the day after Casto issued the challenge, Green sent Nelson Metcalfe's terms. Metcalfe was known to be a crack rifle shot and played to this advantage. Green told Nelson that instead of pistols, the weapon typically used in nineteenth-century duels, the men would fight with Sharps rifles. If Casto could not procure them, the duelists would use five-shot Colt Revolving rifles with one chamber loaded. Or Casto could choose any rifle he wanted and Metcalfe would use a Sharps. Giving Casto the option to choose any rifle showed Metcalfe's confidence about his own marksmanship. The principals would fight the next day, May 8, shooting at each other from sixty yards apart. Green suggested they hold the duel away from Maysville, in either "Charlestown Bottom" or the "bull pasture" on a farm in Aberdeen, Ohio. He also suggested they fight at a nearby fairgrounds or a different place that could be agreed on. When the duel commenced, the participants would hold their rifles at "present arms" (straight in front of their bodies with the muzzles pointing up) until it was time to shoot. To determine who would give the command to fire, the seconds would flip a coin. The loser of that coin toss would choose where his duelist would stand during the fight. When the duel started, the second tasked with giving the word would ask, "Gentlemen, are you ready?" If they were, he would say loudly, "Fire, one, two, three, stop." The duelists could shoot at any time during the number count and could not fire after the word *stop*. Thus, each participant would have about four seconds to aim and fire. Each side could bring ten people to the duel, including the seconds and surgeons. Only the seconds could be armed.[6]

Upon receiving the terms, Isaac Nelson responded at 10:00 p.m. Because news of the duel had spread, Nelson and Respess informed Green that Casto was "in custody in Ohio." Authorities who wanted to prevent the fight had detained him, ending any chance of dueling near Aberdeen. Nelson then suggested the duel take place on the following Saturday in "Egypt Bottom" in Indiana, close to Big Boone Creek. Then, via several notes, Green and Respess argued about which side had the right to name the time and place of the duel. Because Metcalfe wanted to fight quickly and because news of the affair had spread, Casto's seconds said it would be difficult to procure a Sharps or Colt Revolving rifle. Nelson and Respess said that they would "purchase a suitable weapon" but wanted to pick the time and place for the duel. Green, well-versed with the code duello, told Casto's seconds that he was shocked that the Maysville secessionists wanted to pick the time and location. He then referred to the code duello to settle the matter. "According to the usages of the code in this State," Green wrote, "or as I have understood them, the right to fix the time and place, as well as the right to name the weapon and mode of combat, belong to the party challenged, and I do not feel at liberty to waive this right in a case in which the challenge has been so peremptory as that of Mr. Casto." Green said Casto's friends were to blame for any "publicity" and that they would "regret it exceedingly." Later, Green showed Respess a pair of "excellent" Colt Revolving rifles he owned and said they could be used for the duel. When Respess balked at using Green's rifles, Green responded, "Casto had some *months* to be ready for the affair, while Col. Metcalfe had not had forty-eight hours." Finally, Casto agreed to Metcalfe's "right to name the weapon." Respess and Nelson chose one of Green's rifles for Casto and named the nearby "Fishing Shore," outside of Dover, Kentucky, in Bracken County as the duel location. The seconds signed an agreement settling the terms. The fight would commence the next day, May 8, at 4:30 p.m.[7]

First made in 1855, the Colt Revolving rifle was a five-shot, .56 caliber, 50-inch-long weapon that was essentially an oversized rifle version of Colt's famous revolving pistol. Although multiple Civil War regiments contemplated using the gun, firearms historians Earl Coates and Dean Thomas write that "the revolving rifle was considered too complex for military use." Despite this, some units used the weapon. One Union soldier commented that they were "as good or better than any, in the

A Union soldier holding a Colt Revolving rifle, the type of weapon that Casto and Metcalfe used in their duel. *Library of Congress.*

hands of men who are cool and know how to use it." He added that "loading must be done without flurrying" and that it was "a poor weapon to give green troops on this account." Another soldier, a member of the Ninth Illinois Cavalry, wrote, "The Colt's revolving rifle was an excellent arm, and had served us well on many an occasion; but there was one serious objection to them; when being discharged they would shoot splinters of lead into the wrist and hand of the man firing." There was also a more serious risk. The weapon used paper cartridges, which were loaded into five revolving chambers; improper loading techniques or the accidental ignition of excess powder could cause "chain firing" that would shoot all five rounds at once, mauling the arm of anyone holding the rifle. This led one Vermont soldier to exclaim, "They are pretty to look at, but upon examination and test they were found inaccurate and unreliable, prone to get out of order and even dangerous to the user." Since Casto and Metcalfe were only loading one chamber, there was no risk of chain firing. Although the weapon was not popular with the troops, it was most famously used by the green-coated Berdan's Sharpshooters, a unit of Union marksmen. These soldiers, however, eventually exchanged their Colts for the more reliable Sharps rifle. The Colt Revolving rifle was also used with ferocity at the Battle of Chickamauga when members of the Twenty-first Ohio Infantry Regiment repulsed five waves of Confederate attacks. One member of the regiment noted, "One man was like five in shooting power." The Rebels were so stunned by the rapid fire that one captured Southerner said, "I thought you had a whole division here." For those Buckeyes, at least, this "pretty to look at" rifle was an able tool for warfare. It would also prove a reliable instrument for one of the participants in the Casto–Metcalfe duel.[8]

While the seconds chose Colt Revolving rifles because of their accessibility, this weapon was not typically used in duels. At least one other affair of honor, however, was fought with that weapon during the Civil War. In the fall of 1863, C. A. Red killed Richard Copeland near Augusta, Georgia, in a formal duel using Colt Revolving rifles. Their rules, however, were apparently more brutal than those Metcalfe and Casto negotiated. Red and Copeland's agreement stipulated that, separated by just a few yards and armed with fully loaded weapons, the principals could fire and then advance on each other after the first shot. As a crowd of seventy-five spectators watched, both men fired but refused to advance. Red's first shot went through Copeland's hat, but his second struck his antagonist in the chest. The bullet exited behind Copeland's left arm, and he died within a few minutes. Casto and Metcalfe would also learn just how deadly this weapon was.[9]

Further evidence shows that Green's Colt Revolving rifles were chosen out of convenience. In addition, Green contended that Metcalfe had never previously seen the firearm and Metcalfe had only fired about twenty shots with that type of weapon. He was, nonetheless, a more experienced shooter than Casto, who had little familiarity with guns. Green claimed, though, that once Casto returned to Maysville he began preparing for an inevitable showdown. Freed from prison, the secessionist spent time firing pistols and rifles on a quick count. Having practiced for a duel, challenged Metcalfe, and finalized negotiations, Casto would soon get his chance to revenge the dishonor of his confinement.[10]

On the morning of the duel, Casto's inexperience was evident. Respess asked Green if Green could give him some ammunition so that Casto could practice. Green, whose patience had grown thin during the negotiations, told Respess to find his own bullets and powder. Green said he had none and he certainly did not want to tip off authorities by buying ammunition as rumors about the duel ran rampant.[11]

Because authorities were on the prowl for the duelists, the seconds settled on a location ten miles downriver from Maysville. They chose the Fishing Shore outside Dover, a small town on the Ohio River in Bracken County. Like Maysville, during much of the nineteenth century Dover was a shipping center that benefitted from riverine commerce. The first house was built there in 1786, though the area was not surveyed as a town until 1818. Finally incorporated in 1836, it became a major shipping point for tobacco in the region. By 1870, however, the population of Dover was only 159 people. Casto and Metcalfe were heading to a quiet, tranquil spot, away from prying eyes, where they would settle the matter.[12]

Having negotiated the duel, Green bowed out of the proceedings. Although he had set the stage for the engagement, he declined to act as Metcalfe's second on the dueling ground. He did, however, attend the duel. He later wrote that Metcalfe had accepted his reasons, but Green declined to provide the details. Likely, he was hoping to have his law license restored and knew this would be impossible if he participated in another duel. Regardless, Metcalfe accepted Green's excuse and two of Metcalfe's other friends stepped in to serve as his seconds. While Casto retained civilians Isaac Nelson and Thomas Respess, Metcalfe's seconds were two Union officers, Maj. Samuel G. Rogers and Capt. William Oden, who had helped Green with some of the negotiations. The thirty-two-year-old Rogers was a successful Nicholas County farmer, with more than \$5,000 in real estate and \$11,000 in personal property. On December 31, 1861, Rogers had joined the Eighteenth Kentucky (Union) Infantry Regiment and was commissioned captain. The forty-nine-year-old Oden, whose mother was a Metcalfe, was also a Nicholas County farmer, having \$1,400 in real estate, \$6,600 in personal property, and five enslaved African Americans. Oden, who had served with Metcalfe during the Big Sandy Campaign under Bull Nelson, was the soldier who tore the Rebel flag off the Prestonsburg courthouse when that town was liberated. While Oden appears to have led a quiet life after the Civil War, Rogers became embroiled in a terrible struggle that left two of his family members dead. Violence, it seemed, chased several of the men who were involved in the Casto–Metcalfe duel.[13]

Rumors spread quickly throughout Maysville about the impending fight. With the town's former mayor set to duel a controversial Union colonel, talk about the affair must have filled homes, businesses, and sidewalks. Local opinions varied. While some hoped that Metcalfe—who had criticized secessionists, slavery, and enslavers—would pay the ultimate price for his heresy, others condemned the fact that a duel was going to be fought in their neighborhood. One Dover resident blamed the war, as he wrote in a letter to his local newspaper. "This relic of ancient barbarous custom—dueling," he wrote, "for some time on the wane in Kentucky, has been fanned into new life by the war *animus.*" Dover was "thrown into a bubble of excitement." Casto had set the stage, and residents waited for the result.[14]

On the morning of May 8, Casto, his seconds, and several friends boarded the steamboat *Magnolia* and traveled the ten miles to the dueling ground. The atmosphere on the boat was far from funereal. A witness wrote that the party was "jubilant and brave. One would have thought they were out for a picnic." The festivity was heightened because "the day was supremely beautiful," one man wrote. When Casto disembarked, he immediately began practicing with his Colt Revolving rifle. He was determined to master the weapon before he stared down its barrel at Metcalfe.[15]

The colonel appeared with less fanfare. Metcalfe, his seconds, and his surgeons, accompanied by Green and other friends, rode in carriages. When Metcalfe climbed out, he heard Casto's rifle sputtering in the distance. Calm, confident, and collected, Metcalfe lay down on the riverbank and dozed in the sun, occasionally watching the Ohio River lap against the Fishing Shore.[16]

Because word of the affair had spread, the number of spectators far surpassed the ten that had been agreed upon by the seconds. Carriages and horses arrived bearing well-wishers and the macabrely curious. Two hundred spectators soon crowded the Fishing Shore, all waiting to see the Civil War play out along the bank of the Ohio River. The Dover resident reported, "A considerable crowd of friends and sympathizers, many of them rebels, and all loaded down to 'the guards' with arms, was present, to witness the horrid but highly exciting ceremony." The Fishing Shore had been chosen because it was a quiet, out-of-the-way place; in *Famous Kentucky Duels,* J. Winston Coleman calls it "a secluded spot and an ideal place for the affair of honor." On that day, it was far from tranquil.[17]

As the hours ticked by, Metcalfe remained calm. At one point, he rose from the bank and fired a few practice rounds, in one instance striking "the handle of a common pocket knife at 60 yards," one witness wrote. The odds favored the Union colonel. "Casto was wholly unpracticed with the rifle, while Metcalfe has the reputation of being a crack shot," he added. Friends from both parties tried to stop the affair, but to no avail. Neither side wanted to end the duel. Metcalfe hoped to keep his reputation intact and curtail future threats to his life by ending Casto's. As the Dover resident contended, "Mutual friends made an effort to reconcile the *political* antagonists, but a fight alone could heal the wounded honor of the one, and preserve its integrity in the other." While friends tried to intervene, the seconds—Nelson, Respess, Oden, and Rogers—stayed silent. Like the waves rolling onto the Fishing Shore, the conflict was inevitable.[18]

At 4:00 p.m., Nelson and Respess approached Metcalfe's seconds and told them they were ready. The seconds picked the area where the two men would fight and measured off sixty yards. They then tossed a coin to determine who would give the count and call the word to fire, which Nelson won. Under their agreement, Metcalfe had the right to choose the position. Against his seconds' advice, Metcalfe picked the side facing the sun, where it shone in his face. Honor and the code duello dictated that the duel should be a fair match, and Metcalfe followed this convention. Confident and more experienced, he worked to ensure a fair fight; he would at least give Casto a sporting chance.[19]

Shortly after the sides were chosen, Casto appeared. He and Metcalfe greeted each other formally and coldly, then took their places on the shore. While meandering to his spot, Metcalfe reputedly said, "I shall shoot him in the heart. The ball will pass through his left vest pocket." Near 5:00 p.m., the duelists took their positions. The crowd hushed. The sun shone on Metcalfe's brow. Nelson asked if they were ready. Both duelists said yes, and they moved their rifles to the "present arms" position, pointing their rifle barrels skyward.[20]

In an instant, Isaac Nelson said "Fire" in a clear, distinct voice. Both men raised their rifles. "One," Nelson shouted. Casto pulled the trigger. The shot echoed across the Ohio River, and several in the crowd ducked at the report. The bullet whizzed harmlessly past Metcalfe's head. Keeping the game fair as honor dictated, Metcalfe had let Casto shoot first.[21]

"Two," Nelson exclaimed. Metcalfe gazed down the barrel and fired.[22]

As the breeze coming off the river blew the black powder smoke away from the muzzle of Metcalfe's rifle, Casto threw up his arms, arching his hands over his head. He then grabbed his left side, pitched forward, and dropped, face down. One witness recalled, "Casto fell like a log to the beach."[23]

Casto had been shot, a correspondent wrote, "in the left side, just between the lowest rib and the hip bone, passing clear through his body and liver on its way, causing a portion of the substance to protrude." The .56 caliber round, fired at sixty yards, made large entrance and exit wounds. According to another witness, "the ball struck him on the side, just below the range of the heart, and passed completely through him—a splendid center shot." Metcalfe had upheld his reputation as a fine marksman. He had also called his shot, shooting Casto in the left side.[24]

Casto's friends ran to the secessionist's still form. Metcalfe lowered his rifle. "My God!" the colonel exclaimed. "I knew I would kill him—this affair was forced on me—I had nothing against him—I never spoke a word to him in my life—I am a better shot than he was aware of." He added, "Gentlemen, this fight was forced on me. I bore this man no ill will, and gave him no cause of quarrel against me. His blood is on his own head."[25]

A crowd gathered around Casto. He had not brought a surgeon, so Metcalfe's doctor offered to help. Casto's friends assented, but it did no good. Casto died in fifteen minutes, without saying another word. He passed, the Dover resident wrote, with "his blood trickling along the sands into the waters of the Ohio."[26]

That writer knew the cause of Casto's death. "Casto was bent on seeking the recovery of his lost honor and *rights,* and it is the general feeling of a large majority of the people here that he has at last found *them*." Perplexed that the fight had ever taken place, he added, "Casto was insane to challenge such a man." But, one newspaper contended, "Nothing but a resort to arms would satisfy his wounded pride."[27]

Casto had kneeled to none but God. He had been arrested without charges and confined in an out-of-state prison, yet he refused to take the oath of allegiance. He would not bend to the will of Union authorities, and, in the end, he was nearly released upon his own terms. "Take, take my life that heaven gave," Mary E. Wilson Betts penned in her poem "A Kentuckian Kneels to None but God," "and let my heart's blood stain thy sod." Casto was shot in the chest because he was bound to Southern honor culture and bent on revenge, and his heart's blood literally stained the Fishing Shore. Although residents decided he was "insane" to fight the experienced Metcalfe, Casto surely died thinking he was one of "Kentucky's brave" who bent to no one. If she had been alive, one wonders how Wilson would have penned Casto's eulogy.[28]

Metcalfe left the dueling ground and returned to Maysville. One 1877 newspaper article contends that he purchased the rifle that he used to kill Casto. When Metcalfe departed, the large crowd surrounding the Fishing Shore dispersed.[29]

Casto's seconds placed their friend's corpse in a small boat and took it two miles upriver to Dover. The trip back up the river, the waves tossing Casto's corpse about, was a mournful one. The jovial steamboat trip on the *Magnolia* was forgotten. Upon reaching Dover, the Ohio River packet boat *Bostona* delivered Casto's body to Maysville. This was the same steamer that had delivered seven Southern sympathizers to a Cincinnati prison in October 1861. One wonders if the coincidence of Casto's corpse being floated home on a steamboat that had once transported arrested Southern civilians would have been lost on the departed duelist.[30]

Casto was buried in the Maysville cemetery several days later, in section 6, lot 178. A large crowd attended the funeral. A ten-foot-tall marble monument was later erected over his grave. It reads, "W. T. Casto, a patriot, his country's firm unwavering friend, he was willing to die for his principles, and as a man of honor, nobly fell a votary of the sacred and inviolable right of personal liberty." Casto would have been pleased with that epitaph, so perfectly attuned to his code that one wonders if he crafted the lines in preparation for his demise.[31]

In March 1872, another burial took place in the Maysville cemetery that would have, no doubt, were it possible, made Casto roll over in his grave. Although Bull Nelson, the Union officer who had ordered the arrest of Casto and the other Maysville secessionists, had been buried at Camp Dick Robinson after Jefferson C. Davis killed him in the autumn of 1862, the spot of his interment was not peaceful. After the war, as Kentucky took a notable pro-Confederate turn, vandals desecrated Nelson's grave and snapped the flagpole that flew over his tomb. Nelson's body was thus exhumed, transported to his hometown, and reinterred in a friendlier final resting place, the Maysville Cemetery. Metcalfe nearly took a bullet because of Casto's scorn, and Casto held Nelson in equal contempt. Now, these two enemies lie buried in the same ground.[32]

A month after Casto's death, the *Maysville Dollar Weekly Bulletin* ran an administrator's notice: "All persons having claims against the estate of W. T. Casto, (deceased), will please present them, properly authenticated, for payment." Although Casto had died in an event that shocked the community, legal proceedings involving the heirless man's estate continued, despite the civil war raging around them.[33]

The duel bolstered Metcalfe's reputation as a solid unionist whom secessionists should fear. Unionist newspapers lauded him, one writing: "Our informant says the people of that vicinity all rejoice that Col. Metcalf has rid the State of such a traitorous villain." Four days after the fight, the colonel attended a Union meeting at the Nicholas County courthouse in Carlisle. His feelings toward Rebels were even more pronounced. He was named to a committee to draft resolutions, whose statements warned of guerrillas and Southern saboteurs. They called for secessionists to be held financially responsible for damage done to unionists' property. Furthermore, if any loyalists were killed by renegade Rebels, the resolutions stated, "we will retaliate in at least five-fold proportion upon the sympathizing scoundrels in our midst." Like an Old Testament prophet, Metcalfe hoped to bring wrath down upon his enemies.[34]

Lucius Desha, a Southern-leaning state legislator from Harrison County, quickly ran afoul of those Nicholas County resolutions. On May 26, 1862, Union soldiers seized Desha and took him to the camp of Metcalfe's second Capt. Samuel Rogers in Lexington. Desha was quickly paroled, but eleven days later eight of Metcalfe's men approached him and gave him a warning, demanding he conform to the "Nicholas County resolutions." According to Desha, the troops told him he had "to leave this county or you will be shot or otherwise severely dealt with." Eventually, however, a Home Guard unit arrested Desha, and he was imprisoned at Camp Chase.[35]

While Casto's friends mourned and Metcalfe railed against Confederates, authorities sought to punish those involved with the duel. Several months after Metcalfe killed Casto, the Bracken County court indicted Rogers for acting as Metcalfe's second. Rogers appeared for his trial, but prosecutors were "not ready" and asked for a continuance. As the principal witness for the defense, Metcalfe attended the trial, where he planned to claim that Rogers was not his second. Because Metcalfe could not attend a second trial due to his duties as a Union officer, Rogers pled guilty and took a $150 fine. In February 1864, when Rogers's lawyers sought a full pardon and a remittance of his fine from Kentucky's Governor Thomas E. Bramlette (himself a former Union colonel), they told the governor that Rogers "was present only in the character of a friend" at the duel. The attorneys, playing the Union-versus-secessionist card, stated, "If there ever was a Duell justifiable we believe this to be one." Rogers also claimed that he was not the second because he had been in Lexington when Casto issued the challenge to fight Metcalfe. Since Rogers did not handle correspondence, responses, weapons procurement, or any other part of the negotiation, he claimed, he was not Metcalfe's representative. Metcalfe concurred, endorsing the pardon application: "The within statement contains a true statement of the facts of the case concerning Capt. S. G. Rogers." His friend had stood by him on the dueling ground, and now Metcalfe was standing by Rogers. In April 1864, Kentucky's lieutenant governor, Richard T. Jacob, also a former Union colonel, remitted the $150 fine and essentially pardoned Rogers.[36]

In addition to bearing the loss of their friend, Casto's seconds also faced justice. In 1863, Thomas Respess and Isaac Nelson were indicted in the Bracken County court for assisting with the duel. They pled guilty and were each fined $150. That August, fifteen citizens wrote Governor James F. Robinson on behalf of the men and asked for a reprieve. They asked that the fines be remitted, and, to prevent the men from disenfranchisement, requested a full pardon. On September 1, Nelson and Respess wrote Robinson's successor, Governor Bramlette, and enclosed "a petition from Several of the leading and most Influential gentlemen of Bracken & Mason Counties among them Mr. Carpenter the prosecuting attorney." They asked Bramlette to "remit the fine and penalty," which had been handed down by the Bracken County court. Four days later, Bramlette remitted their fine. In pardoning the seconds, authorities again tacitly sanctioned dueling as a way to resolve conflict. This broader cultural attitude, which included officially endorsing the most murderous aspect of Southern honor culture, helped harm the state's reputation for decades after the Civil War. The commonwealth's standing as a violent place was further confirmed when blueblooded Kentuckians replaced dueling with street altercations and unregulated, impromptu violence. Kentucky's "bowie knife and pistol gentry" remained alive and well after the Civil War.[37]

Metcalfe may have won a victory for the Union on the Fishing Shore, but the hearts and minds of Kentuckians wavered. On May 11, 1862, just three days after Metcalfe killed Casto, Ellen Wallace of Hopkinsville wrote, "The recent victories of the Union Army has inspired the patriotick men of this part of the country with confidence that the Union and peace will soon be restored, but should the Republican party continue in power and carry out their wicked designs in opposition to the conservative men North and South, then indeed with the country be shattered into fragments." The wickedness Wallace feared was emancipation. Four months later, President Lincoln issued a preliminary version of the Emancipation Proclamation, which shook Kentucky to its core. Metcalfe, who recognized slavery as the conflict's cause, focused his ire on Rebels and slave owners.[38]

10

Doomed to Exile

The hundreds of witnesses who watched Metcalfe shoot Casto dispersed and told the tale. Among unionists, Metcalfe's reputation soared. Nearly three months after the fight, one newspaper wrote, "The Colonel himself is equal to a regiment. His name is a tower of strength to his soldiers, while it is a terror to the enemies of the country." Metcalfe used his notoriety to benefit the Federal cause. In early June 1862, he began recruiting a new regiment of horsemen from his home region. By the end of July, the organization of that unit, which became the Seventh Kentucky Cavalry, was nearly complete. According to the *New York Times,* the colonel was raising troops "to help clear his part of the State of guerrillas and bushwhackers." Once confronted with regular Confederate soldiers, however, the Seventh Kentucky would wish it had only faced ragtag bands of irregulars.[1]

Comprising men from Mason and Nicholas Counties, the troops surely admired Casto's slayer. They had, however, little time to revel in their commander's success. In July 1862, while the regiment was still undergoing organization, Col. John Hunt Morgan, a Lexington native who became Kentucky's leading Rebel cavalryman, raided the state. Several of Metcalfe's troopers chased Morgan, who cut a swath through the commonwealth. Metcalfe and seventy-three recruits went to Lexington to defend that city, while the balance of his command remained in camp near Cynthiana. Arming and training a new regiment in the face of the enemy was difficult. Weapons were scarce, and those lucky enough to have guns were armed with inferior .50-caliber Gallagher carbines. The men would have done almost anything for a Colt Revolving rifle; in condemning the Gallagher carbine, Capt. William Harris, chief of ordnance for the Department of the Ohio, said, "I have never met an officer who had tried the Gallager carbine in the field, without

Brigadier General John Hunt Morgan, Confederate, defeated Metcalfe's Seventh Kentucky Cavalry at Cynthiana, Kentucky. *Library of Congress.*

pronouncing it unfit for service." Furthermore, only seventy of Metcalfe's two hundred men had horses, and "few had ever been drilled a moment." The troops were not prepared for action, and Metcalfe probably took the mounted men with him to Lexington while the horseless cavalry waited in camp. While Metcalfe was away from the bulk of his regiment, Morgan struck Metcalfe's camp at Cynthiana. Metcalfe's orphaned men—whom Union officers called "raw recruits"—lost fifteen men. The remainder were captured and paroled, including Capt. William Oden, who had been Metcalfe's second in the duel. It was an inauspicious beginning for Metcalfe's Seventh Kentucky Cavalry. Sadly, the regiment's luck would only worsen.[2]

"After this disaster" at Cynthiana, one soldier reported, "Colonel Metcalf went into encampment at Millersburg, Kentucky . . . for the purpose of recruiting." Metcalfe, his reputation still intact, worked to bring his regiment back up to strength. He did complain to his superiors about his command being deployed across different points when Morgan struck the state. Metcalfe bemoaned the lack of unit cohesion during the Rebel raid, and his green troops stood no chance against Morgan's seasoned veterans.[3]

Metcalfe had always talked a good game against secessionists. He had lambasted them, condemned them, and threatened to make them pay for Union financial losses. In the shadow of Morgan's Raid, Metcalfe backed his words with action. Because Morgan's horsemen took horses, food, and other goods from unionists, Metcalfe returned the favor. The colonel scoured the countryside and seized money from secessionists. With these funds, Metcalfe reimbursed loyalists for goods that Morgan had confiscated. One unionist said, "Col. Metcalfe is collecting money off the Southern rights party to pay the damage that was done by Morgan. . . . Innocent men will have to suffer on the account of Morgan coming into Kentucky." Metcalfe told them that if Rebel residents refused to pay, they would be arrested and sent to Camp Chase. "Thus," a newspaper confirmed, "Morgan's friends are paying for the operations of their favorite chieftain." In one instance, Metcalfe supposedly told a secessionist that he would have to pay $1,000 in reparations. The secessionist asked how long he would have to make good on the bill. Metcalfe told him, "Three years or during the war." The secessionist smiled. "Oh, well, well," he responded, "you are not so hard on us, after all. I will have it for you in time." As he started to leave, the colonel told him, "But, we will hold you until it is paid." Wanting to avoid a stay at Camp Chase, the secessionist immediately handed over the cash. Metcalfe deposited the confiscated money in the Bank of Paris and then reimbursed unionists. As part of his reparations project, Metcalfe gave

Cincinnati mayor George Hatch $1,800 to compensate him for eight fire-engine horses that Morgan's men had seized when they attacked Cynthiana.[4]

Metcalfe eventually lost some favor for this unpopular act. In September 1863, Union authorities, pressured by influential Kentucky unionists like the Reverend Robert J. Breckinridge, made him reimburse the Rebel civilians in Bourbon, Nicholas, and Harrison Counties at sixty cents on the dollar. Other Southern sympathizers sued Metcalfe, and a continuance in the lawsuit was granted in the US District Court at Covington in December 1863. In April 1867, a compromise settlement was finally reached in the case. Like Casto, other secessionists whom Metcalfe punished were tenacious and had long memories. Conversely, some unionists condemned Metcalfe for confiscating citizens' money and for killing Casto. Some thought it unseemly for an officer to have engaged in an affair of honor. In fact, several Southern newspapers compared Metcalfe to Gen. Benjamin "Beast" Butler, the Union commander who had treated civilians with a rough hand while occupying New Orleans.[5]

Morgan's Raid had interrupted the organization of Metcalfe's Seventh Kentucky Cavalry, but the colonel continued to recruit troops throughout the summer of 1862. In August, the regiment was officially organized and mustered into the Union army at Paris, Kentucky. Although Metcalfe was enrolled in the regiment and named its colonel, he was never formally mustered into it. Several other men were also not mustered in, a clerical detail emblematic of the regiment's overall disorganization. Hastily organized, abysmally armed, and improperly trained, the troops had little discipline. Historian D. Warren Lambert contends that the regiment "was hardly a paragon of military efficiency. . . . It was green and had a horseplay reputation for fun and games." Although the Kentucky State Military Board purchased Wesson carbines for the regiment, a little-used weapon that was, at least, more reliable than the Gallagher carbine, the troops needed more guns. By August, Metcalfe's ragtag group of horsemen numbered more than 1,200. Soon, these troops—horrifically unprepared—had to fight for their lives.[6]

In August 1862, Maj. Gen. Edmund Kirby Smith invaded the Bluegrass State with his Confederate Army of Kentucky. Smith hoped to draw Union forces away from Chattanooga, Tennessee, a vital railroad

In August 1862, Major General Edmund Kirby Smith invaded Kentucky for the Confederacy. Smith's troops soundly defeated a Union army—which included Metcalfe's cavalry—at Richmond, Kentucky. *Library of Congress.*

junction. He also wanted to recruit Kentuckians to the Southern cause. Stating that his advance was a "bold move, offering brilliant results," Smith led his command into the commonwealth. Shortly thereafter, other Confederate forces, including Gen. Braxton Bragg's Army of the Mississippi, joined him. The Rebels' northern thrust proved to be the largest Confederate offensive made into Kentucky during the war.[7]

Unprepared Union authorities were especially hindered by the lack of cavalry, who were needed to gather intelligence about Rebel movements. Although Metcalfe's men were woefully armed, they were hustled to Lexington "with such arms as they can get." From there, they were ordered to scout out the Confederate advance. William "Bull" Nelson recognized that "the cavalry is miserably armed as far as fire-arms is concerned." Nonetheless, the Seventh Kentucky was ordered forward, because few horsemen were available. On August 21, Metcalfe's superiors sent the regiment toward London, Kentucky, to keep an eye on the advancing Rebels. "The Country is perfectly desolated," Metcalfe reported from Rockcastle County. "How the people are to live here I can't see." He warned that an "overwhelming" number of Confederates were on the move and that "assistance must come quickly or the [Union] position at Cumberland gap will be lost and heavy forces marching on Richmond and Lexington." Metcalfe proved prescient. Outflanked and outnumbered, Federal troops occupying Cumberland Gap retreated into northeastern Kentucky. Kirby Smith's army then advanced toward Richmond. These were, Metcalfe surmised, "stirring times."[8]

Two days later, after falling back in the face of Kirby Smith's army, Metcalfe's regiment and five companies of the Third Tennessee (Union) Infantry deployed fifteen miles south of Richmond to guard a wagon train. They were camped on the north side of Big Hill, a series of ridges where Madison, Jackson, and Rockcastle Counties converge at the southeastern corner of Madison County. Kirby Smith, intent on capturing Lexington, pressed northward toward Richmond, the seat of Madison County. His vanguard, comprising more than 650 veteran cavalrymen led by Col. John Scott, included the First Louisiana Cavalry, First Georgia Cavalry, the Buckner Guards, and a four-gun artillery battery. These Rebels struck Metcalfe's pickets, posted in advance of the Union line to warn of any enemy approach. Overwhelmed, the pickets fell back toward the wagon train. Hoping to stall the Rebel advance, Metcalfe sent skirmishers forward and prepared for battle. The Union colonel gathered four hundred members of the Seventh Kentucky Cavalry and rushed up the hill. Upon nearing the Rebel troopers, Metcalfe dismounted his men and formed a line of battle.[9]

The Southerners struck Metcalfe's position. One company was hit particularly hard: several men were killed, and the unit's captain, still mounted while leading his troops, had two horses shot out from under him. When Scott's four six-pounder mountain howitzers fired into Metcalfe's line, many of the green Kentucky troops fled. "We moved forward on foot," Metcalfe reported, "amid a shower of bullets and shells, which so terrified my raw, undisciplined recruits that I could not bring more than one hundred of them in sight of the enemy." The refusal of his regiment to fight led to the colonel's "mortification." Another soldier wrote that the Rebels "opened such a deadly fire of grape and shell from a chosen position that older troops could not have withstood." The few score who remained with Metcalfe returned fire. One member of the First Louisiana Cavalry wrote that "the firing was hot on both sides for a half hour or more."[10]

The Confederate assault nearly killed Metcalfe. A Rebel artillery shell landed near him, he wrote, "enveloping me completely in smoke and dust." Metcalfe suffered a slight wound to the hand, but, unlike most of his men, he remained on the field. As the Confederate fire intensified, more Union soldiers retreated down Big Hill. Sensing an advantage, Scott went all-in. One of his cavalrymen wrote, "Col. Scott, seeing that that the position of Metcalf in a *stand up* fight was too strong for us, ordered a charge and raising a genuine old Rebel yell, the boys started, and that was the last of Metcalf. His command was scattered in every direction; those keeping the road were chased for nine miles or more." The Union line melted away. One account contended that Metcalfe's troops left their commander alone between the two lines, caught in a dangerous crossfire. Metcalfe, however, escaped.[11]

Metcalfe's troopers streamed down Big Hill and took refuge among the wagons at their camp. The unionist Third Tennessee Infantry, which had remained at the site, formed a battle line and momentarily checked the Rebel advance. Metcalfe attempted to rally his men, but most of the Seventh Kentucky fled toward Richmond. Although the Third Tennessee delayed Scott, the Union soldiers were driven from Big Hill. The wagon train fell into Confederate hands, and Scott captured Metcalfe's horses, coat, personal papers, and recent orders. Scott reported that he drove Metcalfe off "in a complete rout toward Richmond." The Confederates suffered 4 men killed and 12 wounded, while Metcalfe lost 17 killed, 32 wounded (6 of whom died of their injuries), and at least 150 men captured. One member of the Seventh Kentucky noted that "many of the members were captured and paroled."[12]

So many of Metcalfe's soldiers fled that Union authorities deployed troops to arrest stragglers. One cavalryman wrote, "The command was utterly confused and routed, falling back on Richmond, Kentucky." Other Federal officers were disgusted with the Seventh Kentucky. Union officer Lew Wallace, who later earned fame writing the novel *Ben-Hur,* reported, "The enemy moved against Colonel Metcalfe yesterday afternoon. The Colonel led his men to attack them on the Big Hill, but they broke and fled, leaving him and his lieutenant-colonel alone on the field. The conduct of Metcalfe's men was most disgraceful." Another officer commented that the Seventh Kentucky, "at the first cannon-shot, turned tail and fled like a pack of cowards, and are now dispersed over a half dozen counties, some fleeing as far as Paris." Other Federal soldiers were equally dismayed. "Metcalfe's cavalry were defeated by the Rebels and skedaddled in the most cowardly manner you ever heard of," Lt. Samuel Reid of the Sixty-sixth Indiana Infantry wrote. Newspapers also shared their ire. One remarked that Metcalfe's regiment, "in spite of the bravery of their leader and some of the other officers, behaved like poltroons." Some nearby residents, who had heard stories about the regiment's lack of discipline, were not surprised. Ann Clay of Bourbon County told her husband, "As usual Metcalfe's men there [fled] in the greatest disorder." Even youth castigated the regiment. Young diarist Mattie Wheeler, who was outside of Lexington on the Richmond Pike, wrote, "Metcalfe went to Big Hill . . . beyond Richmond where the rebels whipped him all to pieces." Later, she "heard some cavalry come dashing in the Richmond pike & I never heard such swearing, just one oath after another, so we knew instantly what was the matter. It was the home guard of Winchester & a part of Metcalfe's men retreating to Winchester. The whole Federal army was completely routed." For Metcalfe, who obviously put great weight upon honor, discipline, and bravery, the behavior of his regiment was a crushing blow. Having defended his honor in the duel with Casto, he was incensed that his leadership was now sullied.[13]

Bull Nelson was also horrified. Diarist Frances Peter of Lexington wrote, "Nelson was furious at the way Metcalf's men behaved & had the straglers arrested wherever found." She said that those rounded up were "made to run round a stump for 24 hours without stopping." While this punishment may have been exaggerated, Nelson, as a former naval officer, surely meted out stiff discipline to those who fled the fight at Big Hill.[14]

Metcalfe, pursued by Scott's cavalry, fell back to Richmond. The Confederate officer, unsure of the number of Federal troops there, stopped and demanded the town's surrender. "In the event of your refusal," Scott wrote, threatening to attack, "I will give you one hour to remove the women and children." Fortunately for Metcalfe, Union reinforcements arrived. The Federals refused to give up the town.[15]

The action at Big Hill set the stage for a larger battle at Richmond. As Union reinforcements poured in, Kirby Smith's army advanced. The veteran Confederate troops drove the inexperienced Federals from three separate defensive positions, rolling over the Union soldiers and driving them through the streets. Nelson arrived just in time to see the Confederate assault overwhelm his men. Shot in the leg, he barely escaped capture. The 6,500 Union soldiers lost 206 killed, 844 wounded, and 4,303 missing, with most of them captured when Scott's cavalry enveloped their rear. The Rebels lost only 78 killed, 372 wounded, and 1 missing. Following this victory, Smith took Lexington and Frankfort, the only pro-Union state capital to fall into Confederate hands during the war.[16]

When the Battle of Richmond began, Metcalfe had reorganized enough of his command to participate in the early stages of the fight. His troopers fought at Bobtown, just outside of Richmond, but his men were again driven off. In the day's action, the Seventh Kentucky lost an additional 5 men killed, 25 wounded, and 238 captured. Only 150 of the regiment escaped, including Metcalfe. As Kenneth A. Hafendorfer writes, "Metcalfe's cavalry had all but disintegrated." Despite this, Brig. Gen. Mahlon Manson, who had commanded the Federal troops before Nelson's arrival, recognized Metcalfe for gallantry. This was, however, little consolation for Casto's slayer. As news spread about the colonel's defeat, Confederate sympathizers in northeastern Kentucky, who had heard Metcalfe bluster about shooting secessionists and confiscating

Rebel civilians' property, were gleeful. Kentucky native and Confederate soldier Edward O. Guerrant rejoiced: "Metcalf the Infamous" had been bested at Richmond, and, Guerrant incorrectly heard, mortally wounded. "Only hope so," he cackled.[17]

Metcalfe was inconsolable. "The brave boys who did their duty were sacrificed through these cowards," he wrote. He was finished with the Seventh Kentucky. One correspondent wrote, "Col. Metcalfe was so disgusted with his regiment, that he refused to have any thing more to do with such a pack of arrant cowards." Lew Wallace added, "The conduct of Metcalfe's men was most disgraceful. He refuses to command them any longer." Metcalfe resigned his commission. William Oden, who had served as Metcalfe's second in the duel and was lieutenant colonel of the Seventh Kentucky, also left. Although Metcalfe unofficially joined the Eighteenth Kentucky Infantry Regiment for a brief period after the Battle of Richmond (a unit in which his other second, Samuel Rogers, had served), Metcalfe did not lead the Seventh Kentucky or any other regiment for the remainder of the war. Instead, he retired to his farm in Nicholas County.[18]

Metcalfe, however, was soon driven from his home. Shortly after Kirby Smith invaded Kentucky, Gen. Braxton Bragg's Army of the Mississippi also entered the state. The two Southern armies spread their troops across the commonwealth. By late September 1862, much of Kentucky was under Rebel control, including communities in Mason County that were occupied by Rebel cavalry.[19]

When the Confederates neared Carlisle, Metcalfe, feeling threatened by the secessionist neighbors he had previously condemned, moved his family to Cincinnati. Living in exile, he was bitter about the Southern invasion of the state and his loss at the Battle of Richmond. Knowing that Rebels were recruiting men across the commonwealth, he unleashed his ire on a familiar, controversial target: slavery. "If there had been no Slavery there would have been no war," he wrote newspapers. "Peace and Slavery will not amalgamate. Kentuckians! Which will you take?" Speaking of his home state, Metcalfe contended, "Now our peace, safety, and happiness, greatly depend upon getting rid of that demoralizing institution." He urged Kentuckians to accept compensated emancipation, a process encouraged by the Lincoln administration, where slave owners would be paid to free their chattel property. Metcalfe understood—as Lincoln issued a preliminary version of the Emancipation Proclamation on September 22—that slavery was caught in a death spiral. Kentuckians should take payment for their enslaved African Americans and strike down the institution to help end the war.[20]

Metcalfe had previously hammered slavery as the cause of the war. Before the Battle of Richmond, for example, he had written a letter to newspapers blaming the conflict on the peculiar institution. He said that the war, just like Southern attempts to annex Cuba, was started "to conquer a balance of power for the negro owner." He wrote, "*If there had been no n——, there had been no war.*" He added that Southerners "have cried n—— and abolitionist ever since I can remember, to carry any point, and the same cry was gotten up this time to create a war. Thirty years ago they attempted to get up a war upon the tariff, but the public pulse would not vibrate to that call. But now they want a war, and all they have to do is cry out 'N—— is in danger,' and just see what a terrible conflict follows. In the face of all this, will any sane man believe the negro had nothing to do with the war?"[21]

After tying the cause of the conflict to slavery and to Southerners who stoked paranoia about slaves, Metcalfe made an appeal for unionism based on white supremacy; as a slave owner, he was no believer in the equality of the races. After writing that whites were killing each other on the battlefield, he asked, "Shall we go on destroying our own race, killing, slaying, devastating; or shall we remove the cause of the war [slavery] and quit this wicked work."[22]

Metcalfe also made a personal appeal. "I was born a slave owner," he wrote, "and am now a slave owner, and have been a pro-Slavery man until I see plainly that my country is in danger from that institution. My country first. I for one am willing to sacrifice my negroes without compensation if it be required that to save my country or to save our own race from destruction, and he that is not willing to make such a sacrifice has no soul, and is not entitled to the privileges of a free and liberal Government." Kentuckians had two choices: slavery or destruction, and he told residents that abandoning slavery would ultimately help the state's economy by freeing future generations from "this everlasting welfare."[23]

In the aftermath of the 1862 Confederate invasion of Kentucky, Metcalfe was also furious that Rebel armies had forced him and his family out of Kentucky. First, his honor was sullied by his regiment's defeat at Big Hill. Now, Southern troops had driven him into exile. He had been an early unionist and was one of the first to heed to call to Federal service. He had been threatened by Rebel neighbors and had literally placed his life on the line to counteract secessionist threats. He had dueled Casto and embraced incredibly unpopular antislavery views to his own detriment. His had been a life of sacrifice for the Union, and now he was forced from home. Metcalfe and his family, he wrote, "have been doomed to exile without a crime; a home, and peace, and happiness have faded from our view; the invader has possession. . . . My wife and innocent children are now fugitives; have fled from home, kindred, and all the dear associations of our native hills." He blamed slavery and slave owners, whom he saw as desperate oligarchs. With an "overbearing and aggressive disposition" that caused an imbalance of power and undue influence in the nation, slave-owning elites had brought the nation to its knees, to turmoil, and to civil war.[24]

Fortunately for Metcalfe and other Kentucky unionists, the 1862 Confederate invasion of Kentucky ended after the Battle of Perryville. Although Bragg and Kirby Smith had pressed toward Louisville and Cincinnati, Union forces moved against them. On October 8, 1862, Bragg's army fought Union soldiers at Perryville, a small village nearly forty-five miles southwest of Lexington. More than 7,500 men were killed and wounded in the five-hour fight. Although the Confederates won a tactical victory, Union reinforcements were close at hand. With destruction eminent if they remained in the area, and with Chattanooga and other important points farther south threatened, the Southern troops returned to Tennessee. Never again did a Confederate army attempt to hold the commonwealth.[25]

While the Rebel retreat surely thrilled Metcalfe, he still had an axe to grind. Although he had spent months judging secessionists and slave owners, he now turned his pen toward other loyalists. In December 1862, he wrote another letter to newspapers that condemned Kentucky unionists for not acting when John Hunt Morgan raided the state in July, and when Kirby Smith and Bragg invaded a month later. Metcalfe wrote that proslavery unionists were too silent and stood idly by as Rebels seized the state. Many politicians, he argued, treated Confederate sympathizers with kid gloves because they sought reelection. Even more sat on the fence and did nothing.[26]

Metcalfe contended that support of slavery caused unionists' inaction. He complained that the state had been devastated by the recent Confederate occupation, yet proslavery unionists did not care, as long as their slaves "come out of this wreck and crash with the shackles safely riveted." Metcalfe, however, was most indignant that unionists did nothing to Southern sympathizers who had aided Confederate soldiers. He had arrested the Maysville secessionists on flimsier evidence, and had risked his life in a duel because of it. He was dumbfounded that when Union officers from Indiana and Ohio were accused of taking Kentucky slaves to free them, complaints came from unionists. Few protested when civilians aided the Confederacy, Metcalfe lamented, yet when a slave was assisted, the condemnation was deafening. He asked, "Which will we perpetuate—Slavery or the Union?" The nation could not have both, he argued, and the fastest way to defeat the Confederacy was to end slavery.[27]

Metcalfe then committed the ultimate sin in Kentucky: he declared that he also supported President Abraham Lincoln. With the president's small support in the state dwindling after he announced the Emancipation Proclamation, Metcalfe was one of the few Bluegrass State Union officers who vocally supported the president. "The name of Lincoln and universal liberty will forever be as closely allied as the name of Christ and Christianity and will go hand in hand to the throne of Grace," he wrote. Most other Kentuckians, however, disagreed.[28]

Metcalfe's derision of slave owners and his support of the Emancipation Proclamation and President Lincoln was too much for his neighbors to bear. The colonel had burned his last bridge in his hometown, county, and state. Before the Civil War ended, he gave up hope of residing in Nicholas County. He lived in Cincinnati for the remainder of the conflict. There, he sold goods with Metcalfe & Evans, a business located at 312 Sycamore Street. Although he had a new home, he returned to Carlisle and other Kentucky communities to give pro-Union and antislavery speeches. He continued to urge others to take up the banner of emancipation. "We must emancipate ourselves from the rule and control of these traitors," he told a friend in April 1864. "The white race has been really for long years cringing and backing down from the unreasonable demands of this slave oligarchy until we had well nigh become serfs to do their bidding but thank god the people are awakening up to a sense of their real situation and to where the thieving institution is leading us." He added, "We have been cheated and deceived in Ky by pretended union men until the people are now wide awake." Metcalfe was also prescient, telling his friend, "Mark my prediction, that in a few years Lincolns emancipation proclamation will be hailed as the advent of a new era, and the great event of the century, and he the great man of the age." Later, Metcalfe again appalled Kentuckians by supporting the policy of enlisting slaves into the Union army, which many residents saw as being comparable to servile insurrection. He marched to the beat of his own drum, and he did so honestly and without fear. After having faced Casto on the dueling ground and Rebel troops at Richmond, everything else was easy.[29]

When the Civil War ended, Metcalfe continued his business pursuits in Cincinnati. Because the political winds shifted in Kentucky after the Civil War and former Confederate soldiers grasped the reins of power across the state, Metcalfe became a pariah. His success in defending his honor by killing Casto faded from the public mind. Although Metcalfe had upheld his reputation in a formal duel, he had embraced the unholy trinity that postwar Kentuckians most despised: Lincoln, emancipation, and the enlistment of African American Union soldiers. These stances condemned Metcalfe to continued exile after the war.

Metcalfe died from heart disease in Cincinnati on June 7, 1868, at forty-nine years of age, and was buried in that city's Spring Grove Cemetery. The slayer of Casto was not eulogized as a hero in his home state. Upon reporting his death, the *Louisville Daily Courier* wrote that Metcalfe, "by his tyranny and outrages during the late war, established for himself a character scarcely less infamous than that enjoyed by Burbridge." Comparing Metcalfe to Maj. Gen. Stephen Burbridge, the corrupt Union commander of Kentucky who had enacted the hated policy of executing four captured Confederates for every unionist killed by pro-Rebel guerrillas, was a dark condemnation. It also spoke volumes about how postwar Kentucky had embraced Confederate ideals. After the war, Burbridge, called "Butcher" because of his execution policy, was the most reviled former Union officer in Kentucky. To link Metcalfe's name with Burbridge showed the animosity Metcalfe had garnered for forcing cash reparations from secessionists and for pushing Lincoln's policies.[30]

Following the conflict, even emblems associated with Metcalfe riled up animosity toward the Union colonel. A Tennessee newspaper reported that after his duel with Casto, Metcalfe "was accordingly hated by the rebels in that section [near Carlisle] most bitterly, and although he died . . . his flag had sufficient [ire] in it to arouse the infernal rebels where-ever it was thrown to the breeze." Even Metcalfe's banner could stir up controversy. Once, the flag of the Seventh Kentucky Cavalry was flown at a postwar political rally in Carlisle. When ex-Confederates saw it, they threatened to burn down the house where it had flown. Furthermore, at least one man was reportedly killed when he attempted to protect the flag. Although Metcalfe had been victorious in his duel with Casto and his side had won the war, he had certainly lost the hearts and minds of Kentuckians.[31]

11

History Is Written in Blood

The principals of the Casto–Metcalfe duel did not live long enough to reflect on their fight with the benefit of the passing of time. While Casto perished on the dueling ground, Metcalfe died a little more than three years after the end of the Civil War. The lives of the other men who were part of that drama or were arrested during Kentucky's secession crisis spun out in a variety of ways. Some died peacefully in their beds after long careers. Others endured tragedy. Several more became embroiled in their own affairs of honor, which showcased how upper-class Kentuckians changed how they applied violence in the years after the Civil War.

The members of the Kentucky legislature who were suspected of going south to join the Confederacy and were arrested in Harrodsburg by zealous Home Guard members continued their legislative careers, albeit briefly. George Silvertooth, the attorney who represented Fulton and Hickman Counties, returned to the General Assembly. In December 1861, however, Silvertooth was expelled from that body for supporting the Confederacy. He promptly took his legislative experience southward, participating in the Russellville Convention—which set up a provisional Confederate government in Kentucky—and casting his lot with the South.[1]

George Ewing from Logan County was another legislator detained in Harrodsburg. Like Silvertooth, Ewing was expelled from the General Assembly in December 1861. Also like Silvertooth, Ewing transferred his political skills to the Confederacy. He later claimed that he was pro-Union, until Tennessee seceded. Since he was born and lived two miles from the Tennessee state line, he believed his fate was tied to the Volunteer State. Thinking secession would eventually envelop Kentucky, he wrote, "I joined my destiny, though very reluctantly, with the South."

Ewing became a Confederate congressman, representing the Bluegrass State. After the war, when he asked President Andrew Johnson for a pardon, he had already taken a Union loyalty oath. Johnson pardoned him, as he did many Confederate high officials and politicians. He returned to Logan County, where he died in May 1888.[2]

Henry Clay's son James B. Clay was among dozens of Kentuckians arrested while traveling south to join the Confederate army. Although he was prominent quarry for unionists, Clay avoided imprisonment. He paid his $10,000 bond and returned home to Lexington. James's Civil War life, however, was anything but peaceful. When Southern troops invaded Kentucky in 1862, Clay saw an opportunity to strike a blow. Confederate authorities authorized him to raise a regiment of Rebel soldiers, but few recruits appeared. When the Confederates retreated from Kentucky after the Battle of Perryville, Clay joined them. Without a military command, sick with consumption, and unable to return home, he eventually settled in Canada, where he died from tuberculosis in January 1864. Clay had known that the end was near. He wrote a friend, "The greatest distress I shall have in parting with the life is on account of my wife & children whom I shall leave in times of such terrible [adversity]." His remains were sent to Lexington for burial. Historian Lindsey Apple, who chronicled the Clay family history, writes, "The family believed the harsh treatment James Clay received while a prisoner contributed to the rapid onset of tuberculosis." At the time of his death, James was only forty-six years old.[3]

Former governor Charles Morehead, who had been arrested in Louisville with Reuben Durrett and Martin Barr and ultimately imprisoned at Fort Lafayette, was another high-profile prisoner who ended up north of the border. Confined for four months, upon his release Morehead fled to Mexico, Europe, and eventually Canada. In June 1862, he told his friend US Senator John J. Crittenden, "I am a fugitive slave safely landed in Canada." Morehead left the nation for economic reasons. After his release, he was told that he would likely again face arrest unless he took the Union oath of allegiance. Fearful that Confederate authorities would confiscate his Mississippi plantation if he swore fealty to the Federal government, Morehead remained in Canada until the end of the war. After the conflict, he headed south and lived on his Mississippi plantation. Although Morehead managed to keep his Mississippi land, the slaves who once worked the cotton fields were gone. The former governor died on December 21, 1868, and was buried in Frankfort, Kentucky.[4]

Martin W. Barr, the telegrapher who was arrested with Morehead and Durrett and ceaselessly tried to negotiate for his freedom, was also released from Fort Lafayette. Instead of heading north of the border, as Clay and Morehead did, Barr went south. He joined the Confederate army and rose to the rank of major. According to his obituary, upon reaching Rebel lines Barr was immediately employed as a telegrapher, with "his duties being to intercept the news of the northern army." After the war, Barr worked as a telegrapher for the Associated Press. Posted in Washington, DC, he eventually took a job "as proof-reader in the Government printing office." Called "a man of gentle nature and . . . highly esteemed by those who knew him," he died in Washington in May 1911, at age eighty-four.[5]

Newspaper editor Reuben Durrett, who had exchanged gunfire with rival editor George Prentice before the war and was locked in Fort Lafayette with Governor Morehead, eventually became a renowned author and collector. Having an avid interest in Kentucky history, Durrett was one of the founders of what is now Louisville's Filson Historical Society, which met at his home for a time. Durrett's research interests attracted wide attention. When Theodore Roosevelt was writing *The Winning of the West,* he stayed with Durrett and took advantage of the Kentuckian's massive research library and manuscript collection. The publisher of the *National Cyclopedia of American Biography* even asked Durrett, recognized as an authority on Bluegrass State history, to contribute a biography of Prentice to the series. That editor, based in New York, likely did not know about Durrett's scrape with a rival editor. Called "one of Louisville's most honored citizens," Durrett was actively involved in several businesses and community development efforts. He served as the president of the Children's Free Hospital and the Episcopal Orphans' Home and was a director on several bank boards and utility companies and helped bring natural gas to Louisville. After the Civil War, Durrett practiced law, wrote several historical pamphlets, and at the time of his death was called "one of the most learned men in Louisville." Durrett had a stroke on July 10, 1912. As his health declined, he sold his massive collection of rare books and manuscripts to the University of Chicago. He died on September 16, 1913.[6]

Andrew Jackson Morey, the editor of the *Cynthiana News,* served time with Casto at Camp Chase before recanting his secessionist views. Before Morey returned home, however, his wife died. Thus, the editor rejected his Union oath of allegiance. He headed south, where he edited pro-Confederate newspapers. After the Civil War, he returned to Kentucky and again published and edited the *Cynthiana News.* The war only sharpened his critical eye and harsh editorial pen; he spent much of his time refighting the conflict. His articles condemned heavy-handed Union officials who had led Kentucky during the war, and this editorial stance nearly got him killed. One episode involving Morey is emblematic of how bitterness from the Civil War, coupled with Kentucky's propensity for postwar pistol-toting and violence, could be explosive. In November 1867, after writing an editorial critical of the Union's Maj. Gen. Stephen Burbridge, Morey and Burbridge's brother had a shootout on the streets of Covington, Kentucky. Though Burbridge's brother shot Morey in the arm, the editor continued to write blistering attacks on Bluegrass State unionists.[7]

Morey continued in journalism until 1885, when he reported that he was selling the newspaper to practice law. A year later, he retired. In 1896, he ran for congress as a Free Silver Democrat but lost the election. Morey died in November 1907 at age eighty "after a lingering illness from paralysis." Another one of Casto's prison mates had passed on.[8]

While Morey was shot in a violent episode after the Civil War, most of the men arrested with Casto—Richard Stanton, George Forrester, James Hall, B. F. Thomas, Isaac Nelson, and William Hunt—lived quiet lives after the conflict. Several, however, endured great tragedy.

Richard M. Stanton, whom William "Bull" Nelson had called "the soul of the rebellion" in the Maysville area, returned to that town after his release from Fort Lafayette. Nelson had also called Stanton "a man of wonderful intellectual energy," and this assessment held true after the war, as Stanton continued his career in law and politics. In 1867, Stanton was nearly nominated to run for governor of Kentucky. He did not, however, get the call. Despite his incarceration, or, perhaps, thanks to it in postwar, pro-Confederate Kentucky, Stanton served as a circuit court judge for six years. From 1874 until 1885, he practiced law in Maysville and contributed to multiple legal books. He died in Maysville on March 20, 1891.[9]

George Forrester, the editor of the *Maysville Express* who was also arrested with Casto, took the Union oath of allegiance and was released. Instead of returning home, Forrester fled south and became a Confederate officer in John Hunt Morgan's cavalry. Forrester survived the Civil War, despite his having received at least one severe wound. He surrendered at Augusta, Georgia, in May 1865. Federal authorities appeared to have ignored the fact that Forrester disobeyed his oath. With the war over and the nation in shambles, the Federal government was contending with more pressing issues. After Forrester surrendered, he settled in Alabama, where he was a planter for three years. In 1868, he moved to Chicago and worked in sales. Active in veterans' affairs, he was the first commander of a United Confederate Veterans camp in Chicago and served on several Confederate monument commissions. He died in November 1913.[10]

Another one of the arrested Maysville citizens, the plow-maker James H. Hall, continued his business after the Civil War. He ran the James H. Hall Plow Company, later called the Eagle Plow Works, and became "one of Maysville's most substantial and widely-known citizens." His plows, manufactured under the names the Limestone, the Star, the Champion, the Cotton, the Copper, the Lone Star, and more, were sold across the United States and in Central and South America. At the time of his death in February 1886, his company was an expansive, influential business. His funeral in Maysville was reputedly one of the largest ever seen in the city's history.[11]

William Hunt was released from Fort Lafayette after taking a Union oath of allegiance. During the war, his family had another, more tragic encounter with military justice. In 1860, William's son Thomas was a seventeen-year-old who worked for his father making cigars. Thomas studied law, and by the midpoint of the Civil War, he had become a young attorney, practicing in Maysville. At age twenty, Thomas joined the Confederate army. When he was traveling south to enlist, Union authorities captured and imprisoned him in Lexington. Although Thomas never fought for the Confederacy, he and three other men were executed in Frankfort in retaliation for the murder of a Union civilian who had been killed by pro-Confederate guerrillas. This episode overshadowed William's brief confinement in Union prisons. His obituary stated: "This awful fate of his child saddened the rest of his life." He died on January 15, 1892, and was buried in Maysville.[12]

Just as the men who were arrested with Casto resumed their lives, so did the friends of the antagonists who acted as negotiators or seconds during the duel. Some even participated in their own violent confrontations. Isaac Nelson and Thomas Respess, who served as Casto's seconds, lived quietly after the duel. In his later years, Nelson lived in Cincinnati with his daughter. In 1892, at age sixty-six, he fell at her home and shattered his hip. He died "after several days of great pain and suffering."[13]

Respess continued his legal career and became known for his remarkable knowledge of the law. Voters elected him as the Mason County Circuit Court Clerk, a position he held for nearly twenty years. He also served as treasurer and receiver of the Mason County court. Respess lived into his nineties and was one of the last living witnesses of the Casto–Metcalfe duel. He died in March 1919 at age ninety-three and was buried in Maysville. Upon his death, his obituary noted, thus "removes the last man in any way connected with this famous battle."[14]

While Nelson, Respess, and Oden lived peacefully after the Civil War, Metcalfe's second Samuel G. Rogers had a harder path. When he pled guilty in the Bracken County court to acting as Metcalfe's second, he also could have faced a court martial for helping the Union colonel duel. Instead, Rogers's military career continued. Federal authorities, it seemed, cared little that a secessionist had been slain in an illegal duel. After the war, however, Rogers's life took an ominous turn.[15]

On September 27, 1883, Rogers and his son Samuel Rogers Jr. met Rogers's brothers, Thomas and William, at their family farm in Robertson County. This was not a friendly reunion. Samuel and his brothers, all "daring and desperate men," had been at odds over the family estate since their father's death. The men argued and Samuel Jr. pulled a pistol and shot Thomas in the left arm and head, killing him. Rogers and his son then shot William three times, once in the abdomen and twice in the right thigh. William eventually died from the wounds. Samuel Rogers Sr., reputedly armed with two pistols, fired at least ten shots during the fray. A jury later acquitted father and son of murder.[16]

After killing his brothers, Samuel Rogers returned to farming. Ambushing his siblings, however, was not his only violent act after the Civil War. The *Maysville Daily Evening Bulletin,* which reported, "Sam is dead game, cool and self possessed," noted, "He has engaged in several fights and shooting scrapes in his time." This included a fight with a man named Dick Brewer near the Blue Licks battlefield. In 1894, another of his sons, Willis, got involved in legal trouble after shooting a town marshal in Arkansas. In February 1900, poor health necessitated that Samuel Rogers have his leg amputated below the knee. He died shortly thereafter. With his demise, the seconds from the Casto–Metcalfe duel were gone.[17]

While Rogers gunned down his brothers, Thomas M. Green, who had negotiated the terms of the duel for Metcalfe but had refused to serve as second, had his own violent encounter. As evidenced by his artful correspondence, negotiation, and strict adherence to the rules during the Casto–Metcalfe affair, Green was an expert in the code duello. After the Civil War, however, the code and formal duels fell out of favor in Kentucky. Many Kentucky gentlemen now handled their differences immediately with concealed pistols or knives. In 1871, this shocked one Kentucky judge who said "nearly every case of murder or manslaughter" was due "to the pernicious practice of carrying concealed weapons."[18]

Historian Dickson D. Bruce writes that the breakdown of the region's class structure helped take down dueling: "After the Civil War, the hierarchical, carefully ordered world of the Old South lost its strength, and the basic concerns upon which that world had been based no longer had much power to organize life in the region. Despite sporadic attempts to revive dueling, the practice itself died, for all intents and purposes, as antebellum concerns came to seem increasingly irrelevant." Bruce adds that as Kentucky wrestled with upper-class violence after the Civil War, "conflicts between prominent men" also occurred "in all the major Southern cities."[19]

The Civil War did not end violence. Instead, as class lines blurred, it deregulated it among elites. Instead of dueling, these men, like those of the lesser classes, took violent action to the streets. As Dick Steward explains, "the democratization of violence had begun in earnest. By the Civil War and Reconstruction eras, even fewer individual social restraints were in place to curb the destructive and nihilistic forces of vengeance. The duel had kindled the spirit of vengeance, and the killing cult continued unabated long after its demise." Green was among those who embraced public, sporadic violence after the war. Despite his expertise in the code duello, when slighted, he, too, fought his own bloody street skirmish. Green's postwar story is emblematic of how after the Civil

War some upper-class Kentuckians discarded the code duello in favor of direct, violent action.[20]

By the mid-1880s, Green was an influential and prominent citizen, known for his political activism and writing. In modern parlance, he was a public intellectual, a frequent speaker, a prolific writer, respected historian, and commenter on current affairs. In 1866, Green unsuccessfully ran for the US Congress. Despite his failed run, two years later the *Louisville Daily Journal* called him "a very accomplished scholar, an able writer, an eloquent and effective speaker, a patriot without the shadow of suspicion, and a man without fear and without reproach, his influence is great." Another correspondent wrote, "Thomas M. Green is known by reputation at least all over Kentucky." Green wrote several books and by 1887 had become a correspondent for the *Cincinnati Commercial Gazette.* It was this role that tossed the erudite fifty-four-year-old Kentuckian into the world of quick, public violence for which the state was becoming known.[21]

In the fall of 1887, Green wrote an article hinting that Lew Baldwin, a circuit county clerk in Jessamine County, had been involved with election fraud. After exchanging angry letters, on November 16, the two men ran into each other outside of the Phoenix Hotel in Lexington. Baldwin called Green "a liar, a coward, a thief, and a son of a bitch." Green turned and walked away, saying, "Oh, you can curse me as much as you please, or say what you please to me. You are a blackguard and I cannot notice you." He dismissed Baldwin as an insignificant, lower-class bother, which infuriated Baldwin even more. Baldwin drew his revolver; when Green saw the weapon, he rushed forward and grabbed his antagonist by the pistol arm. Baldwin broke free and struck Green in the head several times with his pistol. Green staggered back. As he stumbled nearly ten feet away from Baldwin, he drew his own gun. In the shootout that followed, a bystander was shot twice in the arm, Green was slightly wounded, and Baldwin lay dead, shot in the heart. Green, who had advised Metcalfe prior to the duel with Casto, now had his own victim. Twenty years earlier, the feud with Baldwin likely would have ended with the code duello and a formal duel. Times, however, had changed.[22]

Although Green escaped prosecution for advising Metcalfe in 1862, he was arrested after killing Baldwin. Within a few weeks, he went to trial. Interest in the case was widespread, with one reporter noting that the courtroom was "literally jammed" with spectators. Many were from Maysville, where Green had lived, and others hailed from Nicholasville, Baldwin's hometown. The jury acquitted Green by reason of self-defense, a typical verdict when educated white Kentuckians with means were tried for killing antagonists in street fights in the years after the Civil War. Since 1872, Green had been living in Danville, the home of his alma mater Centre College. He died of diabetes on April 7, 1904, and was buried there. He was sixty-seven years old.[23]

Many of the men involved with the Casto–Metcalfe duel and the 1861 arrests met with tragedy. This is unsurprising; the Bluegrass State was a violent place after the Civil War, and the men's fates reflect Kentucky's postbellum culture. Although the war wiped out the code duello, these Kentuckians continued to embrace violence as a means of conflict resolution. In some cases, as in the shootout between Morey and Burbridge's brother, wartime animosities led to postwar violence. In other instances, including the fight between Green and Baldwin, concealed weapons settled more recent grudges. Many members of the elite who engaged in violence after the Civil War were either acquitted for their brutal acts, as Green was, or were never prosecuted, as Samuel Rogers. Hair-trigger reactions to slights of honor caused much of this upper-class violence after the war, and these responses were typically spontaneous. However, after the Civil War one more noted duel fought in Kentucky followed the code duello. In this final instance, two men settled their antebellum hatred on a commonly used dueling ground.

12

Two Young Bloods

More than seven hundred thousand Union and Confederate soldiers died during the American Civil War. With this much bloodshed, the taste for slaughter had surely grown bitter in most Americans' mouths. Kentucky, which experienced pitched battles and extended irregular warfare, had roughly thirty thousand men fight for the South and seventy-five thousand for the North. After the war, with the state contending with innumerable concerns, upper-class Kentuckians no longer fought formal duels. The war had driven the code duello to obscurity.

In fact, as historian Jack K. Williams writes, dueling waned across the entire South after 1860. Williams argues that a decline in the planter class's political power, together with increased transportation leading to less isolation, a greater exchange of ideas, and a "spreading democratism" that called for equal treatment under the law among gentlemen and common citizens alike, led to fewer duels. As the children of wartime southern gentlemen reached maturity, a generational shift also helped end the practice. Williams writes that for this new generation of southerners, dueling "seemed of little practical value if not outright archaic." Furthermore, the Civil War ushered in societal changes. Williams explains that "social status no longer served as an excuse for breach of the law" and that the war ended "romanticized chivalry" that had formalized violence. Richard Hamm adds that dueling also went extinct because "prominent politicians and newspaper editors . . . refused to duel." For these reasons, and because of war-weariness, Casto's duel with Metcalfe should have been the last fought in Kentucky. However, the code duello was used at least one more time, for honor culture and blueblood touchiness were far from extinct in the Bluegrass State. While formalized dueling was essentially extinguished, violence caused by Kentucky's brand of honor culture lasted for at least another generation. As Richard F. Hamm writes, "honor survived the Civil War."[1]

In 1866, roughly a year after the end of the conflict, another formal duel was fought in Scott County, Kentucky. Although Bluegrass State soldiers had returned home and traded their cavalry saddles for harnesses and their muskets for plows, Kentucky's honor culture remained intact and sparked another formal affair between combat veterans. These antagonists fired their pistols in one of the last formal duels fought in Kentucky; thus, it is important to examine this action, as it reveals how the practice ended. Afterward, violence in the commonwealth became spontaneous and unregulated, even among those who held power.[2]

On the surface, one would assume that a duel fought between a former Union soldier and an ex-Confederate was caused by wartime animosity. The origins of the feud, however, were antebellum. Regardless, the idea of Blue and Gray veterans taking final shots at each another captivated Kentuckians and, in central Kentucky at least, overshadowed the Casto–Metcalfe affair. Joseph Desha and Alexander Kimbrough, "two young bloods of Cynthiana," kept the code duello sputtering one last time.[3]

Like Metcalfe, Joseph Desha had a pedigree steeped in the Bluegrass aristocracy. His grandfather had served as governor of Kentucky, and Metcalfe's father had followed Desha's grandfather into the governor's chair. Governor Desha's family was another prominent Kentucky clan that became entangled in violence and controversy. In 1824, the governor's son Isaac Desha (Joseph's Maysville-born uncle) robbed a man, stabbing and beating him to death in the process. A jury sentenced Isaac, found with the victim's horse and bloodstained property, to hang. Governor Desha, however, pardoned his son, which infuriated Kentuckians. The incident did, however, get Louisville residents talking about the dangers of concealed weapons. At one public meeting, a journal noted, residents condemned the practice and asked for legislative support. They hoped the murder could "be the means of opening the eyes of the people to the barbarity of the practice of carrying about with them weapons of death, and thus familiarizing to their minds the work of murder, some good may result from a deed of the most horrible character." No good came of the murder, however; Kentuckians continued to carry knives and pistols, and Isaac Desha later killed another man in Texas.[4]

In 1866, the thirty-two-year-old Joseph Desha and the twenty-seven-year-old Alexander Kimbrough were both veterans of the American Civil

War. Desha had been a major in the Confederate army while Kimbrough had served as a sergeant for the Union. Both men were reared in Harrison County, but this common upbringing did little to temper their enmity. While their mutual animosity had its roots in their school years, the specific cause of their bitterness remains lost to history. Warren Smith, who witnessed the duel, simply said, "They attended school together when boys, but were never fond of each other." The war, and honor culture, twisted this antipathy into something much more deadly.[5]

Desha, born in Harrison County on May 22, 1833, was the grandson of his namesake, who had ridden his War of 1812 experiences into the governor's mansion, a building Metcalfe's mason father had helped build. Just as Metcalfe had been born at Forest Retreat, his father's home, Desha was born on family property just north of Cynthiana. Like Metcalfe, Desha was the descendant of a Kentucky governor who embraced Southern honor culture and respected the code duello.[6]

Jo Desha attended local schools (where he presumably tangled with Kimbrough) before studying at the Kentucky Military Institute and the University of Virginia. In 1860, Jo worked as the surveyor of Harrison County. When the Civil War erupted a year later, he raised a company of Confederate troops and joined the First Kentucky Infantry Regiment. He fought with that unit in Virginia as a company commander and was wounded at Dranesville. When Desha's term of enlistment expired, he briefly joined John Hunt Morgan's cavalry. Preferring the infantry over cavalry service, he left Morgan's command and in 1862 raised another infantry company, which became Company I of the Ninth Kentucky Infantry. His brother Ben was also a Confederate officer, and both served with distinction in the Orphan Brigade, Kentucky's most famous Rebel infantry unit. Secession fever evidently ran in the family. Desha's father, Lucius, was a prominent Kentucky legislator and secessionist who was arrested by Federal authorities in July 1862. Like Casto, Lucius was temporarily confined at Camp Chase.[7]

Jo Desha's dedication to the cause showed itself at the Battle of Stones River, at Murfreesboro, Tennessee. When Desha was clipped in the head by a cannonball, his troops thought he was dead. Johnny Green, a soldier in the unit, wrote, "A cannon ball passed through our earth works, struck him on the head & tore a great gash in his scalp. He was carried to the rear for burrial but by the time the ambulance driver had gotten there & called for some one to help him lift out the dead body the Captain sat up & told them to bring the Surgeon." One Orphan Brigade doctor later commented, "Desha was brought to my ambulance corps like a dead man from a shell wound." Despite this injury, Desha returned to his unit that night. About ten months later, while fighting with the Fifth Kentucky Infantry Regiment, Desha was seriously wounded in the arm at the Battle of Chickamauga. Again, despite the injury, the officer stayed with his unit and finished the battle. Toward the end of the war, he suffered another wound, at Dallas, Georgia. There, his left arm was "badly shattered." It never fully healed, disabling him from further service. After the war, he could hardly use his left arm.[8]

Desha ended the conflict as a well-respected Rebel officer. One writer contended that he was "noted for his dauntless courage while serving in the Southern army." Desha's service was further recognized when he visited Richmond in February 1864. There, President Jefferson Davis reputedly presented the officer with a pistol. When the war ended, Desha was seen as "an unusual man and a splendid example of the typical Kentucky gentleman." Kimbrough would find that a "typical Kentucky gentleman" was more than willing to defend his honor on the dueling ground. In a letter he wrote from Virginia early in the war, Desha admonished his brothers to "fear no man." He took this maxim to heart.[9]

Although Desha and Kimbrough were both "young bloods of Cynthiana," Kimbrough's blood was only slightly less blue than Desha's. Born on January 21, 1839, in Harrison County, Kimbrough was the son of John and Susan Jones Kimbrough. Before the Civil War, John had been a well-to-do farmer, with $20,000 in real estate and $8,700 in personal property. In 1860, the twenty-one-year-old Alexander Kimbrough helped his father as a farmhand, aided by his father's seven enslaved African Americans. Kimbrough may not have been descended from a governor, but the family was exceedingly well off.[10]

On August 16, 1861, Kimbrough enlisted in the Fourth Kentucky (Union) Infantry Regiment at Cynthiana. Five months later, the regiment fought with distinction at the Battle of Mill Springs, Kentucky. Kimbrough mustered into service at Camp Dick Robinson and became sergeant of Company K. Like Desha, he was severely wounded at the September 1863 Battle of Chickamauga. Kimbrough's right leg was badly fractured, and he spent weeks recovering in hospitals in Louisville and Lexington. He was finally discharged for disability on December 6, 1864. Thus, the two young bloods returned home from the war physically broken. The idea of these two men fighting a formal duel after enduring such horrors on the battlefield is absurd, yet honor culture prevailed.[11]

In February 1866, Desha and Basil Duke, a former Confederate general who was also the late John Hunt Morgan's brother-in-law, were socializing at a hotel in Cynthiana. The front door swung open, and Kimbrough walked in, limping on his battered leg. Desha eyed his antagonist but was determined to forget past grievances. Warren Smith, a friend of Desha's, later recalled, "Desha told me that during the war he felt that it was time to forget past annoyances and as he and . . . Kimbrough had never had serious trouble with each other he formed the resolution, if both should come home again, he would meet . . . Kimbrough half way." The war was over, and, although the two men had fought on opposite sides, Desha was determined to make peace.[12]

Desha stood, approached Kimbrough, and extended his right hand. The former Union sergeant, unbound to reconciliation, glared. "How dare you offer to shake hands with me, you scoundrel!" Kimbrough said. Desha would no longer bury the hatchet. Instead, he would use a chair: he picked one up and smashed it over Kimbrough, who fell to the floor. The two disabled veterans then started brawling, their shouts filling the hotel. Several men stepped in to break up the fight, but Basil Duke, sitting a few feet away, pulled a revolver from under his coat and waved the peacemakers away. "They are equally matched," he said, "and let them have it out." Despite Desha's injured left arm, he won the brawl, but his right hand was injured in the fray. Considering he had pummeled Kimbrough with a chair, it is not surprising that the former Confederate came away the victor. The two bloodied and bruised veterans then went their separate ways. The conflict, however, was far from over.[13]

The next day, Kimbrough sent Desha a challenge note, delivered by his friend Maj. William Long of Covington, Kentucky. Desha immediately accepted the offer to duel. He chose the traditional weapons and distance: pistols at ten paces. The code duello called for the fight to be completely fair; because Desha's hand had been badly sprained in the brawl, the duel was delayed until sunrise on March 26. "Even at this time he could use his hand very little," Warren Smith said. "He hardly had strength in his finger to pull a trigger."[14]

While Casto and Metcalfe each had two seconds, Desha and Kimbrough were more streamlined in their adherence to the code duello. They each had only one second. Major Long, a former Union officer, served Kimbrough. Desha had first asked Basil Duke to be his second, but Duke declined, citing an illness that had overcome his wife. Duke, a Rebel general who was under the watchful eye of federal authorities, likely wanted to avoid a legal entanglement. Desha then asked his cousin Hervey McDowell, a physician and former Confederate lieutenant colonel, to serve. McDowell was related to Ephraim McDowell, Kentucky's most famous surgeon, who in 1809 performed the world's first successful ovariotomy. Hervey was born near Lexington on April 15, 1835, and graduated from the Kentucky Military Institute and the St. Louis Medical College. He practiced medicine in Cynthiana immediately before the Civil War and raised what became Company F of the Second Kentucky (Confederate) Infantry. Severely wounded at Fort Donelson, he was captured and imprisoned at Camp Chase and Johnson's Island. Exchanged, he returned to his regiment and fought in most of the major battles of the western theater, from Stones River, where he was "shot through both arms, and wounded in three other places," to Chickamauga and the battles of the Atlanta Campaign, where he was wounded a seventh time at Resaca. After the war, Hervey practiced medicine in Cynthiana. Thomas Marshall Green, who included McDowell in his book *Historic Families of Kentucky*, wrote, "In prison, in camp, on the march, in the hottest fights of the bloody war; in victory and in defeat; always uncomplaining, calm, energetic and daring, he exhibited the best qualities of a soldier." While only one surgeon attended the Casto–Metcalfe duel, Kimbrough and Desha also brought their own physicians to the field, in addition to Hervey McDowell. W. B. Kean of Georgetown represented Kimbrough, while Desha's surgeon was John Burk of Lexington. Unlike the Casto–Metcalfe affair, no crowd gathered. Instead, only a handful of witnesses attended, including Warren K. Smith, who lived near the dueling ground; Desha's uncle John Desha; and two other men, George Spake and George W. Downing of Georgetown.[15]

Although Duke did not participate in the duel, he suggested the fight's location. Duke recommended his childhood home, the farm of James K. Duke, five miles southeast of Georgetown, on the Fayette County–Scott County line. Because of that location, it was difficult for authorities to determine a prosecutorial jurisdiction if a duel was fought there. Therefore, J. Winston Coleman contended, the Duke farm was "the favorite dueling ground of central Kentucky." The place had witnessed several affairs of honor. In August 1818, the Dudley–Richardson duel, in which one doctor shot another before saving his wounded opponent's life, was fought there. Nearly a decade later, in 1829, George Trotter killed Charles Wickliffe on the farm while fighting with pistols at eight feet. On September 6, 1848, William O. Smith and Thomas H. Holt fought there. And, on October 5, 1852, two students from Transylvania University in Lexington fought a duel on the farm with shotguns, loaded with slugs, at forty yards. In that episode, Benjamin Thompson killed Thomas White at the first fire, shooting him through the head. These hotheaded and honor-bound Kentuckians had made the Duke property a dark and bloody ground.[16]

When rumors about the duel spread, newspapers wrongly stated that the antagonists were each to be armed with a pistol and a "six pound bowie knife." The report contended that the men were to stand ten paces apart, fire, and then advance to finish "the struggle by a hand to hand encounter with the cleavers." While this would have been a personal, brutal way to end their hatred, this was inaccurate. Instead, Desha and Kimbrough followed the recommendations John Lyde Wilson set forth in *Code of Honor:* pistols at ten paces. Moreover, adding historical flair to the episode, the firearms to be used were a set of dueling pistols owned by Henry Clay, which the "Great Compromiser" had reputedly used in his fight with John Randolph. The large caliber, smoothbore weapons had flintlock firing mechanisms that had been converted to percussion cap. Made in Sheffield, England, then noted for its steel foundries and knife-making, they were "finely finished and silver mounted." The duelists' seriousness was further shown by the fact that each brought an extra set of pistols in case the Clay relics did not operate correctly.[17]

On the morning of the duel, the antagonists, their seconds, surgeons, and witnesses met at the Duke farm. The seconds tossed a silver coin to determine where each man would stand while shooting. McDowell, Desha's second, won the toss. They also flipped a coin to see who would give the call to fire. McDowell also won that honor. One witness said that after the duelists lined up, they "stood in their positions with the utmost composure, pistols in hand, body erect, and ready to receive the other's fire."[18]

McDowell asked the men if they were ready. Each gave his assent, and McDowell called them to fire. Clay's dueling pistols operated flawlessly, and black powder smoke ringed the men as they pulled the triggers. Both shooters, however, missed. The seconds asked if honor had been satisfied. Both men said no, they wanted to continue. Clay's pistols were reloaded and handed back to the antagonists. McDowell again gave the call to fire.[19]

Before the second pistol shots cracked across Duke's pasture, Kimbrough's bullet passed through Desha's coat pocket. Desha then pulled the trigger. His aim was true, and Kimbrough dropped like a stone, falling face forward to the ground. The bullet had struck Kimbrough just below the hip, passed through his body, and exited near his other hip. It was a dangerous wound. The former Union sergeant, who had endured a debilitating leg wound during the Civil War, was in agony.[20]

With Kimbrough writhing on the ground, Desha and his party departed, leaving Kimbrough's friends to take care of the wounded duelist. Kean attended to the injured man, who was taken to the home of former governor James F. Robinson in Georgetown. Kimbrough survived, and after being bedridden for nearly six weeks (at the governor's home and then at his father's house), he began to walk with a cane. Kimbrough had, however, a permanent reminder of the duel. The limp from his Civil War wound was accentuated for the rest of his life.[21]

Several years after the fight, the disabled Kimbrough sought a pension from the federal government for his wartime service in the Union army. In his pension application he wrote, "I was shot by a pistol in the hands of ex-Captain De Shay of the Rebel army. The wound was very serious and cripples me now so I can not walk in plowed ground, but very little. It hurt my spine and hips." According to Kimbrough, the duel was not fought because of antebellum antagonism. Instead, it "was caused by ill feeling of war times and I could not well have avoided it." While prewar arguments may have kindled the duel, Kimbrough's refusal to shake Desha's hand sparked it. Although Desha and Kimbrough had fought on opposite sides during the war, the duelists' shared concept of honor ultimately drove them to Duke's farm.[22]

After the duel, Kimbrough moved west. While it is unknown whether he left Kentucky because of the fight, he may have done so to avoid prosecution. By the fall of 1869, he lived in Texas and later moved to Phoenix, Arizona, where he remained for twenty-seven years.

Disabled from his wartime wounds and the injury caused by the duel, he spent the rest of his life moving from one disabled soldiers' home to another. By 1910, he was in Malibu, California, at the Pacific Branch National Home for Disabled Volunteer Soldiers. He died in Leavenworth, Kansas, on August 22, 1921. His body was sent home for burial in Cynthiana's Battle Grove Cemetery. He was eighty-five years old.[23]

The duel sent Desha and McDowell into exile. To elude prosecution, immediately after the fight, both men slipped away to Canada, where they remained for nearly ten years. Finally, on January 28, 1875, Kentucky governor James B. McCreary, a former Confederate officer who likely knew both men, pardoned them. Upon Desha's return to the state, he was a farmer in Harrison County and earned some renown raising thoroughbred horses. He died of pneumonia on May 8, 1902. Like Kimbrough, he was interred at Battle Grove Cemetery. He was eighty-eight years old. Later, a local chapter of the United Daughters of the Confederacy and a commandery of the United Confederate Veterans were named in his honor. Warren Smith wrote, "Desha was never proud of the notoriety the fighting of that duel occasioned."[24]

The duel, fought in March 1866, was among the last affairs of honor fought in Kentucky under the formalities of the code duello. It illustrates that, despite the ravages of the Civil War, Southern honor culture still held sway over many elite white male Kentuckians. The conflict may have been over, and some Kentuckians may have returned from the war broken, but Desha and Kimbrough and others like them still had a propensity to fight when their honor had been maligned. Still, code duello was in decline. In forthcoming years, Kentuckians rejected honor-bound formalities and used concealed weapons and impulsive violence. And, instead of fleeing to Canada to avoid justice, men who engaged in honor-bound killings were often acquitted on claims of self-defense.

Leonidas Metcalfe, Casto's slayer, was alive when Desha and Kimbrough dueled. One wonders whether newspaper articles about Kimbrough falling face down in the mud with a bullet through his hips stirred in Metcalfe feelings of regret for killing Casto. It is doubtful. As he sat by the fire in his home in Cincinnati, in self-imposed exile, away from his home state, he likely set his jaw, frowned, and threw the newspaper in the fire before stoking the flames.[25]

Conclusion

In 1892, thirty years after Metcalfe killed Casto, the *Maysville Daily Public Ledger* reported that someone had loaned the publication photographs of the two duelists. It displayed the images at its office so "the curiously inclined can see pictures of both." Within a month, a rival newspaper wrote that the Maysville Public Library had displayed several historical paintings, including portraits of Casto and Metcalfe. Although three decades had passed since the affair, the duel between the Union colonel and the secessionist civilian still held public interest.[1]

That notice stirred more memories about the duel. Soon, relics related to the fight were pulled out of closets and drawers. After running the piece, the *Daily Public Ledger* reported that its staff was "allowed to examine the right hand glove that Col. Metcalfe wore in his duel with W. F. Casto on the fishing shore just below town. It was made of buckskin of the gauntlet pattern, and shows a wonderful state of preservation to be 30 years old." Today, one of the gloves Casto wore during the duel is in the collection of the Gateway Museum Center in Maysville.[2]

The Colt Repeating rifles used in the duel were also displayed in the area. In the 1960s, the Civil War centennial brought a resurgence of local interest in the duel, and the rifles were exhibited at Blue Licks State Park, a Revolutionary War battlefield south of Maysville. Unfortunately, later that decade, both weapons were stolen from the park museum and have not been seen since. Thus, the two most important artifacts from this duel are lost.[3]

Like those rifles, the importance of what the Casto–Metcalfe duel represents has been lost over time. However, deconstructed and contextualized, the duel is emblematic of an important broader narrative.

First, the duel shows that Civil War violence went beyond the battlefield. It saturated Kentucky society. Casto and Metcalfe, surrounded by the bloodshed of the war and shrouded by the state's Southern honor culture, were willing to kill each other to preserve their reputations. Violence, as historian James C. Klotter notes, was embedded in the timeline of Kentucky history and permeated its culture. The duel at the Fishing Shore was another black mark in the account book of Bluegrass State violence.

Second, the duel had its roots in the secession crisis and explains how political and military policies could lead to bloodshed. When Casto was arrested in the fall of 1861, Union authorities were determined to remove secessionists from critical Kentucky communities. Maysville, a vital location on the Ohio River with roads and rail lines stretching into central Kentucky, was an important location for offloading troops and military supplies, including William "Bull" Nelson's "Lincoln guns." Maysville was also an important strategic point for controlling northeastern Kentucky. By sending men like Casto and Stanton out of state before beginning the Union military campaign into the Big Sandy Valley of Eastern Kentucky, Federal authorities removed potential trouble from behind their lines. Furthermore, unionists' ability to arrest and exile prominent Kentuckians, like former governor Charles Morehead and Henry Clay's son, showed secessionists that no one was safe from unionist control. An unforeseen consequence of those arrests was Casto's challenge to Metcalfe.

The events surrounding the Casto–Metcalfe duel also detail the enmity caused by the unionist arrests made during the fall of 1861. His honor bruised from his confinement, the stubborn Casto, the only Maysville prisoner to not take the oath of allegiance, set his mind on revenge. Metcalfe, a hated, visible unionist in the region, became his ready target. Further, not only was Metcalfe advocating unionism, he also called for the exile or death of local secessionists. Even more extreme to Kentuckians, he blamed slavery and slave owners for causing the war. Metcalfe refused to be "browbeaten" by these men, and the duel and Casto's death were the results.

Metcalfe's self-imposed exile after the Confederate invasion of Kentucky during the fall of 1862 also showcases the hatred in the region that was caused by the secession crisis and the Civil War. After leaving the Union army following the collapse of his cavalry regiment at the Battle of Richmond, threats to his person and local support for the Rebel invasion of Kentucky pushed Metcalfe to move across the Ohio River. Kentuckians despised him after the Civil War. The luster of his having defended his honor against the Maysville secessionist faded quickly as Metcalfe condemned slavery, blamed enslavers, endorsed Lincoln, supported African American enlistments into the Union army, and levied fines against secessionist civilians. After the war, the sight of Metcalfe's regimental flag in a Kentucky community was enough to spark a riot and a shooting. So perhaps Metcalfe made a wise choice in living his few remaining years in Ohio.

The duel also shows that despite the carnage of the Civil War, Southern honor culture thrived in the Bluegrass State. Although formalities tied to the state's honor culture, like the code duello, disappeared after the conflict, Kentuckians' determination to uphold their reputations or avoid public shame—and using violence to do so—remained intact. Although the Civil War raged around them, Metcalfe and Casto followed the conventions of the code duello; they formalized their own civil war on the banks of the Ohio River. The weight of this honor culture meant that Metcalfe, the privileged son of a Kentucky governor, was willing to risk a court martial, prison, and death to defend his character. Conversely, Casto was willing to gamble everything—despite Metcalfe's known proficiency with rifles—because he believed Metcalfe had unjustly arrested him. Metcalfe did not know Casto and after seizing him did not give Casto's confinement a second thought. Yet the logic of fighting a duel to settle the matter made perfect sense to these men; honor culture and the need to defend one's reputation and avoid shame outweighed any risks. This was paramount within their upper-class society, even as war raged around them.

The Casto–Metcalfe duel also represents a pivot point in Kentucky history, highlighting a cultural change pertaining to interpersonal violence. After the Civil War, even though Southern honor culture remained intact, Kentucky gentlemen dropped the formality of the code duello. There was no longer a regulated, formalized, dispassionate way of settling disputes. Instead, the use of violence as a tool for defending one's honor changed after the Civil War. While bruised honor, shattered egos, and the need to protect one's reputation continued to drive some Kentuckians to violence, the street fight replaced the formal duel. As thousands of men were killed on battlefields around them, many Kentuckians surely noted the absurdity of fighting formal duels. After the war, the elite decided that they no longer needed to adhere to the antiquated conventions of the code duello. Casto was dead, Metcalfe lived in self-imposed exile, and the duel was fading from blue-blood favor. Except for a few additional fights, such as the Desha–Kimbrough duel, the Civil War ended formalized violence in Kentucky. Thus, the Casto–Metcalfe duel—fought during the war—exemplifies the cultural shift that ended regulated violence among the upper classes. The Desha–Kimbrough duel, fought after the war between former Union and Confederate soldiers, was a last dying gasp of that practice.

After 1866, with the formal duel having gone out of fashion, the white Bluegrass elite embraced impulsive, spontaneous violence that was fuel-injected by the commonwealth's brand of honor culture. Instead of brooding over an offense, consulting with friends, and writing challenge notes, insulted gentlemen relied on concealed weapons and quick action. Violence became a great equalizer, as men of all classes immediately resolved differences by pulling pistols or knives. With the decline of the duel, one southerner lamented, "But now the silver-mounted, smooth bore duelling pistols have given away to the rifle barreled revolvers, and quick snap shooting on the street superseded the old fashioned ten paces. . . . The formality of a challenge is now out of fashion and the hip pocket [pistol] is now inserted in every man's trousers. Both methods are barbarous, but I am inclined to think that the old time method was the least so, as it gave one time to make his will and hope for an apology."[4]

Spontaneous gunfights also became easier in Kentucky after the Civil War because of the prevalence of weapons. In 1879, Speed S. Fry, a Danville merchant and attorney who had been a Union brigadier general, was called to testify as a witness in a murder trial. He commented on the number of firearms that were available. "After the war army guns of all kinds were scattered all over the country," Fry said. This meant it was easier for Kentuckians to access—and use—guns to end conflicts.[5]

The 1887 fight between Metcalfe's advisor Thomas M. Green and Lew Baldwin personifies this shift of upper-class Kentuckians discarding formal duels for impromptu fights. Had Baldwin taken offense at Green's newspaper articles twenty-five years earlier, he would not have confronted Green on the street. Instead, he would have sent a challenge to duel. And Green, who served as Metcalfe's first advisor in his duel with Casto, surely would have assented.

By the time Green and Baldwin encountered each other, Kentucky's culture had changed to such an extent that both men were primed to fight in public. Baldwin had a pistol in his pocket, and Green, on learning that his antagonist was in town, easily borrowed a revolver. With their honor already bruised and threats and insults bandied about, these men would avoid the public shame of cowardice at all costs. By the time they met in Lexington, they considered only violence as the means of settling their differences. In the ensuing encounter, Green killed Baldwin, leaving six children orphaned and a spectator wounded. Although duels were barbaric, antiquated, and illegal, in this instance a formal affair would have been better than two men blazing away at each other while a crowd surrounded them. In addition to endangering their own lives, Green and Baldwin put scores of others at risk.

The combination of this postwar cultural shift, dozens of street fights across the state, well-publicized feuds in Eastern Kentucky, the assassination of Governor William Goebel (shot on January 30, 1900), and widespread poverty sent Kentucky's national reputation into a downward spiral. The state also contended with postwar vigilantism and broad racial violence, including depredations by the Ku Klux Klan and self-styled Regulators who targeted African Americans and white Republicans. Moreover, lynch mobs involved hundreds of participants. In the fall of 1866, for example, massive crowds in Lebanon lynched both white and Black victims. Lynchings involving smaller numbers were just as prevalent. At Stamping Ground in January 1871, for example, seventeen Klan members killed a Black shoemaker before raiding a nearby African American township. Nearly two years later, twenty-five men took an African American man named Sam Bascom out of the Owingsville jail and hanged him. Bascom had been charged with arson, and, the *Louisville Courier-Journal* complained, "the crime [the lynching] committed in this little interior town reflects upon the whole commonwealth." Historian Anne Marshall contends that because of this violence, "between 1865 and 1885, Kentucky emerged as one of the most lawless states in America."[6]

Murders and street fights existed in Kentucky before and during the Civil War, but the state's national reputation plummeted after the conflict when the commonwealth's politicians and upper-class residents engaged in violent public affrays. Out-of-state newspapers were quick to publish the violent escapades of the state's political leaders and wealthy residents, whose actions, a generation earlier, would have

Philip B. Thompson Jr., his brothers, and his father had a shootout with the Daviess family in the Harrodsburg courthouse in 1873. *Library of Congress*.

resulted in formal duels. By engaging in curbside shootings and spontaneous public violence, these prominent Kentuckians were essentially endorsing gunplay and knife fights as a legitimate way to settle disputes. Illegally carrying concealed weapons, which, if convicted, only resulted in low fines, and using them to shoot down one's political enemies seemed to sanction bloodletting. It also ended lives.[7]

Instances of legislators and prominent Kentuckians engaging in public violence are plentiful, and several led to harsh criticism against the practice of carrying concealed pistols. During an 1873 trial at the Harrodsburg courthouse, for example, attorney Phil B. Thompson and his sons engaged in a shootout with the Daviess family. Dozens of shots were fired in just a few seconds, riddling the courtroom with bullets. The Thompsons killed three Daviesses.[8]

Although eyewitnesses contradicted one another, Thompson was charged with murder because he chased one of Daviess's sons outside and shot him in the back. During the subsequent trial—held in the bullet-pockmarked courtroom—a reporter became incensed that these prominent lawyers had engaged in gunplay in the place where they fought for justice. The journalist blamed concealed firearms: "I thought I had never witnessed a more fearful illustration of the silly and barbarous practice of carrying concealed weapons, a practice which is converting even our temples of justice into slaughterhouses." He added, "Human life is held to-day more cheaply than ever before. Courts and juries too often wink at crime, and on the rising generation we seem to be fostering an array of young 'bloods' whose chief reliance for future honors is on the pistol and the bowie knife."[9]

The murder of John Milton Elliott, one of the state senators who had investigated the Civil War arrests of the legislators in Harrodsburg, highlights how postwar Kentuckians had become desensitized to violence. During the war, Elliott abandoned his post in the Kentucky General Assembly and became a Confederate congressman. He later became a judge on the Kentucky Court of Appeals. In 1879, Thomas Buford, a man from another prominent Kentucky family, approached Elliott on the streets of Frankfort. Buford promptly killed the judge with a double-barreled shotgun. Elliott had ruled against one of Buford's relatives in a property case, and Buford took revenge. Authorities later judged the killer insane and sentenced him to an asylum.[10]

Elliott's brutal death showed how Kentuckians had become inured to acts of violence. One man traveling through Kentucky wrote of the shooting: "I passed through Frankfort the following day. To show you how indifferent they are about killing, let me say that a few miles from Frankfort I asked a man living there what was the feeling? 'To tell you the truth, sir, I didn't know that the Judge had been shot. There is so much of that thing done among us that unless we lose a brother, a father or some close kin it don't excite us much.'"[11]

Some residents, however, worked to end violence. On February 6, 1900, shortly after Governor William Goebel was assassinated in Frankfort, "the Women of Louisville" held a mass meeting to express their indignation. Several ministers and other presenters spoke at the meeting, and attendees called on the General Assembly to support laws providing stiffer penalties for those convicted of assault with a deadly weapon and carrying concealed weapons. Those present also passed resolutions, including one stating that "the carrying of deadly weapons is largely responsible for the moral disorder and resultant crime prevalent in our State."[12]

Sadly, the calls of the ladies of Louisville went unheeded as street fights and shootouts among men in power remained in the news. Several years after the mass meeting, former state senator Charles Bronston shot Lexington funeral homeowner W. R. Milward on the street because Bronston believed Milward had been sticking his nose into his domestic matters. Milward survived because Bronston's bullet struck some heavy brass keys in Milward's pocket. Bronston never received jail time, but he was fined $50. Using the episode to note racial disparities in the prosecution of violent crimes in Kentucky, the *Maysville Daily Public Ledger* wondered, "By the way, wonder what would have been done to a N——— if one had shot at MILWARD instead of BRONSTON." Unprosecuted street fights remained the privilege of upper-class white males.[13]

One of the most shocking incidents involving politicians engaging in street battles occurred at the Lexington post office on November 9, 1889. Armistead Swope and William Cassius Goodloe were Kentucky Republican Party operatives who had become bitter rivals. Swope, a Lincoln County native who had lived in Bourbon County for several years, served as a collector of internal revenue in central Kentucky. Goodloe, the nephew of Kentucky emancipationist firebrand Cassius

Marcellus Clay, was born in Madison County and graduated from Transylvania University in 1861. Goodloe followed his uncle to St. Petersburg, Russia, after President Abraham Lincoln appointed Clay as the US minister there. Upon his return to the United States, Goodloe became a Union officer and was captured at the Battle of Richmond, Kentucky. After the Civil War, he practiced law in Lexington, edited the *Kentucky Statesman*, unsuccessfully ran for Kentucky attorney general, and was a member of the Republican National Committee.[14]

Tensions between Swope and Goodloe emerged from Republican Party politics in the mid-1880s. Both were vying to become party leaders, and they had a public argument when the Republican state convention met in Louisville in 1888. Later, they nearly came to blows in Lexington after a spat at the Phoenix Hotel. Friends tried to make peace, but to no avail. While party politics certainly played a role, Goodloe's aversion to Swope may have come from his own snobbery. According to one writer, who showed that lines separating social and economic classes had become blurred after the Civil War, "Goodloe was a member of an aristocratic family; he was proud of his ancestry, proud of his family relation, and he evidently resented the idea of Col. Swope's elevation to a position over him; and it was still more humiliating to him to be forced to recognize his own intellectual inferiority to the man whom he most heartily despised."[15]

Because Kentucky's culture embraced violence as a means of settling disputes, both men expected a fight and armed themselves. Despite the adage to never bring a knife to a gun fight, Goodloe carried what the *New York Times* called "a long bladed clasp knife." Another witness said "the knife was a terrible weapon, sharpened to a razor's edge on both sides of the point, with a blade five inches long and with a rough bone grip handle." For Goodloe, knife fighting was a family affair; his uncle, Cassius M. Clay, was a renowned bowie knife fighter who had successfully defended himself on multiple occasions with a blade. In an August 1844 instance, Cassius hacked the nose, eye, and ear from one opponent who had shot him. Swope's armament, however, was more modern. He carried a nickel-plated .38 caliber Smith & Wesson revolver.[16]

On November 9, 1889, Swope and Goodloe met at the Lexington post office, where they argued and then drew weapons. Swope fired as

Goodloe opened his large switchblade. The round struck Goodloe in the abdomen, "three inches to the right of the navel." Despite the bullet's impact, Goodloe grabbed Swope by the right arm and plunged the knife into his chest, back, abdomen, and arm. The men engaged in a macabre dance, circling around the post office, blood flowing from their wounds. Swope fired another round, which missed and struck a post office box. As Goodloe's knife slashed into Swope's arm, one witness said Swope dropped "his pistol by reason of a wound on his wrist which almost severed the hand from the arm."[17]

Goodloe stabbed Swope at least thirteen times. Eighteen additional cuts were made across his overcoat. Each time Goodloe plunged the knife into Swope's body, Swope yelled "Oh!" or "Help!" The postmaster, who saw the fight, said that "Swope was backing away and uttering loud exclamations, and Goodloe rapidly stabbing him all the time." After Swope dropped his gun, Goodloe let go him, and he immediately fell face-first to the floor. One stab wound under Swope's left arm went nearly six inches deep and cut into Swope's heart. The man died within seconds. Standing over Swope's lifeless form, Goodloe cried, "He bellowed like a calf!"[18]

Goodloe turned away, told onlookers he was shot, and asked for a doctor. He was hustled off to a nearby physician. L. F. Johnson wrote that on reaching the doctor's office, "his clothes were still burning from the effects of the powder, showing that Col. Swope's pistol must have been almost against him when the shots were fired." The doctor examined the wound, which went deep into Goodloe's abdomen. He was taken to a room at the Phoenix Hotel. When one of his six daughters arrived and saw her father's state, she promptly fainted. Despite an operation, Goodloe died forty-eight hours later. According to one physician, Goodloe's good luck charm, a coin he carried in his pocket, killed him. Swope's bullet struck the coin and pushed it far into Goodloe's body, causing the peritonitis that led to his demise.[19]

According to the *New York Times*, William O. Bradley, who would in 1895 become the first Republican governor of Kentucky, said that the loss of the two men "would be one of the saddest blows the Republican Party in Kentucky ever had to bear." Goodloe was buried in the Lexington Cemetery. Swope was taken to Lincoln County, where he was interred in a family plot.[20]

Again, as politicians became embroiled in vicious street fights—even into the early twentieth century—one could conclude that the state sanctioned violence as a way to resolve personal difficulties. Further, as political squabbles dusted with Kentucky's honor culture led to violence, more politicians began carrying concealed arms, which begat additional shootings. This created a vicious cycle. After state senator William Goebel shot and killed bank cashier John Sanford in 1895 over a political issue (Goebel had pushed legislation that hurt Sanford's business interests), one reporter wrote that because of political feuding, "Personal encounters and convention fights were numerous. It is not an exaggeration to say that a hundred prominent citizens have constantly carried pistols for the past three years, expecting an attack any moment."[21]

Widespread violence and the lack of prosecutions led to the national image of a bourbon-soaked Kentucky "colonel," pockets stuffed with pistols and belt laden with bowie knives. This became a familiar theme in out-of-state newspaper articles and political cartoons. Kentucky was no longer viewed as a cultured place where men like Henry Clay raised thoroughbreds and sipped mint juleps; instead, it was a backward, feudal backwater where alcohol-fueled rage and violence were the norm. Prior to World War II, this image certainly harmed the commonwealth's reputation. It also hindered economic development by discouraging outside investments and the relocation of businesses to the state.

Journalists and forward-thinking political leaders believed violence, and the subsequent loss of the state's reputation, hurt Kentucky's economy. "The damage that acts of violence in Kentucky do the State outside can not be calculated," the *Bourbon News* wrote in 1883. "They deter immigration; they intimidate capital; they make the name of Kentucky a reproach. All sensible men, as well as all good men, should combine to beat down and destroy the swaggering spirit which gives rise to them."[22]

These arguments did little to change Kentucky's culture, and violence continued throughout the late nineteenth and early twentieth centuries. Newspaper editors across the country grimly reported on Bluegrass State violence, one writing that there were "more homicides in Kentucky in 1878 than in the eight states of Maine, New Hampshire, Vermont, Massachusetts, Rhode Island, Connecticut, Pennsylvania, and Minnesota with an aggregate population of ten millions." In fact, stories of murders and shootings across the state and "ambushes" in Eastern Kentucky were so widely reported that newspapers ran summaries of deadly encounters. The Associated Press, for example, compiled violent acts occurring in Kentucky on one day, October 22, 1892. It distributed the piece under the headline "A Day's Record of Deeds of Violence in Kentucky." The accounting included violence in Greenwood, near Somerset, where Jim Patterson and Joe Haynes argued "and resorted to fire arms." Haynes shot first and missed, but his bullet struck an African American spectator and killed him. Another stray bullet wounded a railroad station agent. Finally, Patterson killed Haynes with his Winchester rifle and surrendered to authorities. On the same day, near Lebanon, in Marion County, a man named Dan Horton shot his wife and young child. To the northeast in Grayson, a town in Carter County, J. D. Bennett shot and killed Sylvester Adams and wounded Adams's nephew Oscar, who had been "beating Bennett with clubs." The men had argued "over a right-of-way." Even if violence equaled that of other states, once Kentucky's reputation plummeted, newspapers were quick to report on shootings, stabbings, and other mayhem that made good headlines. Readers lapped up the articles and likely shook their heads in disbelief and superiority over the backwardness of the once-sophisticated commonwealth.[23]

These accounts, coupled with the Tobacco Wars and Night Riders in Western Kentucky, and Goebel's assassination in Frankfort, painted Kentucky as one of the most violent states in the nation. This lasted several more years. When Judge Charles A. Hardin addressed the Boyle County Circuit Court in 1910, he lamented Kentucky's bloody record: "The United States is the most lawless nation in the civilized world; Kentucky ranks fifth in the percentage of law violation among the states in the Union; Lexington is the second city in the nation in homicides and other forms of lawlessness, and Danville ranks with Lexington." The murder rates, and the state's reputation, were equally terrible.[24]

With national newspapers listing Bluegrass State deeds of violence, some twentieth century writers who recounted the Casto–Metcalfe duel recognized that Kentucky had fallen into a pattern of cyclical violence. The writer of a 1903 piece about Metcalfe's fight with Casto concluded, "Such was the duel of other days. Thank God it has been abolished! But, with all its cruelties, it was braver, more manly and better far than the modern method of 'getting the drop' on your opponent and shooting him down with no chance for defense. . . . Let us hope that modern so-called 'duels' may ever become as obsolete as the duels of old, and that all differences may be settled under the guidance of sound, sober sense and kindly judgment." However, it took at least one additional generational change, a major shift in the state's culture, and increased penalties for those who carried hidden weapons for Kentuckians to end their reliance on concealed revolvers and violence as the first option to settle squabbles.[25]

In his landmark book *Southern Honor,* Bertram Wyatt-Brown reveals that some victorious duelists expressed guilt at having killed their opponent. Not Metcalfe. He never felt remorse for killing Casto. The fight at the Fishing Shore was a transformation of the battlefield to the dueling ground for Metcalfe, who had to kill Casto to preserve his honor, protect his reputation, and cull future threats. It was an extension of his personal and military duty. When, a few years after the duel, someone asked Metcalfe if he had been worried to fight the Maysville secessionist, the former Union colonel "smiled grimly and remarked that he feared more for the life of his antagonist."[26]

While Metcalfe was confident that he would defeat his opponent, we will never know if Casto feared Metcalfe. Casto was determined, however, to kneel to none but God. In the end, on the Fishing Shore, Metcalfe gave him that opportunity.

Acknowledgments

Many wonderful people have encouraged and assisted me with writing this book.

I first thank the staff and advisory board of the University Press of Kentucky for supporting this project. This includes Patrick O'Dowd, senior acquisitions editor; Brooke Raby, director of sales and marketing; Sarah A. Olson, project editor; and Trish Murphy, sales assistant. All have been incredibly helpful and supportive. I am also appreciative of the press's anonymous readers, who helped make this a better book. I am also thankful for the conscientious work of copyeditor Erin Holman, whose efforts greatly improved every chapter.

Friends Matt Cassady, Keith Jackson, Patrick Lewis, Jim Prichard, Don Rightmyer, Phillip Seyfrit, and Tim Talbott read either sections of the book or the entire manuscript. They offered valuable suggestions, and I am thankful for their important insights and continuing conversations about Kentucky history, honor, the Civil War, and interpersonal violence.

While writing the book, I was fortunate to collaborate with colleagues at the Kentucky Historical Society (KHS) on a temporary exhibition about dueling that was installed in Kentucky's Old State Capitol. Working with Carol Bolton Easterly, Julie Kemper, Megan Sauter, and Jake Turner on that exhibition was a wonderful experience that helped me think more deeply about the subject. I'm also appreciative of my colleagues on the library and archives staff who pulled archival materials, and Digital Archivist Alyssa Ollier, who helped procure several important illustrations. Although they are too many in number to thank individually, I am grateful for all of my wonderful coworkers at KHS, past and present.

I am thankful to the staff of the Filson Historical Society in Louisville for assistance and hospitality, including Emma Bryan, Hannah Costelle, Jennie Cole, Abby Glogower, and Heather Potter. Sue Ellen

Acknowledgments

Grannis at the Kentucky Gateway Museum Center in Maysville generously provided several critical illustrations.

Jim Parrish gave me important information about the Colt Revolving rifle. Friends John Barnes, Brett Gentzel, Chris Goodlett, Brian Grimmer, Greg Hardison, Anna Goodman Hoover, Erik Ingmundson, Wendell Neeley, and Erik Olson either offered encouragement or threatened me with "pistols at dawn." Steve and Amy Isola were, as always, wonderful friends during the writing of this book. Madison Silvert, Jason Williams, and Chris Workman also provided a great support network.

I am also thankful to have known my late friend Michael S. Johnson of Lexington, Virginia. Our visits to the museum at the Virginia Military Institute when we were in elementary school first introduced me to the Colt Revolving rifle and that weapon's proclivity for "chain firing." I have thought about him often while researching and writing this book. He was interested in the Civil War and loved a good story, and I think he would have liked this one. I am honored to have been his friend, and I cherish the memories of our childhood ramblings throughout our hometown.

I also thank my wife, Jenny, and my wonderful children, John, Anne, and Elizabeth, for their love, support, and patience as I worked on this project.

My father, Taylor Sanders, a retired history professor, and my mother, Barbara W. Sanders, a former English teacher, have read just about everything I have written, including this book. My love of history and interest in writing comes from them. Grateful for their constant love and support and thankful to them for being wonderful parents, I dedicate this book to them with much love.

Notes

Introduction

1. April 7, 1862, Jesse Hyde diary, SC1274_1, Special Collections, Kentucky Historical Society (KHS), Frankfort. After the war, one soldier wrote, "After Shiloh, then dawned upon the minds of thinking men the knowledge that the war would last so long as the rebels had an army in the field, or a fortification garrisoned; and thereafter, our military operations became destructive as well as offensive; a war of annihilation, so far as every defensive or aggressive element of the Confederacy was concerned." "Six Weeks in the Mud," *Overland Monthly* 2 (March 1869): 217.

2. Bertram Wyatt-Brown, *Southern Honor: Ethics and Behavior in the Old South* (Oxford: Oxford University Press, 2007), 356; Joanne B. Freeman, *The Field of Blood: Violence in Congress and the Road to Civil War* (New York: Farrar, Straus & Giroux, 2018), 88–89; Dickson D. Bruce, *Violence and Culture in the Antebellum South* (Austin: University of Texas Press, 1979), 35; Lorien Foote, *The Gentlemen and the Roughs: Violence, Honor, and Manhood in the Union Army* (New York: New York University Press, 2010), 78; Todd Hagstette, "Writing the Duel: Rhetorical Negotiation and the Language of Honor in the Nineteenth Century South," in *The Field of Honor: Essays on Southern Character and American Identity,* ed. John Mayfield and Todd Hagstette (Columbia: University of South Carolina Press, 2017), 80.

3. Tourgée quoted in James M. McPherson's introduction to David J. Eicher, *The Longest Night: A Military History of the Civil War* (New York: Simon & Schuster, 2001), 17.

4. "Monthly Record of Current Events," *Harper's New Monthly Magazine,* November 1861, 832; William W. Freehling, *The South vs. the South: How Anti-Confederate Southerners Shaped the Course of the Civil War* (Oxford: Oxford University Press, 2001), 52; Luke E. Harlow, *Religion, Race, and the Making of Confederate Kentucky, 1830–1880* (Cambridge: Cambridge University Press, 2014), 6.

5. Ireland and Klotter ably explain this cultural shift and honor's role in fomenting violence in Robert M. Ireland, "Homicide in Nineteenth Century

Kentucky," *Register of the Kentucky Historical Society* 81 (Spring 1983): 134–53; and James C. Klotter, *Kentucky Justice, Southern Honor, and American Manhood: Understanding the Life and Death of Richard Reid* (Baton Rouge: Louisiana State University Press, 2003).

6. Edward Mills John, *The American Notary and Commissioner of Deeds Manual* (Chicago: Callaghan & Co., 1904), 302; and Oath of Allegiance for Brown Anderson, 1876, Kentucky State Guard Records, 2008SC02, KHS. *Bowie-knife-and-pistol-gentry* was coined by Kentucky lawyer Benjamin Hardin, who used the term during an 1838 murder case. Lucius P. Little, *Ben Hardin: His Times and Contemporaries* (Louisville: Courier-Journal Job Printing Co., 1887), 307; also quoted in A. B. Carlton, *The Law of Homicide* (Cincinnati: Robert Clarke & Co., 1882), 182.

7. "The Last Duel Fought in Kentucky," *Louisville Courier-Journal*, March 12, 1877.

1. A Scene of Desolation

1. It was reported that "the whole body of water in the Ohio river surged toward the Ohio shore, rising suddenly on that shore several feet." Lewis Collins and Richard H. Collins, *History of Kentucky,* 2 vols. (Covington: Collins & Co., 1882), 1:73.

2. "Terrible Explosion at Maysville," *Eaton (OH) Democrat*, August 17, 1854; "The Maysville Explosion," *Evansville (IN) Daily Journal*, August 22, 1854; "Terrible Explosion at Maysville of Eleven Hundred Kegs of Gunpowder," *Louisville Daily Courier*, August 16, 1854, "The Maysville Explosion—Some of the Incidents," *Meigs County Telegraph* (Pomeroy, OH), August 29, 1854; "The Explosion at Maysville," *Spirit of Democracy* (Woodsfield, OH), August 30, 1854; "Miscellaneous," *New York Herald*, August 15, 1854; "The Maysville Explosion," *Gallipolis (OH) Journal*, August 24, 1854.

3. "Terrible Explosion," *Louisville Daily Courier;* "Maysville Explosion," *Evansville Daily Journal;* "Explosion at Maysville," *Spirit of Democracy;* "Terrible Explosion," *Eaton Democrat; Louisville Daily Courier*, August 23, 1854.

4. For a list of many buildings damaged in the explosion, see "The Maysville Eagle—Extra," 1854 broadside, Kentucky Historical Society Broadside Collection, 2008M04, Kentucky Historical Society, Frankfort. Property damage estimates varied from $50,000 to more than $200,000. "Miscellaneous," *New York Herald;* "Incidents," *Louisville Daily Courier;* "Maysville Explosion," *Louisville Daily Courier.* Value of damage in today's dollars calculated from Morgan Friedman, "The Inflation Calculator," *Ceci n'est pas une homepage,* https://westegg.com/inflation/, accessed August 25, 2022.

5. Animal casualties from "Incidents," *Louisville Daily Courier;* "Miscellaneous," New *York Herald;* "Death of a Poetess," *Washington Daily Evening Star,* October 7, 1854.

6. Collins and Collins, *History of Kentucky,* 1:584; John Wilson Townsend, *Kentucky in American Letters, 1784–1912,* 2 vols. (Cedar Rapids, IA: Torch Press, 1913), 1:238.

7. Nathaniel Cheairs Hughes, *Yale's Confederates: A Biographical Dictionary* (Knoxville: University of Tennessee Press, 2008), 37; "Old Killings Recalled," *Hazel Green (KY) Herald,* May 23, 1895; "The Last Duel Fought in Kentucky," *Louisville Courier-Journal,* March 12, 1877, 1; William T. Casto, Memorial ID 9607014, Find a Grave, accessed February 20, 2023, https://www.findagrave.com/memorial/9607014/william-thomas-casto; Abijah Casto, Memorial ID 114096132, Find a Grave, accessed February 20, 2023, https://www.findagrave.com/memorial/114096132/abijah-casto; *Statistics of the Class of 1845 in Yale College, From 1845 to 1850* (New Haven: J. H. Benham, 1851), 7, 10, 18; "Letter from Kentucky," *Caledonian* (St. Johnsbury, VT), May 23, 1862; Dick Steward, *Duels and the Roots of Violence in Missouri* (Columbia: University of Missouri Press, 2000), 42; "Anti-Duelling Society," *Pensacola Gazette,* April 4, 1828.

8. Hughes, *Yale's Confederates,* 37; "Maysville," *Louisville Daily Courier,* January 7, 1853; *Louisville Daily Courier,* January 6, November 9, 1854; "Democratic Meeting in Mason," *Louisville Daily Courier,* November 13, 1858; "Last Duel Fought in Kentucky," *Louisville Courier-Journal;* "List of Delegates to the Democratic State Convention," *Louisville Daily Courier,* January 12, 1860.

9. Hughes, *Yale's Confederates,* 37; Kenneth H. Williams and James Russell Harris, eds., "Kentucky in 1860: A Statistical Overview," *Register of the Kentucky Historical Society* 103 (Autumn 2003): 749; "Election Returns," *Louisville Daily Courier,* August 13, 1861. In November 1849, the steamboat *Herman* arrived in Maysville loaded with enslaved African Americans who were being sent to Lexington. *Maysville Eagle,* November 4, 1849. See Marion B. Lucas, *A History of Blacks in Kentucky: From Slavery to Segregation, 1760–1891* (Frankfort: Kentucky Historical Society, 2003), 96.

10. "Duel of Other Days," *Maysville Evening Bulletin,* December 8, 1903; "Fatal Duel in Kentucky," *Evansville (IN) Daily Journal,* May 13, 1862; "Last Duel Fought in Kentucky," *Louisville Courier-Journal;* J. Winston Coleman Jr., *Famous Kentucky Duels* (Lexington: Henry Clay Press, 1969): 120.

11. Williams and Harris, "Kentucky in 1860," 762, 761, 749; J. T. Dorris, "President Lincoln's Treatment of Kentuckians," *Filson Club History Quarterly* 28 (January 1954): 5; "Election Returns," *Lancaster Gazette,* November 8, 1860.

12. John Klee, "Maysville," in *The Encyclopedia of Northern Kentucky,* ed. Paul A. Tenkotte and James C. Claypool (Lexington: University Press of

Kentucky, 2009), 595, 594; Lewis Collins and Richard H. Collins, *History of Kentucky*, 2 vols. (Covington: Collins & Co., 1878), 2:546, 548; Jean W. Calvert, "Maysville," in *The Kentucky Encyclopedia*, ed. John E. Kleber (Lexington: University Press of Kentucky, 1992), 621.

13. Calvert, "Maysville," 621; Lowell H. Harrison and James C. Klotter, *A New History of Kentucky* (Lexington: University Press of Kentucky, 1997), 103; Klee, "Maysville," 595; Collins and Collins, *History of Kentucky*, 1:539, 36, 62. For the Maysville Road, see Karl Raitz and Nancy O'Malley, *Kentucky's Frontier Highway: Historical Landscapes along the Maysville Road* (Lexington: University Press of Kentucky, 2012), and Craig Thompson Friend, *Along the Maysville Road: The Early American Republic of the Trans-Appalachian West* (Knoxville: University of Tennessee Press, 2005). For descriptions of antebellum Maysville, see Charles Wolf to "My Dear Father," June 10, 1830, and E. A. Butterfield to Dr. Israel Lathrop, October 12, 1843, both in Filson Historical Society, Louisville.

14. Williams and Harris, "Kentucky in 1860," 749, 751, 756; Klee, "Maysville," 595. For details about Maysville businesses and churches, see Collins and Collins, *History of Kentucky*, 2:546.

2. All to Lose and Nothing to Gain

1. Union meetings noted in Lewis Collins and Richard H. Collins, *History of Kentucky*, 2 vols. (Covington: Collins & Co., 1882), 1:84. Slavery was extensive across the state; as Luke Harlow notes, "more Kentuckians per capita owned slaves by 1850 than did whites in any other slaveholding state except Georgia or Virginia." Of Kentucky's population of 1.1 million people, about 225,000 were enslaved African Americans. Harlow, *Religion, Race, and the Making of Confederate Kentucky, 1830–1880* (Cambridge: Cambridge University Press, 2014), 6. Aaron Astor writes that slave hiring, a "vital component of the slave system," meant that white Kentuckians who did not own slaves also relied heavily upon the institution. Aaron Astor, *Rebels on the Border: Civil War, Emancipation, and the Reconstruction of Kentucky and Missouri* (Baton Rouge: Louisiana State University Press, 2012), 25–28.

2. Bruce S. Allardice and Lawrence Lee Hewitt, introduction to *Kentuckians in Gray: Confederate Generals and Field Officers of the Bluegrass State*, ed. Bruce S. Allardice and Lawrence Lee Hewitt (Lexington: University Press of Kentucky, 2008), 2; Gary R. Matthews, "Beleaguered Loyalties: Kentucky Unionism," in *Sister States, Enemy States: The Civil War in Kentucky and Tennessee*, ed. Kent T. Dollar, Larry H. Whiteaker, and W. Calvin Dickinson (Lexington: University Press of Kentucky, 2009), 11; William W. Freehling, *The South vs. the South: How Anti-Confederate Southerners Shaped the Course of the Civil War* (Oxford: Oxford University Press, 2001), 52; Astor,

Rebels on the Border, 41–42. Berry Craig explains that the Jackson Purchase region of Western Kentucky was, as far as trade was concerned, more closely linked to the South, and this was a primary factor in Western Kentucky containing strong support for the Confederacy. Berry Craig, *Kentucky Confederates: Secession, Civil War, and the Jackson Purchase* (Lexington: University Press of Kentucky, 2014), 9. Benjamin Franklin Cooling also notes that "Kentucky's human ties to the South [slavery] were more than offset by commercial and economic linkages northward." Benjamin Franklin Cooling, *Fort Donelson's Legacy: War and Society in Kentucky and Tennessee, 1862–1863* (Knoxville: University of Tennessee Press, 1997), 35.

3. Mark V. Wetherington, "Three Central Kentuckians, the 'Bone' of Political Office, and the Kentucky Exodus, 1792–1852," in *Bluegrass Renaissance: The History and Culture of Central Kentucky, 1792–1852,* ed. James C. Klotter and Daniel Rowland (Lexington: University Press of Kentucky, 2012), 163; Lowell H. Harrison and James C. Klotter, *A New History of Kentucky* (Lexington: University Press of Kentucky, 1997), 94; Lowell H. Harrison, *The Civil War in Kentucky* (Lexington: University Press of Kentucky, 1975), 2; James C. Klotter, "Kentucky, the Civil War, and the Spirit of Henry Clay," *Register of the Kentucky Historical Society* 110 (Summer–Autumn 2012): 247; Albert D. Kirwan, *John J. Crittenden: The Struggle for the Union* (Lexington: University Press of Kentucky, 1962), 427, 429; Elizabeth D. Leonard, *Lincoln's Forgotten Ally: Judge Advocate General Joseph Holt of Kentucky* (Chapel Hill: University of North Carolina Press, 2011), 134.

4. Starling quoted in Lowell H. Harrison, *Lincoln of Kentucky* (Lexington: University Press of Kentucky, 2000), 147. Christopher Phillips notes that Warner Underwood, a former Kentucky congressman, also knew that, "should war come, the border slave states . . . would inevitably bear its brunt." Christopher Phillips, *The Rivers Ran Backward: The Civil War and the Remaking of the American Middle Border* (Oxford: Oxford University Press, 2016), 115.

5. Patrick A. Lewis, *For Slavery and Union: Benjamin Buckner and Kentucky Loyalties in the Civil War* (Lexington: University Press of Kentucky, 2015), 54, 65; Jacob F. Lee, "Unionism, Emancipation, and the Origins of Kentucky's Confederate Identity," *Register of the Kentucky Historical Society* 111 (Spring 2013): 208, 208n33. For information about the "proslavery capacity" of Kentucky unionists, also see Patrick A. Lewis, "'All Men of Decency Ought to Quit the Army': Benjamin F. Buckner, Manhood, and Proslavery Unionism in Kentucky," *Register of the Kentucky Historical Society* 107 (Autumn 2009): 513–49; and Astor, *Rebels on the Border,* 34. Christopher Phillips notes that "most white Kentuckians . . . believed the status quo—loyalty to the federal government—was the best protection for their property." Phillips, *Rivers Ran Backward,* 121, 125; Lee, "Unionism, Emancipation," 209; April 19, 1861, Ellen Kenton McGaughey Wallace journal, 1849–1865, transcribed by

James T. Killebrew, Special Collections, and Robert H. Earnest to James H. Earnest, December 12, 1860, Robert H. Earnest Papers, SC 90, both in Kentucky Historical Society (KHS), Frankfort. For Kentucky's "halting" allegiances, also see Cooling, *Fort Donelson's Legacy*, xvi.

6. Ann Hagedorn, *Beyond the River: The Untold Story of the Heroes of the Underground Railroad* (New York: Simon & Schuster, 2002), 10, 14–15; "Runaways," *Louisville Daily Courier*, January 9, 1860; "Runaway Slaves," *Asheville News*, January 26, 1860; "Fugitive Slaves," *Louisville Daily Courier*, July 1, 1861; Harold D. Tallant, *Evil Necessity: Slavery and Political Culture in Antebellum Kentucky* (Lexington: University Press of Kentucky, 2003), 124.

7. James C. Klotter, *Henry Clay: The Man Who Would Be President* (New York: Oxford University Press, 2018), 355; J. Blaine Hudson, *Fugitive Slaves and the Underground Railroad in the Kentucky Borderland* (Jefferson, NC: McFarland, 2002), 137; J. Blaine Hudson, "Edward James 'Patrick' Doyle," in *Encyclopedia of the Underground Railroad* (Jefferson, NC: McFarland, 2006), 82; Marion B. Lucas, *A History of Blacks in Kentucky: From Slavery to Segregation, 1760–1891* (Frankfort: Kentucky Historical Society, 2003), 73. For Doyle, see James M. Prichard, "This Priceless Jewell—Liberty," in *Slavery and Freedom in the Bluegrass State: Revisiting My Old Kentucky Home*, ed. Gerald L. Smith (Lexington: University Press of Kentucky, 2023), 79–102.

8. *Maysville Eagle* quoted in "The Right Spirit," *Highland Weekly News* (Hillsboro, OH), March 21, 1861; "Saturday Night's Report," *Fremont (OH) Daily Journal*, May 6, 1861; and *Spirit of Democracy* (Woodsfield, OH), May 8, 1861; "Pleasant Courtesy Accepted," *Cincinnati Daily Press*, June 25, 1861; "The Glorious Ninth," *Spirit of Democracy*, July 10, 1861; Thomas Speed, *The Union Cause in Kentucky: 1860–1865* (New York: G. P. Putnam & Sons, 1907), 178; Wadsworth background information from "Wm. H. Wadsworth," *Maysville Evening Bulletin*, April 3, 1893. Wadsworth's presence during Nelson's Big Sandy campaign is noted in November 7, 1861, Winchester Byron Rudy Civil War Diary, 1998ms003, University of Kentucky Special Collections (UK), Lexington; "The Maysville Eagle—Extra," 1854 broadside in Kentucky Historical Society Broadside Collection, 2008M04.

9. "My dear Weller" letter, June 16, 1861, Jacob F. Weller Letters, 1860–1869, Weller Family Papers, Filson Historical Society, Louisville; Speed, *Union Cause in Kentucky*, 178.

10. Enlistment numbers from Allardice and Hewitt, *Kentuckians in Gray*, 4; Craig, *Kentucky Confederates*, 8; Freehling's "71 percent" from Freehling, *South vs. the South*, 54; May 31, 1861 entry, George Washington Smith Diary Transcript, Smith Family Papers, 64M142, UK.

11. Kenneth H. Williams and James Russell Harris, eds., "Kentucky in 1860: A Statistical Overview," *Register of the Kentucky Historical Society* 103 (Autumn 2003): 749; Edwin Porter Thompson, *History of the Orphan Brigade*

(Cincinnati: Caxton Publishing, 1868), 505, 620, 639, 640, 722–29, 747, 895, 898, 899; "My dear Weller" letter, June 16, 1861, Jacob F. Weller Letters, 1860–1869, Weller Family Papers; Leslie Combs to Abraham Lincoln, August 16, 1861, Abraham Lincoln Papers, Library of Congress, transcribed and annotated by the Lincoln Studies Center, Knox College, Galesburg, IL, online at memory.loc.gov (Lincoln Papers, LC); William C. Harris, *Lincoln and the Border States: Preserving the Union* (Lawrence: University Press of Kansas, 2011), 39. For Cynthiana during the Civil War, see William A. Penn, *Kentucky Rebel Town: The Civil War Battles of Cynthiana and Harrison County* (Lexington: University Press of Kentucky, 2016). For African Americans from Mason County who joined the Union army, see United States Colored Troops Muster and Descriptive Roll for Kentucky, the 7th, 8th, and 9th Districts, FF1.153, KHS.

12. Harrison, *Lincoln of Kentucky,* 131; Williamson Murray and Wayne Wei-Siang Hsieh, *A Savage War: A Military History of the Civil War* (Princeton, NJ: Princeton University Press, 2016), 73–74.

13. *The War of the Rebellion: A Compilation of the Official Records of the Union and Confederate Armies* (Washington, DC: GPO, 1880–1901), ser. 3, vol 1:70 (*OR;* unless noted, all citations to ser. 1); Magoffin also quoted in Harrison, *Civil War in Kentucky,* 8; and Harrison, *Lincoln of Kentucky,* 131; *Journal of the House of Representatives of the Commonwealth of Kentucky, Begun and Held in the Town of Frankfort, on Monday, the Second Day of September, in the Year of our Lord 1861* (Frankfort: Yeoman Office, 1861), 33; Judith M. Jacob, *The Washington Monument: A Technical History and Catalog of the Commemorative Stones* (Washington, DC: National Park Service, 2005), 165; and Klotter, "Kentucky, the Civil War, and the Spirit of Henry Clay," 246.

14. Brian D. McKnight, *Contested Borderland: The Civil War in Appalachian Kentucky and Virginia* (Lexington: University Press of Kentucky, 2006), 25; Harrison, *Civil War in Kentucky,* 9; Harrison, *Lincoln of Kentucky,* 135; Speed, *Union Cause in Kentucky,* 45; Freehling, *South versus the South,* 52–53; R. M. Kelly, "Holding Kentucky for the Union," in *Battles and Leaders of the Civil War,* ed. Robert Underwood Johnson and Clarence Clough Buel, 4 vols., repr. ed. (Secaucus, NJ: Castle Books, 1887), 3:374; *OR,* vol. 4:192; George of Meadville to Hal, May 29, 1861, SC 1062, KHS.

15. July 28, 1861, Ellen Kenton McGaughey Wallace journal; H. M. Pearce to Beriah Magoffin, May 28, 1861, Office of the Governor, Beriah Magoffin, Governor's Official Correspondence File Military Correspondence, 1859–1862, MG5-107 to MG5-108, Kentucky Department for Libraries and Archives, Frankfort (KDLA), accessed via the *Civil War Governors of Kentucky Digital Documentary Edition,* Kentucky Historical Society, http://discovery.civilwargovernors.org/document/KYR-0001-019-0057.

16. Albert D. Kirwan, *John J. Crittenden: The Struggle for the Union* (Lexington: University Press of Kentucky, 1962), 443, 444; Harrison, *Civil War in*

Kentucky, 11; Harrison, *Lincoln of Kentucky*, 146; Collins and Collins, *History of Kentucky*, 1:92; "Monthly Record of Current Events," *Harper's New Monthly Magazine*, November 1861, 832, 833.

17. Donald A. Clark, "Major General William 'Bull' Nelson," in *The Encyclopedia of Northern Kentucky*, ed. Paul A. Tenkotte and James C. Claypool (Lexington: University Press of Kentucky, 2009), 648; John E. Stanchak, "William Nelson," Patricia L. Faust, ed., *Historical Times Illustrated Encyclopedia of the Civil War* (New York: Harper Perennial, 1986), 523; Ezra J. Warner, *Generals in Blue: The Lives of the Union Commanders* (Baton Rouge: Louisiana State University Press, 1992), 343; Mark M. Boatner III, "William Nelson," in *The Civil War Dictionary* (New York: Vintage, 1988), 586.

18. Boatner, *Civil War Dictionary*, 586; Clark, "Major General William 'Bull' Nelson," 648; William Nelson to John B. S. Todd, April 18, 1861, and Nelson to Todd, April 22, 1861, both in Lincoln Papers, LC.

19. Daniel Stevenson, "General Nelson, Kentucky, and Lincoln Guns," *Magazine of American History* 10 (July–December 1883): 128; Kelly, "Holding Kentucky for the Union," 3:375; Harris, *Lincoln and the Border States*, 89; "Hamilton Gray," in *Biographical Encyclopaedia of Kentucky of the Dead and Living Men of the Nineteenth Century* (Cincinnati: J. M. Armstrong & Co., 1878), 303; "Distressing Accident," *Maysville Dollar Weekly Bulletin*, September 17, 1863; Joshua Speed to Lincoln, May 29, 1861, Lincoln Papers, LC; "My dear Weller" letter, June 16, 1861, Jacob F. Weller Letters, 1860–1869, Weller Family Papers. In 1860, the forty-five-year-old Hamilton Gray held $46,000 in real estate and $40,000 in personal property. 1860 US Federal Census, Maysville, Mason County, accessed via Ancestry.com. It was reported that twenty-five hundred guns went to Hamilton Gray. "Army Correspondence," *Louisville Daily Courier*, May 22, 1861.

20. For correspondence between Lincoln and Magoffin, see Harrison, *Civil War in Kentucky*, 11–12; Harrison, *Lincoln of Kentucky*, 148; Frank Moore, ed., *The Rebellion Record: A Dairy of American Events*, 12 vols. (New York: G. P. Putnam, 1862), 3:29–30; Magoffin to Lincoln, August 19, 1861, and Lincoln to Magoffin, August 24, 1861, both in Lincoln Papers, LC; *Journal of the House of Representatives of the Commonwealth of Kentucky*, 37–38, 39–40. For the Battle of Wildcat Mountain, see Kenneth A. Hafendorfer, *The Battle of Wild Cat Mountain* (Louisville: KH Press, 2003). For the Battle of Mill Springs, see Kenneth A. Hafendorfer, *Mill Springs: Campaign and Battle of Mill Springs, Kentucky* (Louisville: KH Press, 2001); and Stuart W. Sanders, *The Battle of Mill Springs, Kentucky* (Charleston, SC: History Press, 2013).

21. Speed to Lincoln, September 1, 1861, Anderson to Lincoln, September 13, 1861, and Lincoln to Orville Browning, September 22, 1861, all in Lincoln Papers, LC; Mark E. Neely Jr. *The Fate of Liberty: Abraham Lincoln and Civil Liberties* (New York: Oxford University Press, 1991), 34. For

Frémont's order, also see Harris, *Lincoln and the Border States,* 98–106. The Kentucky legislature worried that Frémont had assumed "extraordinary powers." *Journal of the House of Representatives of the Commonwealth of Kentucky,* session beginning September 2, 1862, 58.

22. *OR,* vol. 4:256; A. James Fuller, *Oliver P. Morton and the Politics of the Civil War and Reconstruction* (Kent: Kent State University Press, 2017).

23. Phillips, *Rivers Ran Backward,* 142; Kelly, "Holding Kentucky for the Union," 378–79; Cooling, *Fort Donelson's Legacy,* 36; Harrison, *Lincoln of Kentucky,* 149–50; *OR,* vol. 4:175, 257; Moore, *Rebellion Record,* 3:67; John G. Nicolay and John Hay, "Abraham Lincoln: A History, Tennessee and Kentucky," *Century* 36 (August 1888): 568; *OR,* vol. 52, 2:141.

24. *Journal of the House of Representatives of the Commonwealth of Kentucky,* session beginning September 2, 1862, 81, 101–2; *Journal of the Senate of the Commonwealth of Kentucky, Begun and Held in the Town of Frankfort, on Monday, the Second Day of September, in the Year of Our Lord 1861* (Frankfort: Yeoman Office, 1861), 99–100; Nicolay and Hay, "Abraham Lincoln," 568, 567; Collins and Collins, *History of Kentucky,* 1:93, 94, 95; Harrison, *Civil War in Kentucky,* 13, 16–17; *OR,* vol. 4:175; Harrison, *Lincoln of Kentucky,* 159; September 25, 1861, Ellen Kenton McGaughey Wallace journal.

25. Morton to Lincoln, Lincoln Papers, LC; Gary R. Matthews, *Basil Wilson Duke: The Right Man in the Right Place* (Lexington: University Press of Kentucky, 2005), 36; Harrison, *Civil War in Kentucky,* 13; Kenneth W. Noe, *Perryville: This Grand Havoc of Battle* (Lexington: University Press of Kentucky, 2001), 8; *Journal of the Senate of the Commonwealth of Kentucky,* for the session beginning September 2, 1861, 130–32.

26. *OR,* ser. 2, vol. 4:199; E. Merton Coulter, *The Civil War and Readjustment in Kentucky* (Gloucester, MA: Peter Smith, 1966), 146.

3. When Men Talk Politics Now They Whisper

1. *The War of the Rebellion: A Compilation of the Official Records of the Union and Confederate Armies* (Washington, DC: GPO, 1880–1901), vol. 4:199 (*OR;* unless noted, all citations to ser. 1); Gary R. Matthews, *Basil Wilson Duke: The Right Man in the Right Place* (Lexington: University Press of Kentucky, 2005), 36; Frank Moore, ed., *The Rebellion Record: A Dairy of American Events,* 12 vols. (New York: G. P. Putnam, 1862), 3:145; William A. Penn, *Kentucky Rebel Town: The Civil War Battles of Cynthiana and Harrison County* (Lexington: University Press of Kentucky, 2016), 39; "No true son" from *OR,* vol. 52, pt. 1:191; and quoted in Thomas B. Van Horne, *History of the Army of the Cumberland,* 2 vols. (Cincinnati: Robert Clarke & Co., 1875), 1:34.

2. *OR,* ser. 2, vol. 2:74–75; Anderson proclamation quoted in "Affairs in Kentucky," *New York Times,* September 28, 1861; E. Merton Coulter,

The Civil War and Readjustment in Kentucky (Gloucester, MA: Peter Smith, 1966), 147–48; Lewis Collins and Richard H. Collins, *History of Kentucky* (Covington: Collins & Co., 1882), 1:95; Porter quoted in Matthews, *Basil Duke*, 35. For Anderson's initial command in Kentucky, also see Mark Grimsley, *The Hard Hand of War: Union Military Policy toward Southern Civilians, 1861–1865* (Cambridge: Cambridge University Press, 1995), 62.

3. Speed to Lincoln, September 1, 1861, and Holt to Lincoln, September 2, 1861, both in Abraham Lincoln Papers, Library of Congress, transcribed and annotated by the Lincoln Studies Center, Knox College, Galesburg, IL, online at memory.loc.gov (Lincoln Papers, LC); *OR*, vol. 4:197, 270; September 8, 1861, Journal by Ellen Kenton McGaughey Wallace, 1849–1865, transcribed by James T. Killebrew, Special Collections, Kentucky Historical Society (KHS), Frankfort. For Holt, see Elizabeth D. Leonard, *Lincoln's Forgotten Ally: Judge Advocate General Joseph Holt of Kentucky* (Chapel Hill: University of North Carolina Press, 2011).

4. Morton to Lincoln, September 10, 1861, Lincoln Papers, LC; *OR*, vol. 4:267–68, 273, 274.

5. Hambleton Tapp and James C. Klotter, eds., *The Union, the Civil War, and John W. Tuttle* (Frankfort: Kentucky Historical Society, 1980), 31.

6. *OR*, vol. 4:272, 262; Anderson to Lincoln, September 20, 21, 1861, Lincoln Papers, LC.

7. *OR*, vol. 4:266, 275, 269, 266; A. C. Badger to James Speed and Joshua Speed, September 23, 1861, Lincoln Papers, LC.

8. September 13, 1861, Ellen Kenton McGaughey Wallace journal, KHS, September 13, 1861.

9. November 1, 10, 1861, George Washington Smith diary transcript, Smith Family Papers, 64M142, University of Kentucky Special Collections, Lexington.

10. Holt to Lincoln, September 2, 1861, Lincoln Papers, LC.

11. *OR*, ser. 2, vol. 2:894, 895, 889, 884; Coulter, *Civil War and Readjustment*, 149; John Lafferty Civil War Narrative, SC934, KHS; Guy C. Shearer, "William Armstrong Cooper, 1813–1909," *Filson Club History Quarterly* 25 (April 1951): 145; Aaron Astor, *Rebels on the Border: Civil War, Emancipation, and the Reconstruction of Kentucky and Missouri* (Baton Rouge: Louisiana State University Press, 2012), 89. For Union loyalty oaths, also see Christopher Phillips, *The Rivers Ran Backward: The Civil War and the Remaking of the American Middle Border* (Oxford: Oxford University Press, 2016), 189–92; and Christopher Phillips, "Netherworld of War: The Dominion System and the Contours of Federal Occupation in Kentucky," *Register of the Kentucky Historical Society* 110 (Summer–Autumn 2012): 339–46. For the Federal government's initial conciliatory policy toward southerners, see Grimsley, *Hard Hand of War*, 23–35. For shame and Southern honor, see Bertram Wyatt-Brown, *Southern Honor: Ethics and*

Behavior in the Old South (Oxford: Oxford University Press, 2007), 155; Anna Koivusalo, "He Ordered the First Gun Fired & He Resigned First," in *The Field of Honor: Essays on Southern Character and American Identity*, ed. John Mayfield and Todd Hagstette (Columbia: University of South Carolina Press, 2017), 197.

12. Coulter, *Civil War and Readjustment in Kentucky*, 147; *OR*, ser. 2, vol. 2:747–49, 889, 234, 882, 883, 881. For an example of a Union oath of allegiance, see Freeland Culley Oath of Allegiance, Freeland Culley Papers, FF1-43-1, KHS.

13. *OR*, ser. 2, vol. 2:893, 882; John Wesley Robards obituary, *Harrodsburg Herald*, October 22, 1909; "Revolver Duel at Harrodsburg," *Louisville Courier-Journal*, October 13, 1909; "Robards Dies from Wounds," *Louisville Courier-Journal*, October 17, 1909.

14. Coulter, *Civil War and Readjustment in Kentucky*, 147–48; Collins and Collins, *History of Kentucky*, 1:94, 95; *OR*, vol. 4:278, ser. 2, vol. 2:81.

15. *OR*, ser. 2, vol. 2:886, 887, 894.

16. Mark E. Neely Jr., "The Lincoln Administration and Arbitrary Arrests: A Reconsideration," *Journal of the Abraham Lincoln Association* 5, no. 1 (1983): 8, 13, 23; *OR*, ser. 2, vol. 2:882. Seward also quoted in Mark E. Neely Jr., *The Fate of Liberty: Abraham Lincoln and Civil Liberties* (New York: Oxford University Press, 1991), 30, 7, 26. Neely calls civilian arrests primarily a "border-state problem" (75). For the effectiveness of arrests in Maryland, see 29–30. For an overview of Seward's role in civilian arrests, see 19–24.

17. *Journal of the House of Representatives of the Commonwealth of Kentucky*, session beginning September 2, 1861, 222; Collins and Collins, *History of Kentucky*, 1:94; Brutus J. Clay to Ann Clay, September 24, 1861, *Voices from the Century Before: The Odyssey of a 19th Century Kentucky Family*, ed. Mary Clay Berry (New York: Arcade, 1994), 263.

18. *Journal of the House of Representatives of the Commonwealth of Kentucky*, session beginning September 2, 1861, 222, 194, 196, 223, 221; *Acts of the General Assembly of the Commonwealth of Kentucky*, passed at September 1861, November 1861, February 1862, August 1862, and January 1863 sessions (Frankfort: John R. Major & W. R. Hughes, 1861–1863), 111; *Journal of the Senate of the Commonwealth of Kentucky*, session beginning September 2, 1861, 155–56; Collins and Collins, *History of Kentucky*, 1:94. The committee's report was also reprinted in "House of Representatives," *Frankfort Commonwealth*, September 26, 1861. The arrest of the Kentucky legislators was not unique. In Maryland in September 1861, several pro-Confederate legislators were detained. See Neely, *Fate of Liberty*, 15.

19. Neely, *Fate of Liberty*, 20.

20. *Journal of the House of Representatives of the Commonwealth of Kentucky*, session beginning September 2, 1861, 222, 223; Collins and Collins, *History of Kentucky*, 1:94.

21. Lindsey Apple, *The Family Legacy of Henry Clay: In the Shadow of a Kentucky Patriarch* (Lexington: University Press of Kentucky, 2011), 19–20, 27, 28, 41, 61, 100, 107, 108, 109; Collins and Collins, *History of Kentucky,* 1:8, 86, 217, 358; George W. Ranck, *History of Lexington, Kentucky: Its Early Annals and Recent Progress* (Cincinnati: Robert Clarke & Co., 1872), 390; August 1, 1861, George Washington Smith diary transcript.

22. Apple, *Family Legacy of Henry Clay,* 104, 107, 278n67; Collins and Collins, *History of Kentucky,* 1:79; "Domestic," *New York Observer and Chronicle,* February 25, 1858; "Washington Correspondence," *Christian Inquirer,* February 27, 1858; James B. Clay to Major Alexander, Ashland, July 18, 1855, Henry Clay Memorial Foundation Papers, 96M2, UK.

23. *OR,* ser. 2, vol. 2:884, 886; Collins and Collins, *History of Kentucky,* 1:95; Ranck, *History of Lexington, Kentucky,* 390; Apple, *Family Legacy of Henry Clay,* 114; Eastham Tarrant, *The Wild Riders of the First Kentucky Cavalry* (Louisville: R. H. Carothers, 1894), 37. One Bourbon County resident who was at Camp Dick Robinson wrote his aunt, "I find a good deal of excitement here. James B. Clay is here a prisoner." Christopher Clay to Ann Clay, September 1861, in Berry, *Voices from the Century Before,* 262.

24. "Arrest of James B. Clay," *New York Times,* September 28, 1861.

25. Anderson to Lincoln, September 28, 1861, Lincoln Papers, LC; *OR,* ser. 2, vol. 2:885; Apple, *Family Legacy of Henry Clay,* 113.

26. Brian McGinty, *The Body of John Merryman: Abraham Lincoln and the Suspension of Habeas Corpus* (Cambridge, MA: Harvard University Press, 2011), 1; James F. Simon, *Lincoln and Chief Justice Taney* (New York: Simon & Schuster, 2006), 186, 189, 196–97; Neely, *Fate of Liberty,* 10, 12; Williamson Murray and Wayne Wei-Siang Hsieh, *A Savage War: A Military History of the Civil War* (Princeton, NJ: Princeton University Press, 2016), 79–80; Kentucky legislative resolution from *Journal of the House of Representatives of the Commonwealth of Kentucky,* session beginning September 2, 1862, 200.

27. *OR,* ser. 2, vol. 2:885, 890; Anderson to Lincoln, September 28, 1861, Lincoln Papers, LC; Apple, *Family Legacy of Henry Clay,* 114; James Guthrie and Robert Anderson to Abraham Lincoln, September 30, 1861, Lincoln Papers, LC.

4. Beyond the Reach of Law or Liberty

1. *The War of the Rebellion: A Compilation of the Official Records of the Union and Confederate Armies* (Washington, DC: GPO, 1880–1901), ser. 2, vol. 2:805 (*OR;* unless noted, all citations to ser. 1); William C. Harris, *Lincoln and the Border States: Preserving the Union* (Lawrence: University Press of Kansas, 2011), 109; Lewis Collins and Richard H. Collins, *History of Kentucky,* 2

vols. (Covington: Collins & Co., 1882), 1:95; James A. Ramage, "Charles Slaughter Morehead," in *Kentucky's Governors: 1792–1985*, ed. Lowell H. Harrison (Lexington: University Press of Kentucky, 2004), 77; E. Merton Coulter, *The Civil War and Readjustment in Kentucky* (Gloucester, MA: Peter Smith, 1966), 148; *Richmond Daily Dispatch*, September 27, 1861.

2. *OR*, ser. 2, vol. 2:806.

3. *OR*, ser. 2, vol. 2:812.

4. *Journal of the House of Representatives of the Commonwealth of Kentucky*, session beginning September 2, 1862, 208–9.

5. Transcription of nine volumes of writing by Capt. Leland Hathaway after the Civil War, Hathaway Family Papers, 5M113, University of Kentucky Special Collections, Lexington.

6. *OR*, ser. 2, vol. 2:823, 825, 826, 827, 806, 828.

7. *OR*, ser. 2, vol. 2:805; *Richmond Daily Dispatch*, September 24, 1861; *Cincinnati Daily Press*, September 21, 1861; A. H. Smead to Lincoln, September 20, 1861, and George D. Prentice to Lincoln, January 1, 1862, both in Abraham Lincoln Papers, Library of Congress, transcribed and annotated by the Lincoln Studies Center, Knox College, Galesburg, IL, online at memory. loc.gov (Lincoln Papers, LC); Collins and Collins, *History of Kentucky*, 1:95.

8. *OR*, vol. 52, 2:153.

9. "Charles S. Morehead," in *The Biographical Cyclopedia of the Commonwealth of Kentucky* (Chicago: John M. Gresham Company, 1896), 285, 286; Ramage, "Charles Slaughter Morehead," 75, 76, 77; George W. Ranck, *History of Lexington, Kentucky: Its Early Annals and Recent Progress* (Cincinnati: Robert Clarke & Co., 1872), 371; Harris, *Lincoln and the Border States*, 16; 1860 US Federal Census—Slave Schedule, Jefferson County, Kentucky, available at Ancestry.com; "Kentucky Rebels at Fort Lafayette," *New York Times*, September 22, 1861; "The Voice of Kentucky," *New York Times*, November 10, 1860; Coulter, *Civil War and Readjustment in Kentucky*, 34; *OR*, ser. 2, vol. 2:805, 806.

10. "Kentucky Rebels at Fort Lafayette," *New York Times*, September 22, 1861; Chapman Coleman, *The Life of John J. Crittenden*, 2 vols. (Philadelphia: J. P. Lippincott & Co., 1873), 2:342.

11. *OR*, ser. 2, vol. 2:818; "*Louisville Daily Democrat*, January 11, 1862; Breckinridge quoted in Coulter, *Civil War and Readjustment in Kentucky*, 148.

12. "Distinguished Arrivals in New York," *Richmond Daily Dispatch*, October 1, 1861; "Monthly Record of Current Events," *Harper's New Monthly Magazine*, November 1861, 833; *OR*, ser. 2, vol. 2.

13. Coleman, *Life of John J. Crittenden*, 2:334, 335, 342, 333; "Parallels between Robespierre and Lincoln," *Old Guard* 1 (August 1863): 208; *OR*, ser. 2, vol. 2:230, 819.

14. Charles S. Morehead, "The Habeas Corpus," *Old Guard* 1 (June 1863): 128; J. T. Dorris, "President Lincoln's Treatment of Kentuckians," *Filson Club History Quarterly* 28 (January 1954): 8.

15. *OR*, ser. 2, vol. 2:809; Mark E. Neely Jr., *The Fate of Liberty: Abraham Lincoln and Civil Liberties* (New York: Oxford University Press, 1991), 63. Lincoln could be magnanimous toward political prisoners. When the president learned that Kentuckians William S. Pryor of Henry County and J. O'Hara of Covington, both of whom had been imprisoned at Camp Chase, were in Cincinnati "on parole, without permission to leave the State of Ohio," Lincoln told Secretary of War Edwin Stanton to leave them alone, writing "let their parole stand, but allow them to go at large generally." Abraham Lincoln to Secretary of War Edwin Stanton, January 9, 1863, SC 1083, KHS. Neely also notes that of the approximately 13,000 civilian arrests carried out during the Civil War, Seward "presided over the arrest of only 864 civilians." Neely, *Fate of Liberty,* 23.

16. *OR*, ser. 2, vol. 2:813, 824, 819; Prentice to Lincoln, January 1, 1862, Lincoln Papers, LC; Charles J. Bussey, "James Guthrie," in *The Kentucky Encyclopedia*, ed. John E. Kleber (Lexington: University Press of Kentucky, 1992), 396; Thomas Speed, *The Union Cause in Kentucky: 1860–1865* (New York: G. P. Putnam & Sons, 1907), 73.

17. *OR*, ser. 2, vol. 2:807. Prentice also asked Lincoln to release Barr, who "is a poor man" who "has a very lovely wife dependent upon him." For Prentice's support for Morehead's release, also see Harris, *Lincoln and the Border States,* 110–11.

18. *OR*, ser. 2, vol. 2:825; 805, 223, 824; *Lexington Observer and Reporter*, January 11, 1862; Morehead to Crittenden quoted in Coleman, *Life of John J. Crittenden,* 2:349.

19. *OR*, ser. 2, vol. 2:820, 805; "Col. Reuben T. Durrett," in *Biographical Cyclopedia of the Commonwealth of Kentucky,* 344; "Reuben T. Durrett," in *The Biographical Encyclopaedia of Kentucky of the Dead and Living Men of the Nineteenth Century* (Cincinnati: J. M. Armstrong & Co., 1878), 337; Fannie Porter Dickey, *Blades O' Bluegrass* (Louisville: John P. Morton & Co., 1892), 305, 306; 1860 US Federal Census—Slave Schedule, Louisville, Jefferson County, available at Ancestry.com.

20. *OR*, ser. 2, vol. 2:806, 805; Collins and Collins, *History of Kentucky,* 1:94. For other editors arrested by the federal government, see Neely, *Fate of Liberty,* 28.

21. *OR*, ser. 2, vol. 2:821, 820, 810.

22. *OR*, ser. 2, vol. 2:808.

23. *OR*, ser. 2, vol. 2:811.

24. George D. Prentice to Lincoln, September 24, 1861, Lincoln Papers, LC; *OR,* ser. 2, vol. 2:807.

25. *OR,* ser. 2, vol. 2:809.

26. Coulter, *Civil War and Readjustment in Kentucky,* 452; Leslie Ann Harper, "Lethal Language: The Rhetoric of George Prentice and Louisville's Bloody Monday," *Ohio Valley History* 11 (Fall 2011): 25; Polk Johnson, *A History of Kentucky and Kentuckians,* 3 vols. (Chicago: Lewis Publishing Co., 1912), 1:180; from, *Autobiography of Samuel D. Gross, M.D.,* 2 vols., ed. Samuel W. Gross (Philadelphia: W. B. Saunders, 1893), 2:353.

27. "The Editorial Street Affray at Louisville," *Washington Evening Star,* July 25, 1857; "Cause of the Street Fight in Louisville, Ky.," *Wheeling Daily Intelligencer,* July 23, 1857; "Editorial Affray," *Nashville Union and American,* July 25, 1857. For Durrett-Prentice correspondence, see "Prentice's Statement of the Difficulty Between Himself and the Editor of the Courier," *Wheeling Daily Intelligencer,* July 24, 1857. Durrett-Prentice correspondence also from "Miscellany," *Weekly Clarksville (TN) Chronicle,* July 31, 1857; "The Shooting Affair Yesterday," *Nashville Union and American,* July 24, 1857. Some admirers approved of Durrett's fight with Prentice. See Ogden Fontaine to Col. R. C. Durrett, December 14, 1895, Reuben T. Durrett Added Papers, Correspondence, 1895, Filson Historical Society, Louisville. For editors participating in formal duels, see Jack K. Williams, *Dueling in the Old South: Vignettes of Social History* (College Station: Texas A&M University Press, 1980), 29–33. While editors appeared as frequent participants in duels, historian Matthew A. Byron notes that from 1800 to 1810 most duelists were either soldiers or lawyers. Doctors were the third-highest profession to engage in duels during this period. Matthew A. Byron, "An Honorable Death? The Stuart-Bennett Duel of 1819," in *The Field of Honor: Essays on Southern Character and American Identity,* John Mayfield and Todd Hagstette (Columbia: University of South Carolina Press, 2017), 104.

28. *OR,* ser. 2, vol. 2:821, 822, 823, 806.

5. The Soul of the Rebellion

1. Lewis Collins and Richard H. Collins, *History of Kentucky,* 2 vols. (Covington: Collins & Co., 1882), 1:94; *The War of the Rebellion: A Compilation of the Official Records of the Union and Confederate Armies* (Washington, DC: GPO, 1880–1901), ser. 1, vol. 4:280, ser. 2, vol. 3:914. (*OR;* unless noted, all citations to ser. 1); "The Maysville Union Barbeque," *Cincinnati Daily Press,* September 19, 1861; "Union Barbeque," *Cincinnati Daily Press,* September 24, 1861; "Words and Work," *Cincinnati Daily Press,* September 25, 1861; "Soldiers' Letters," *Highland Weekly News,* October 10, 1861; J. Winston Coleman Jr., *Famous Kentucky Duels* (Lexington: Henry Clay Press, 1969), 107; Jean W. Calvert, "Maysville," in *The Kentucky Encyclopedia,* ed. John E. Kleber (Lexington: University Press of Kentucky, 1992), 622; E. Merton

Coulter, *The Civil War and Readjustment in Kentucky* (Gloucester, MA: Peter Smith, 1966), 127; C. Glenn Clift, *History of Maysville and Mason County* (Lexington: Transylvania Printing, 1956), 218.

2. Coleman, *Famous Kentucky Duels,* 110, 110n1; Genealogy of the Metcalfe Family, Metcalfe Family Papers, SC1272, Kentucky Historical Society (KHS), Frankfort; "The Last Duel Fought in Kentucky," *Louisville Courier-Journal,* March 12, 1877.

3. Genealogy of the Metcalfe Family; Frank M. Mathias, "Thomas Metcalfe," in *Kentucky's Governors: 1792–1985,* ed. Lowell H. Harrison (Lexington: University Press of Kentucky, 2004), 33; Robert Peter, *History of Bourbon, Scott, Harrison, and Nicholas Counties, Kentucky* (Chicago: O. L. Baskin & Co., 1882), 397, 396; Karl Raitz and Nancy O'Malley, *Kentucky's Frontier Highway: Historical Landscapes along the Maysville Road* (Lexington: University Press of Kentucky, 2012), 219; History of Forest Retreat Farm, Metcalfe Family Papers, SC1272, KHS; J. Winston Coleman, *Historic Kentucky* (Lexington: Henry Clay Press, 1967), 130, 182, 82.

4. Mathias, "Thomas Metcalfe," 33, 34–35, 36; Genealogy of the Metcalfe Family; Robert Peter, *History of Bourbon, Scott, Harrison, and Nicholas Counties, Kentucky* (Chicago: O. L. Baskin & Co., 1882), 396, 397; Raitz and O'Malley, *Kentucky's Frontier Highway,* 219; "Thomas Metcalfe to Valentine Peers, September 17, 1826, MSS6, box 1, folder 4, Valentine Peers Papers, KHS.

5. Raitz and O'Malley, *Kentucky's Frontier Highway,* 219; Peter, *History of Bourbon, Scott, Harrison, and Nicholas Counties,* 397.

6. Z. F. Smith, "Dueling, and Some Noted Duels in Kentucky," *Register of the Kentucky Historical Society* 8 (September 1910): 80–81; "McDuffie and Metcalfe," *National Banner and Nashville Whig,* March 24, 1827; and "From the National Intelligencer, of Feb. 28," *Niles' Weekly Register,* March 3, 1827; *Newbern (NC) Sentinel,* March 10, 1827; "A Challenge But No Duel," *New-England Galaxy and United States Literary Advertiser* 10 (March 9, 1827): 2; "An Essay Towards a Duel," *Western Recorder* 4 (March 13, 1827): 43; Roger Lane, "Murder in America: A Historian's Perspective," *Crime and Justice* 25 (1999): 199. In her study about violence in the US Congress, Joanne B. Freeman found "more than *seventy* violent incidents between congressmen in the House and Senate chambers or on nearby streets and dueling grounds." Several of these involved elected officials from Kentucky. Joanne B. Freeman, *The Field of Blood: Violence in Congress and the Road to Civil War* (New York: Farrar, Straus & Giroux, 2018), 5.

7. Raitz and O'Malley, *Kentucky's Frontier Highway,* 221; Mathias, "Thomas Metcalfe," 36; Coleman, *Historic Kentucky,* 82; Peter, *History of Bourbon, Scott, Harrison, and Nicholas Counties,* 397; Genealogy of the Metcalfe Family; History of Forest Retreat Farm.

8. *List of Cadets Admitted into the United States Military Academy, West Point, N.Y.* (Washington, DC: GPO, 1902), 67; "Last Duel," *Louisville Courier-Journal.*

9. E. Polk Johnson, *A History of Kentucky and Kentuckians,* 3 vols. (Chicago: Lewis Publishing Co., 1912), 1:594; Genealogy of the Metcalfe Family; Mayor E. C. Phister to Captain Leonidas Metcalfe, September 28, 1847, John Metcalfe Family Papers, SC1273, KHS.

10. Thomas Metcalfe to Leonidas Metcalfe, January 20, 1848, John Metcalfe Family Papers, SC1273, KHS; "Last Duel," *Louisville Courier-Journal*; Charles K. Gardner, *A Dictionary of All Officers, Who Have Been Commissioned, or Have Been Appointed and Served, in the Army of the United States* (New York: D. Van Nostrand, 1860), 548.

11. "Last Duel," *Louisville Courier-Journal*; 1860 US Federal Census, Nicholas County, available at Ancestry.com; 1860 US Federal Census—Slave Schedule, Nicholas County, District 2, available at Ancestry.com; Kenneth H. Williams and James Russell Harris, eds., "Kentucky in 1860: A Statistical Overview," *Register of the Kentucky Historical Society* 103 (Autumn 2003): 749.

12. "Last Duel," *Louisville Courier-Journal.*

13. "Last Duel," *Louisville Courier-Journal*; Garrett Davis to Simon Cameron, July 15, 1861, William Nelson to Leonidas Metcalfe, undated, and William Nelson to Salmon P. Chase, July 18, 1861, all in John Metcalfe Family Papers, SC1273, KHS.

14. "Army Correspondence," *Louisville Daily Courier,* May 22, 1861; "Last Duel," *Louisville Courier-Journal*; Thomas Speed, *The Union Cause in Kentucky: 1860–1865* (New York: G. P. Putnam & Sons, 1907), 102, 103.

15. *OR*, vol. 4:332; "Liability of Military Officers," *Evansville (IN) Daily Journal,* April 28, 1864. This was likely the Canadian-born James McKrell, a forty-four-year-old farmer who in 1860 owned $9,500 in real estate and $5,000 in personal property. He also owned six slaves, three female and three male, ages four months old to twenty-six years. 1860 US Federal Census, Mason County, District 2, and 1860 US Federal Census—Slave Schedule, Mason County, District 2, both available at Ancestry.com. McKrell lived near Mayslick in Mason County. "Sale of Mules," *Louisville Daily Courier,* February 3, 1861.

16. Coleman, *Famous Kentucky Duels,* 110, 107–8; "Letter from Kentucky," *Caledonian* (St. Johnsbury, VT), May 23, 1862; John A. Marshall, *American Bastille: A History of Illegal Arrests and Imprisonment of American Citizens during the Civil War* (Philadelphia: Evans, Stoddart, & Co., 1871), 236; *OR*, ser. 2, vol. 2:913, 914; Clift, *History of Maysville,* 219; "Arrests in Kentucky—Proclamation of Gen. Anderson," *Louisville Daily Courier,* October 14, 1861; Collins and Collins, *History of Kentucky,* 1:97; *Lexington Observer and Reporter,* May 10, 1862.

17. *OR,* ser. 2, vol. 2:915; Marshall, *American Bastille,* 238.

18. "Secession Sympathizers," *Cincinnati Daily Press,* October 3, 1861; "Arrest of Alleged Secessionists in Kentucky," *Philadelphia Inquirer,* October 5, 1861; "The Habeas Corpus Case," *Cincinnati Daily Press,* October 3, 1861.

19. Marshall, *American Bastille,* 236; "Last Duel," *Louisville Courier-Journal;* "Arrests in Kentucky," *Louisville Daily Courier; Louisville Daily Courier,* October 14, 1861; "Another Arrival of Rebel Sympathizers," *Cincinnati Daily Press,* October 10, 1861; *Louisville Daily Courier,* October 17, 1861; "General News," *Raleigh Semi-Weekly Standard,* October 5, 1861.

20. "Union Camps," *Evansville (IN) Daily Journal,* September 16, 1861; Collins and Collins, *History of Kentucky,* 1:96; "A Rebel Commander from Covington Retreats," *Cincinnati Daily Press,* November 8, 1861; "Last Duel," *Louisville Courier-Journal;* T. R. C. Hutton, *Bloody Breathitt: Politics and Violence in the Appalachian South* (Lexington: University Press of Kentucky, 2013), 43; *OR,* vol. 4:225; November 8, 10, 1861, Winchester Byron Rudy Civil War diary, 1998ms003, University of Kentucky, Lexington.

21. Dennis W. Belcher, *The Cavalry of the Army of the Cumberland* (Jefferson, NC: McFarland, 2016), 69; "Rebel Outrage in Nicholas County," *Cincinnati Daily Press,* December 18, 1861.

22. Clift, *History of Maysville,* 219; "Dead at Maysville," *Louisville Courier-Journal,* March 21, 1891; Charles W. Kent, "Henry Throop Stanton," *Library of Southern Literature,* ed. Edwin Anderson Alderman and Joel Chandler Harris (New Orleans: Martin & Hoyt Co., 1907), 11:5083; "Hon. Richard H. Stanton," in *Biographical Encyclopaedia of Kentucky of the Dead and Living Men of the Nineteenth Century* (Cincinnati: J. M. Armstrong & Co., 1878), 101; 1850 US Federal Census, Maysville, Mason County, available at Ancestry.com; "Owes Its Name to Judge Stanton," *Maysville Evening Bulletin,* July 20, 1891.

23. *Biographical Directory of the United States Congress, 1774–2005* (Washington, DC: GPO, 2005), 143; "Dead at Maysville," *Louisville Courier-Journal;* "Democratic Meeting in Maysville," *Louisville Daily Courier,* May 14, 1859; "Hon. Richard H. Stanton," 101; 1850 US Federal Census—Slave Schedule, East Maysville, Mason County, 1860 US Federal Census—Slave Schedule, East Maysville, Mason County, and 1860 US Federal Census, East Maysville, Mason County, all available at Ancestry.com; Marshall, *American Bastille,* 236, 237; William C. Davis, *Breckinridge: Statesman, Soldier, Symbol* (Lexington: University Press of Kentucky, 1974), 281; *OR,* ser. 2, vol. 2:914; Kent, "Henry Throop Stanton," 5083–84; J. Stoddard Johnston, "Biographical Sketch of Major Henry T. Stanton," *Register of the Kentucky Historical Society* 14 (May 1916): 9–11; Henry Gannett, *The Origins of Certain Place Names in the United States* (Washington, DC: GPO, 1905), 289.

24. *OR,* ser. 2, vol. 2:916; Clift, *History of Maysville,* 219.

25. Johnson, *History of Kentucky and Kentuckians*, 3:1282, 1283; "James H. Hall, Sr.," Memorial ID 111935707, Find a Grave, accessed February 20, 2023, https://www.findagrave.com/memorial/111935707/james-h-hall; 1860 US Federal Census—Slave Schedule, East Maysville, Mason County; 1860 US Federal Census, East Maysville, Mason County; "James H. Hall," in *Biographical Encyclopaedia of Kentucky*, 372; "Eagle Plow Works," *Maysville Evening Bulletin*, March 13, 1882; Marshall, *American Bastille*, 237.

26. 1860 US Federal Census, Maysville, Mason County; 1850 US Federal Census, Maysville, Mason County; "Important Enterprise," *Maysville Daily Evening Bulletin*, December 21, 1881; "William Hunt," *Maysville Evening Bulletin*, January 15, 1892; Carrie Westlake Whitney, *Kansas City, Missouri: Its History and Its People*, 2 vols (Chicago: S. J. Clarke Publishing Co., 1908), 2:312; "Arrests in Kentucky," *Louisville Daily Courier*; John C. Underwood, *Report of the Proceedings Incidental to the Erection and Dedication of the Confederate Monument* (Chicago: William Johnston Printing Co., 1896), 85; "Forrester," *Bourbon News* (Paris, KY), November 21, 1913.

27. Marshall, *American Bastille*, 238, 239, 240; Coleman, *Famous Kentucky Duels*, 108; "Arrests in Kentucky," *Louisville Daily Courier*.

28. "Change of Name," *Cleveland Morning Leader*, June 22, 1861; "Atrocious Treatment of Our Prisoners—The 'Pens' at Camp Chase in Ohio," *Daily Nashville Patriot*, October 10, 1861; "Local Matters," *Daily Ohio Statesman* (Columbus), October 8, 1861; *OR*, ser. 2, vol. 2:917. N. S. Offutt, a Kentucky Confederate soldier confined at Camp Chase for two months, said, "We were treated and fed as well [as] a soldier should ask." N. S. Offutt to his father, December 1867, N. S. Offutt Letter, SC 226, KHS. For additional descriptions about conditions and provision at Camp Chase, see "From Columbus," *Cleveland Morning Leader*, October 29, 1861, and "The Political Prisoners at Camp Chase, Columbus," *Cleveland Morning Leader*, November 19, 1861.

29. "Horrible Barbarities," *Nashville Patriot*, December 15, 1861. For another Kentucky prisoner's view of Camp Chase, see "My Own Dear Mother" from "son Willie," January 1, 1862, Corlis-Respess Family Papers, Correspondence, 1860–1864, Filson Historical Society, Louisville.

30. "A Secession Editor's Confession," *Gallipolis (OH) Journal*, October 17, 1861; "Veteran Editor Dead," *Maysville Daily Public Ledger*, November 30, 1907; William A. Penn, *Kentucky Rebel Town: The Civil War Battles of Cynthiana and Harrison County* (Lexington: University Press of Kentucky, 2016), 69; "Latest By Telegraph," *Louisville Daily Courier*, April 17, 1861; "The Opinion of a Unionist," *Fayetteville Observer*, June 6, 1861.

31. Penn, *Kentucky Rebel Town*, 65, 66, 69; "Covington News," *Cincinnati Daily Press*, October 1, 1861.

32. Morey's letter from "Secession Editor's Confession," *Gallipolis Journal*; "The Great Rebellion," *Weekly Perrysburg Journal*, October 10, 1861; "A

Secession Editor Recants," *Cincinnati Daily Press,* October 5, 1861; "A Craven," *Memphis Daily Appeal,* October 16, 1861.

33. "Released," *Cincinnati Daily Press,* October 28, 1861; *Evansville (IN) Daily Journal,* March 3, 1862; "Horrible Barbarities," *Nashville Patriot*; Penn, *Kentucky Rebel Town,* 70; "Veteran Editor Dead," *Maysville Daily Public Ledger,* 4.

34. Tolle, a twenty-eight-year-old blacksmith, had been arrested for raising $200 to equip a secessionist company. Bull Nelson asked US Secretary of the Treasury Salmon P. Chase to release Tolle, whose "wife is a good Union woman of a good Union family." Congressman W. H. Wadsworth had promised "to be responsible for his future conduct." Tolle took the Union loyalty oath and was released on October 17, 1861, two months before most of the other Maysville prisoners were freed. Nelson said he would "have him kept under surveillance" and would arrest him again if needed. Nelson, however, believed that Tolle's confinement "will take away his power to do harm and make him afraid to attempt it." 1860 US Federal Census, Mason County, Maysville East precinct, available at Ancestry.com; *OR,* ser. 2, vol. 2:915–16.

35. Marshall, *American Bastille,* 239, 240; *OR,* ser. 2, vol. 2:917, 913, 931, 155; Clift, *History of Maysville,* 220; "Last Duel," *Louisville Courier-Journal*; *Ohio Statesman* quoted in Alfred Emory Lee, *History of the City of Columbus, Capital of Ohio* (New York: Monsell & Co., 1892), 2:102; Collins and Collins, *History of Kentucky,* 1:97; "A Card," *Cincinnati Daily Press,* October 5, 1861.

6. Down with Them

1. "'Seceshers' in the Clutches of Uncle Sam," *Altoona (PA) Tribune,* November 7, 1861; "More Prisoners for Fort Lafayette," *Daily Nashville Patriot,* November 20, 1861; Lonnie R. Speer, *Portals to Hell: Military Prisons of the Civil War* (Lincoln: University of Nebraska Press, 1997), 35; "The Political Prisoners," *New York Times,* September 24, 1861. The *Cincinnati Daily Press* said that when Casto, Stanton, and the other Maysville men were sent to Fort Lafayette, it was "to be a sort of Bastille for captured rebels." "Inklings," *Cincinnati Daily Press,* November 6, 1861.

2. Paul G. Pierpaoli Jr., "Fort Lafayette, New York," in *American Civil War: The Definitive Encyclopedia and Document Collection,* 6 vols., ed. Spencer C. Tucker (Santa Barbara: ABC-CLIO, 2013), 1:677; Speer, *Portals to Hell,* 35, 36; *Washington Evening Star,* July 19, 1861; "The Political Prisoners," *New York Times,* September 24, 1861; "News of the Day," *New York Times,* August 29, 1861; "Fort Lafayette," *Washington Evening Star,* September 19, 1861; Burke to Cameron, *The War of the Rebellion: A Compilation of the Official Records of the Union and Confederate Armies* (Washington, DC: GPO, 1880–1901), ser. 2, vol. 2:91 (*OR*; unless noted, all citations to ser. 1); Levi C. Turner to John

G. Nicolay, November 17, 1862, Abraham Lincoln Papers, Library of Congress, transcribed and annotated by the Lincoln Studies Center, Knox College, Galesburg, IL, online at memory.loc.gov (Lincoln Papers, LC).

3. Pierpaoli, "Fort Lafayette," 677; Speer, *Portals to Hell*, 36–37, 38, 36; "Political Prisoners," *New York Times*; *OR*, ser. 2, vol. 2:998.

4. *OR*, ser. 2, vol. 2:776, 155.

5. Holt to Seward, *OR*, ser. 2, vol. 2:891–92; vol. 4:296; "Arrests in Kentucky—Proclamation of Gen. Anderson," *Louisville Daily Courier*, October 14, 1861; E. Merton Coulter, *The Civil War and Readjustment in Kentucky* (Gloucester, MA: Peter Smith, 1966), 148.

6. *OR*, ser. 2, vol. 2:91, 92, 920, 125–26; *OR*, vol. 4:296, 327; "Arrests in Kentucky," *Louisville Daily Courier*; Coulter, *Civil War and Readjustment*, 149; Lewis Collins and Richard H. Collins, *History of Kentucky*, 2 vols. (Covington: Collins & Co., 1882), 1:96. For Judge Bullitt's arrest, see Felix G. Stidger, *Treason History of the Order of Sons of Liberty* (Chicago: By the author, 1903), 106, 172; Elizabeth R. Bullitt and Joshua F. Speed to Abraham Lincoln, August 26, 1864, Lincoln Papers, LC. Mark Grimsley writes that Sherman "continued [Anderson's] mild policy after taking over in early October." He did so "from the simple conviction that it was morally just and best for military discipline, not from any faith that conciliation would undermine Confederate resistance." Mark Grimsley, *The Hard Hand of War: Union Military Policy Toward Southern Civilians, 1861–1865* (Cambridge: Cambridge University Press, 1995), 62, 63.

7. Francis T. Hood and H. Taylor to Abraham Lincoln, November 18, 1861, quoted in C. Glenn Clift, *History of Maysville and Mason County* (Lexington: Transylvania Printing Co., 1956), 220.

8. *OR*, ser. 2, vol. 2:913–14, 918, 919.

9. J. Winston Coleman Jr., *Famous Kentucky Duels* (Lexington: Henry Clay Press, 1969), 109; Clift, *History of Maysville*, 220–21; *OR*, ser. 2, vol. 2:919.

10. *OR*, ser. 2, vol. 2:923.

11. *OR*, vol. 4:214, 225, 534; Thomas D. Matijasic, "Battle of Ivy Mountain," in *The Kentucky Encyclopedia*, ed. John E. Kleber (Lexington: University Press of Kentucky, 1992), 457, 458; William Ely, *The Big Sandy Valley: A History of the People and Country* (Catlettsburg, KY: Central Methodist, 1887), 298; Henry M. Cist, *The Army of the Cumberland* (New York: Charles Scribner's Sons, 1885), 4, 5; Frank Moore, ed., *The Rebellion Record: A Dairy of American Events*, 12 vols. (New York: G. P. Putnam, 1862), 3:276; Hendrick and Oden taking the flag from "Introductory to the Fight," *Louisville Daily Journal*, November 15, 1861. For the Sixteenth Kentucky Infantry, see *Report of the Adjutant General of the State of Kentucky*, 2 vols. (Frankfort: Kentucky Yeoman, 1866), 1:936. Union soldier Winchester Rudy called the flag taken at

Prestonsburg "the three striped flag of Rebellion or Secession." November 3, 1861, Winchester Byron Rudy Civil War diary, 1998ms003, University of Kentucky, Lexington.

12. *OR*, vol. 4:226, 227, 354. Matijasic, "Battle of Ivy Mountain," 458; Ely, *Big Sandy Valley*, 298; Cist, *Army of the Cumberland*, 5; Moore, *Rebellion Record*, 3:338. For the Big Sandy Campaign, see James M. Prichard, "John Stuart Williams" in Bruce S. Allardice and Lawrence Lee Hewitt, *Kentuckians in Gray: Confederate Generals and Field Officers of the Bluegrass State* (Lexington: University Press of Kentucky, 2008), 273–74; Brian D. McKnight, *Contested Borderland: The Civil War in Appalachian Kentucky and Virginia* (Lexington: University Press of Kentucky, 2006), 49–52; Donald A. Clark, *The Notorious "Bull" Nelson: Murdered Civil War General* (Carbondale: Southern Illinois University Press, 2013), 73–77; John David Preston, *The Civil War in the Big Sandy Valley of Kentucky* (Baltimore: Gateway Press, 2008), 36–51; and Julius Christopher Miller Diary, SC 1601, Kentucky Historical Society, Frankfort.

13. *OR*, ser. 2, vol. 2:921; Coleman, *Famous Kentucky Duels*, 108; Clift, *History of Maysville*, 221. Maysville native and Union soldier Winchester Rudy said that after the Big Sandy campaign the troops went back to Maysville, where they "were welcomed home with the greatest pleasure." November 18, 1861, Winchester Byron Rudy Civil War Diary, 1998ms003, UK.

14. *OR*, ser. 2, vol. 2:914, 916, 921; Clift, *History of Maysville*, 221; Coleman, *Famous Kentucky Duels*, 108. As an example, Forrester's oath said that he would not enter a seceded state, correspond with anyone in a seceded state "without permission of the Secretary of State," or "do anything hostile to the United States during the present insurrection." George Forrester, Civil War Service Records, Confederate Records, Miscellaneous, available at Fold3. com.

15. "Forrester," *Bourbon News* (Paris, KY), November 21, 1913; John C. Underwood, *Report of the Proceedings Incidental to the Erection and Dedication of the Confederate Monument* (Chicago: William Johnston Printing Co., 1896), 85; George Forrester Compiled Service Record, Third Kentucky Cavalry, available at Fold3.com.

16. *OR*, ser. 2, vol. 2:927, 929, 914; Stanton to Lincoln, December 17, 1861, quoted in Clift, *History of Maysville*, 221.

17. *OR*, ser. 2, vol. 2:930, 919, 931, 932; Clift, *History of Maysville*, 221; Coleman, *Famous Kentucky Duels*, 109.

18. Clift, *History of Maysville*, 222; *OR*, ser. 2, vol. 2:239, 933, 240, 221; Coleman, *Famous Kentucky Duels*, 110, 111.

19. "Municipal Election at Maysville," *Highland Weekly News*, January 30, 1862.

20. Collins and Collins, *History of Kentucky,* 1:95, 96–97; *OR,* vol. 4:205; J. T. Dorris, "President Lincoln's Treatment of Kentuckians," *Filson Club History Quarterly* 28 (January 1954): 6–7; J. F. Speed to Lincoln, October 7, 1861, John Catron to William T. Carroll, October 9, 1861, both in Lincoln Papers, LC. For Camp Wildcat, see Kenneth A. Hafendorfer, *The Battle of Wild Cat Mountain* (Louisville: KH Press, 2003).

21. Collins and Collins, *History of Kentucky,* 1:97; Lowell H. Harrison, *The Civil War in Kentucky* (Lexington: University Press of Kentucky, 1975), 20; Lowell H. Harrison, *Lincoln of Kentucky* (Lexington: University Press of Kentucky, 2000), 152; Thomas Speed, *The Union Cause in Kentucky: 1860–1865* (New York: G. P. Putnam & Sons, 1907), 206; "George W. Johnson, 1861–1862," *Civil War Governors of Kentucky Digital Documentary Edition,* http://discovery.civilwargovernors.org/george-w-johnson-1861-1862, accessed February 22, 2021; and Lowell H. Harrison, "George W. Johnson and Richard Hawes: The Governors of Confederate Kentucky," *Register of the Kentucky Historical Society* 79 (Winter 1981): 3–39.

22. *Lexington Observer and Reporter,* January 1, 1862.

23. *OR,* vol. 7:159–61, 424–25; James Lee McDonough, *War in Kentucky: From Shiloh to Perryville* (Knoxville: University of Tennessee Press, 1994), 14–16; Benjamin Franklin Cooling, *Forts Henry and Donelson: The Key to the Confederate Heartland* (Knoxville: University of Tennessee Press, 1897), 212–13, 237; Collins and Collins, *History of Kentucky,* 1:99, 100.

24. "Union Meeting in Kentucky," *Highland Weekly News* (Hillsborough, OH), May 1, 1862. Unionists controlled Kentucky polls for much of the Civil War. In Bourbon County in August 1865, for example, authorities in Millersburg maintained a list of Confederate sympathizers who were banned from voting. Confederate Sympathizers List, FF2.5, Kentucky Historical Society (KHS), Frankfort.

25. "Union Meeting in Kentucky," *Highland Weekly News.* Black Hawk was a Sauk Native American leader who fought against white settlers in the present-day American Midwest. This included the Black Hawk War of 1832. See Patrick J. Jung, *The Black Hawk War of 1832* (Norman: University of Oklahoma Press, 2007). Antonio Lopez de Santa Anna, or Santa Anna, led Mexican forces at the Battle of the Alamo and during the Mexican-American War. See Will Fowler, *Santa Anna of Mexico* (Lincoln: University of Nebraska Press, 2007).

26. "Union Meeting in Kentucky," *Highland Weekly News.*

27. "Union Meeting in Kentucky," *Highland Weekly News.* Nathaniel Harris, a former Confederate soldier from Kentucky, was among those imprisoned at Camp Morton in Indiana. Harris informed his wife, "i am well and have ben well and very well treated here." He was later sent to Johnson's Island, off Sandusky Bay in Lake Erie. Nathaniel Harris to his wife and children, October 17, 1862, Nathaniel Harris Papers, SC 1013, KHS.

28. "Union Meeting in Kentucky," *Highland Weekly News*.
29. "Union Meeting in Kentucky," *Highland Weekly News*.
30. "Union Meeting in Kentucky," *Highland Weekly News*.
31. "Union Meeting in Kentucky," *Highland Weekly News*.

7. A Matter of Honor

1. J. Winston Coleman Jr., *Famous Kentucky Duels* (Lexington: Henry Clay Press, 1969): 110, 111; "The Last Duel Fought in Kentucky," *Louisville Courier-Journal*, March 12, 1877; "To the Public," *Frankfort Tri-Weekly Commonwealth*, May 21, 1862. For the Lee House, see "Lee House," in *The Encyclopedia of Northern Kentucky*, ed. Paul A. Tenkotte and James C. Claypool (Lexington: University Press of Kentucky, 2009), 543.

2. "Death of Capt. Isaac Nelson," *Maysville Daily Public Ledger*, April 26, 1892; 1860 US Federal Census, Maysville, Mason County, available at Ancestry.com; "Proved Fatal," *Maysville Evening Bulletin*, April 26, 1892; advertisement, *Maysville Dollar Weekly Bulletin*, August 7, 1862.

3. "Death of Capt. Isaac Nelson," *Maysville Daily Public Ledger*; *The War of the Rebellion: A Compilation of the Official Records of the Union and Confederate Armies* (Washington, DC: GPO, 1880–1901), ser. 2, vol. 2:914 (*OR*; unless noted, all citations to ser. 1).

4. William T. Casto to Col. Leonidas Metcalfe, May 6, 1862, challenging him to a duel, accompanied by Col. Metcalfe's letter of acceptance, May 6, 1862, Filson Historical Society, Louisville; and "Last Duel," *Louisville Courier-Journal*; and "To the Public," *Tri-Weekly Commonwealth*, 2; and Coleman, *Famous Kentucky Duels*, 111–12. Correspondence pertaining to the duel can also be found in *Frankfort Tri-Weekly Commonwealth*, May 21, 1862.

5. Kenneth S. Greenberg, "The Nose, the Lie, and the Duel in the Antebellum South," *American Historical Review* 95 (February 1990): 58; Christopher G. Kingston and Robert E. Wright, "The Deadliest of Games: The Institution of Dueling," *Southern Economic Journal* 76 (April 2010): 1097.

6. *Lexington Observer and Reporter*, May 10, 1862; Caroline R. Miller, "Casto–Metcalfe Duel," in Tenkotte and Claypool, *Encyclopedia of Northern Kentucky*, 165; "Old Killings Recalled," *Hazel Green (KY) Herald*, May 23, 1895; Coleman, *Famous Kentucky Duels*, 119; "Last Duel," *Louisville Courier-Journal*, 1.

7. Coleman, *Famous Kentucky Duels*, 112.

8. John Wilson Townsend, *Kentucky in American Letters, 1784–1912*, 2 vols. (Cedar Rapids, IA: Torch Press, 1913), 1:310; Stella Pickett Hardy, *Colonial Families of the Southern States of America* (Baltimore: Southern Book Co., 1958), 243; "From Lincoln County," *Louisville Daily Courier*, February 27, 1854; "Yields to Death," *Louisville Courier-Journal*, April 8, 1904. For the

Centre College class of 1855, see *The Thirty-First Annual Catalog of the Officers and Students of Centre College at Danville, Kentucky, for the Year Ending June 30, 1855* (Frankfort: Frankfort Commonwealth, 1855), 4.

9. L. F. Johnson, "Franklin County: Chapter Ten, From 1850 to 1860," *Register of the Kentucky Historical Society* 8 (September 1910): 60; Thomas M. Green to James Harlan, June 4, 1862, Office of the Governor, Beriah Magoffin, Governor's Official Correspondence File, Petitions for Pardons and Remissions, 1859–1862, MG23-470, Kentucky Department for Libraries and Archives, Frankfort, accessed via *Civil War Governors of Kentucky Digital Documentary Edition*, http://discovery.civilwargovernors.org/document/KYR-0001-020-1999.

10. Timothy Bennett, executed on September 3, 1821, in Illinois, was reputedly the only American ever condemned for killing a man in a duel. Matthew A. Byron, "An Honorable Death? The Stuart-Bennett Duel of 1819," in *The Field of Honor: Essays on Southern Character and American Identity*, ed. John Mayfield and Todd Hagstette (Columbia: University of South Carolina Press, 2017), 93, 99.

11. James C. Klotter, *Kentucky Justice, Southern Honor, and American Manhood: Understanding the Life and Death of Richard Reid* (Baton Rouge: Louisiana State University Press, 2003), 48; Edward L. Ayers, *Vengeance and Justice: Crime and Punishment in the Nineteenth-Century American South* (Oxford: Oxford University Press, 1984), 13; Bertram Wyatt-Brown, *Southern Honor: Ethics and Behavior in the Old South* (Oxford: Oxford University Press, 2007), 360, 350, 400. For an example of a caning and class differences, see Dick Steward, *Duels and the Roots of Violence in Missouri* (Columbia: University of Missouri Press, 2000), 37. Steward also notes the push and pull of honor and shame: "Honor and shame had always been at the opposite poles of social evaluation. But honor, unlike its opposite, shame, could be remedied by satisfaction alone" (101).

12. Richard F. Hamm, *Murder, Honor, and Law: Four Virginia Homicides from Reconstruction to the Great Depression* (Charlottesville: University of Virginia Press, 2003), 21; Mayfield, "Marketplace of Values," 5, 8, 10; Lorien Foote, *The Gentlemen and the Roughs: Violence, Honor, and Manhood in the Union Army* (New York: New York University Press, 2010), 79.

13. William Faux, *Memorable Days in America: Being a Journal of a Tour to the United States* (London: W. Simpkin & R. Marshall, 1823), 187.

14. Mayfield notes that "slavery ossified honor into a set of defensive postures against modernity; the wide gap between planter and poor white and between white and black made 'mastery'—a term loaded with racial and class control—absolutely nonnegotiable." John Mayfield, "The Marketplace of Values: Honor and Enterprise in the Old South," in Mayfield and Hagstette, *Field of Honor*, 14, 15.

15. Mayfield, "Marketplace of Values," 11; Ayers, *Vengeance and Justice*, 20.

16. Joanne B. Freeman, *Affairs of Honor: National Politics in the New Republic* (New Haven: Yale University Press, 2001), 168, 168–69. For dueling being more common in the Deep South, see Jack K. Williams, *Dueling in the Old South: Vignettes of Social History* (College Station: Texas A&M University Press, 1980), 7–8. Lorien Foote explains that Northerners had their own version of honor culture regardless of social standing: "Few northern men dueled, but they would fight and kill for honor." While historians tend to focus on Southern honor, Foote notes that "honor was contested but still evident in the Civil War north. Its rituals and spoken expressions retained a hold even over those men who did not claim honor." This means "Northern men tended to avoid the formal rituals of dueling. Instead, they engaged in altercations that borrowed forms and phrases from the duel." Foote's work provides examples of other Union soldiers, like Metcalfe, who followed the code duello. Foote, *Gentlemen and the Roughs*, 83, 72, 78–79; 117, 96, 102–3. Richard F. Hamm writes, "Honor had once been present all across the nation, but by the middle of the nineteenth century, it was increasingly being seen as a distinctive aspect of Southern society." Hamm, *Murder, Honor, and Law*, 19

17. "History and Practice of Duelling," *Christian Register* 29 (February 16, 1850): 28. Regarding the legal system refusing to enforce the law for the upper classes, Steward writes, "Its sectional beatification was evidenced by the nonenforcement of the anti-dueling laws and by the host of politicians, editors, lawyers, and other professionals who supplanted the ranks of the planters." Steward, *Duels and the Roots of Violence in Missouri*, 9. In "Mob Violence in the Old South," *Mississippi Valley Historical Review* 29 (December 1942), Clement Eaton writes, "Although most Southern states passed severe laws against dueling, public opinion nullified these laws and sanctioned dueling as a proper means of a gentleman to protect his honor" (352).

18. Steward, *Duels and the Roots of Violence in Missouri*, 23. Dickson Bruce notes that dueling was also imported to California during the 1850s. Dickson D. Bruce, *Violence and Culture in the Antebellum South* (Austin: University of Texas Press, 1979), 5.

19. Steward, *Duels and the Roots of Violence in Missouri*, 34; Howard L. Conard, *Encyclopedia of the History of Missouri*, 5 vols. (New York: Southern History Company, 1901), 2:229–30, 423; Robert Sidney Douglass, *History of Southeast Missouri* (Chicago: Lewis Publishing Co., 1912), 190; Floyd C. Shoemaker, "Missouri History," *Sikeston Standard*, October 5, 1934; Bonnie Stepenoff, *From French Community to Missouri Town: Ste. Genevieve in the Nineteenth Century* (Columbia: University of Missouri Press, 2006), 94; "Cincinnati," *Long Island Star*, November 20, 1811; William E. Railey, *History of Woodford County, Kentucky* (Frankfort: Published by the author, 1938), 51;

Lewis Collins and Richard H. Collins, *History of Kentucky*, 2 vols. (Covington: Collins & Co., 1882), 1:350; Thomas Marshall Green, *Historic Families of Kentucky* (Cincinnati: Robert Clarke & Co., 1889), 248. The duel even made the *London Evening Chronicle* in England: "Ship News," December 28, 1811.

20. Kenneth H. Winn, "Benjamin Gratz Brown," *Dictionary of Missouri Biography*, ed. Lawrence O. Christensen et al. (Columbia: University of Missouri Press, 1999), 121, 122; Albert Castel, *General Sterling Price and the Civil War in the West* (Baton Rouge: Louisiana State University Press, 1968), 8; Andrew Rolle, *The Lost Cause: The Confederate Exodus to Mexico* (Norman: University of Oklahoma Press, 1965), 146; Walter B. Stevens, *St. Louis: The Fourth City, 1764–1909* (St. Louis: S. J. Clarke Publishing Co., 1909), 537, 538; Steward, *Duels and the Roots of Violence in Missouri*, 152, 160, 120; "A Fearful Death Plunge," *New York Times*, March 31, 1887.

21. John Lyde Wilson, *The Code of Honor; Or, Rules for the Government of Principals and Seconds in Dueling* (Charleston: James Phinney, 1858), 6. Ayers writes that *intentional* insult was the key cause of duels. Ayers, *Vengeance and Justice*, 19.

22. Wilson, *Code of Honor*, 4; Military Department of Kentucky, *Military History of Kentucky* (Frankfort: State Journal, 1939), 148; Bruce, *Violence and Culture*, 5. For militia units, see John Hope Franklin, *The Militant South: 1800–1861* (Chicago: University of Illinois Press, 2002), 73–74; and Harry S. Laver, *Citizens More Than Soldiers: The Kentucky Militia and Society in the Early Republic* (Lincoln: University of Nebraska Press, 2007).

23. Robert M. Ireland, "Dueling," in *The Kentucky Encyclopedia*, ed. John E. Kleber (Lexington: University Press of Kentucky, 1992), 272; Klotter, *Kentucky Justice*, 49; Wyatt-Brown, *Southern Honor*, 355; John Mayfield and Todd Hagstette, "Honor, Violence, and the Law," in Mayfield and Hagstette, *Field of Honor*, 75; "Steward, *Duels and the Roots of Violence in Missouri*, 6; Joanne B. Freeman, "Understanding the Burr-Hamilton Duel," *History Now* 44 (Winter 2016), available at the Gilder Lehrman Institute of American History, https://www.gilderlehrman.org/history-by-era/Hamilton/essays/understanding-burr-hamilton-duel. Some Southerners used dueling as a means of raising their status; see Byron, "Honorable Death," 93. However, as Todd Hagstette asserts, one could not gain honor through dueling. See Hagstette, "Writing the Duel," in Mayfield and Hagstette, *Field of Honor*, 81.

24. Williams, *Dueling in the Old South*, 72, 26, 27; Wyatt-Brown, *Southern Honor*, 355; Freeman, *Affairs of Honor*, xxii. Freeman writes, "Because only equals were supposed to duel, canings displayed the victim's inferior status" (172). In *Vengeance and Justice*, Ayers connects Southerners' "propensity for violence" to slave-owning societies and a general "lack of restraint" (10–11). Bruce notes, in *Violence and Culture*, that whipping a white man was insulting because it was "the kind of violence reserved for inferiors and slaves" (85).

25. Freeman, *Affairs of Honor*, xv; Foote, *Gentlemen and the Roughs*, 96, 78; Greenberg, "Nose, the Lie, and the Duel," 58. In *Murder, Honor, and Law*, his study of four Virginia murders, Richard F. Hamm writes, "Homicide trials . . . showed the existence of honor among white men who were not socially prominent" (63).

26. James Lee McDonough, *Nashville: The Western Confederacy's Final Gamble* (Knoxville: University of Tennessee Press, 2004), 140. For violence at the University of Virginia, see Rex Bowman and Carlos Santos, *Rot, Riot, and Rebellion: Mr. Jefferson's Struggle to Save the University That Changed America* (Charlottesville: University of Virginia Press, 2013). The authors write that at the university, "students repeatedly used the code not as a restraint but as a license for violence" and that "with a sense of honor easily bruised, they were reflexively violent" (6, 4).

27. Freeman, *Affairs of Honor*, 170–71; Wyatt-Brown, *Southern Honor*, 351, 356; Lewis Collins and Richard H. Collins, *History of Kentucky*, 2 vols. (Covington: Collins & Co., 1882), 2:353; L. F. Johnson, *Famous Kentucky Tragedies and Trials* (Louisville: Baldwin Law Book Company, 1916), 24–25; Jon Meacham, *American Lion: Andrew Jackson in the White House* (New York: Random House, 2008), 26; H. W. Brands, *Andrew Jackson: His Life and Times* (New York: Anchor, 2005), 138. In *Affairs of Honor*, Freeman also notes how duels could take weeks, if not months, to finally play out (167). Conflicts under the code duello did not always lead to bloodshed. Before being killed by Aaron Burr, Alexander Hamilton was involved in eleven challenges that ended peaceably. David O. Stewart, *American Emperor: Aaron Burr's Challenge to Jefferson's America* (New York: Simon & Schuster, 2011), 27. For duels curbing passion and violence, see Joanne B. Freeman, *The Field of Blood: Violence in Congress and the Road to Civil War* (New York: Farrar, Straus & Giroux, 2018), 88–89. For a detailed example of a negotiation, see Recollections by Thomas Jessup of the Clay–Randolph Duel, March 5, 1853, Henry Clay Memorial Foundation Papers, 96M2, University of Kentucky Special Collections, Lexington.

28. Wilson, *Code of Honor*, 10.

29. Wilson, *Code of Honor*, 12, 14.

30. Hagstette, "Writing the Duel," 78, 80. Hagstette adds that challenges were "an exercise in civility—evidence of cultivation, breeding, and literacy, all within the large landscape of a rather uncultivated, crossbred, half illiterate world." Correspondence between duelists was used "to prove their elite status" in what was equal parts "performance" and serious challenge (89).

31. Wilson, *Code of Honor*, 10, 12, 13, 14. For duels being designed to be dispassionate, see Bruce, *Violence and Culture*, 32, 35.

32. Wilson, *Code of Honor*, 17, 19, 20. Dickson Bruce also notes "that one should never fight with a social inferior." Bruce, *Violence and Culture*, 40. Rex

Bowman and Carlos Santos write, "To 'post' someone was to accuse an opponent of dishonorable behavior in writing and then to post the note in public." This brought community shame. Bowman and Santos, *Rot, Riot, and Rebellion*, 49. Also see Freeman, *Affairs of Honor*, 172–73.

33. Wilson, *Code of Honor*, 20.

34. Wilson, *Code of Honor*, 21, 22, 30; "To the Public" handbill, George Claiborne Thompson Papers, Filson Historical Society. Jack K. Williams writes that a challenged blacksmith reputedly chose sledgehammers as his dueling weapons. His challenger wisely called off the fight. Williams, *Dueling in the Old South*, 52. While pistols were typically used, rifles were not uncommon. When William Graves fought Jonathan Cilley in 1838, the antagonists used rifles at eighty yards, a choice similar to the Casto–Metcalfe duel. Robert S. Levine, "'The Honor of New England': Nathaniel Hawthorne and the Cilley–Graves Duel of 1838," in Mayfield and Hagstette, *Field of Honor*, 152. For the Graves–Cilley duel, see Freeman, *Field of Blood*, 75–111. University of Virginia students Louis Wigfall (a future Confederate senator) and Charles Hamer once planned to duel at ten paces "with rifles mounted on rests," but the suicidal fight was averted. Bowman and Santos, *Rot, Riot, and Rebellion*, 64. In 1854, Deveraux J. Woodlief and Achilles Kewen fought a duel with rifles in California. This was one of several such duels fought in California from 1853 to 1854. "Fatal Duel in California," *Evansville (IN) Daily Journal*, December 11, 1854.

35. Wilson, *Code of Honor*, 29, 22, 24.

36. Wilson, *Code of Honor*, 26, 27; Burr Harrison broadside, October 20, 1819, Mss CH, Filson Historical Society; "Kentucky Legislature," *Kentucky Gazette* (Lexington), December 24, 1819; John Walter Wayland, *A History of Shenandoah County, Virginia* (Baltimore: Genealogical Publishing, 2006), 606; Collins, *History of Kentucky*, 2:645; "Nathaniel Wickliffe," in *The Biographical Encyclopaedia of Kentucky of the Dead and Living Men of the Nineteenth Century* (Cincinnati: J. M. Armstrong & Co., 1878), 128; Minnie S. Wilder, ed., *Kentucky Soldiers of the War of 1812* (Baltimore: Genealogical Publishing, 1969), 310.

8. Kentucky and the Code Duello

1. Bertram Wyatt-Brown, *Southern Honor: Ethics and Behavior in the Old South* (Oxford: Oxford University Press, 2007), 350; John Hope Franklin, *The Militant South: 1800–1861* (Chicago: University of Illinois Press, 2002), 49. For more on "rough and tumble" fighting, see Elliott J. Gorn, "Gouge and Bite, Pull Hair and Scratch: The Social Significance of Fighting in the Southern Backcountry," *American Historical Review* 90 (February 1985): 18–43. Gorn writes, "The code of honor offered a genteel, though deadly, way to

settle personal disputes while demonstrating one's elevated status. Ceremony distinguished antiseptic duels from lower-class brawls" (22).

2. Wyatt-Brown, *Southern Honor*, 351, 353; "A Duel in the Dark," *Sunbury (PA) American*, October 16, 1852; Lewis Collins and Richard H. Collins, *History of Kentucky*, 2 vols. (Covington: Collins & Co., 1882), 2:112. Anti-dueling societies also noted in Franklin, *Militant South*, 59–60. Richard Bell writes, "The American anti-dueling movement first emerged in the wake of Alexander Hamilton's duel with Aaron Burr." Richard Bell, "The Double Guilt of Dueling: The Stain of Suicide in Anti-Dueling Rhetoric in the Early Republic," *Journal of the Early Republic* 29 (Fall 2009): 390. Edward R. Crowther writes that in the South, "the churches directly attacked customs such as dueling through sermons and the pen, challenging directly a basic expression of honor." Edward R. Crowther, "Holy Honor: Sacred and Secular in the Old South," *Journal of Southern History* 58 (November 1992): 629.

3. "Kentucky Peace Association," *Friend of Peace* 2 (January 2, 1821): 24; Z. F. Smith, "Dueling, and Some Noted Duels in Kentucky," *Register of the Kentucky Historical Society* 8 (September 1910): 81; Dick Steward, *Duels and the Roots of Violence in Missouri* (Columbia: University of Missouri Press, 2000), 86.

4. "Intelligence," *Masonic Mirror: and Mechanics' Intelligencer* 3 (June 2, 1827): 183; *Western Luminary* 3 (October 11, 1826): 117; *Kentucky Argus* quoted in "Duel," *Religious Intelligencer* 11 (May 26, 1827): 827; "Honour," *Western Recorder* 4 (June 5, 1827): 91; "Professional Misconduct-Duelling," *United States Intelligencer and Review* 2 (October 1830): 370.

5. J. Winston Coleman Jr., *Famous Kentucky Duels* (Lexington: Henry Clay Press, 1969), 115; "Legislation," *Law Reporter* 2 (February 1840): 316; Lowell H. Harrison and James C. Klotter, *A New History of Kentucky* (Lexington: University Press of Kentucky, 1997), 119; Robert M. Ireland, "Dueling," in *The Kentucky Encyclopedia*, ed. John E. Kleber (Lexington: University Press of Kentucky, 1992), 272. When Governor James F. Robinson took the anti-dueling oath in August 1862, the judge who administered it signed an affidavit that Robinson swore to protect the US Constitution and the state constitution and took the oath of office and "the oath against duelling as prescribed by the 1st sec: of the 8th article of the constitution of this state." J. Swigert, Affidavit, August 18, 1862, Office of the Governor, James F. Robinson: Appointments by the Governor, Civil Appointments, 1862–1863, R1-411, Kentucky Department for Libraries and Archives, Frankfort, accessed via *Civil War Governors of Kentucky: Digital Documentary Edition*, Kentucky Historical Society, http://discovery.civilwargovernors.org/document/KYR-0001-031-0326.

6. Edward L. Ayers, *Vengeance and Justice: Crime and Punishment in the Nineteenth-Century American South* (Oxford: Oxford University Press, 1984), 31; Robert M. Ireland, "The Problem of Concealed Weapons in

Nineteenth-Century Kentucky," *Register of the Kentucky Historical Society* 91 (Autumn 1993): 371n2.

7. Hardin quoted in "History and Practice of Duelling," *Christian Register* 29 (February 16, 1850): 28; "The New Constitution of Kentucky," *Western Law Journal* 2 (April 1850): 321; Hardin also quoted in "Duelling," *Lancaster Intelligencer*, January 29, 1850; Matthew A. Byron, "An Honorable Death? The Stuart-Bennett Duel of 1819," in *The Field of Honor: Essays on Southern Character and American Identity*, ed. John Mayfield and Todd Hagstette (Columbia: University of South Carolina Press, 2017), 99, 102. Other states' constitutions also banned dueling. For example, Louisiana's 1845 constitution prohibited duelists or anyone who sent a challenge from voting and holding political office. *Proceedings and Debates of the Convention of Louisiana, Which Assembled at the City of New Orleans, January 14, 1844* (New Orleans: Besancon, Ferguson, & Co., 1845), 958.

8. Rowan quoted in Ireland, "Problem of Concealed Weapons," 372; Todd Hagstette, "Writing the Duel: Rhetorical Negotiation and the Language of Honor in the Nineteenth Century South," in Mayfield and Hagstette, *Field of Honor*, 77; Dickson D. Bruce, *Violence and Culture in the Antebellum South* (Austin: University of Texas Press, 1979), 42; "Steward, *Duels and the Roots of Violence in Missouri*, 44. For anti-dueling laws, also see Kenneth S. Greenberg, "The Nose, the Lie, and the Duel in the Antebellum South," *American Historical Review* 95 (February 1990): 67.

9. *Microscope* 1 (September 4, 1824): 2; "Close of the World's Convention," *New York Evangelist* 14 (August 3, 1843): 122.

10. Ireland, "Dueling," 272; Byron, "Honorable Death?" 99; James C. Klotter, *Kentucky Justice, Southern Honor, and American Manhood: Understanding the Life and Death of Richard Reid* (Baton Rouge: Louisiana State University Press, 2003), 44, 45, 46; Amos Kendall to F. G. Flugel, July 14, 1814, Amos Kendall Letters, Filson Historical Society, Louisville. Matthew G. Schoenbachler writes that "decades of warfare . . . had inured the Kentuckians to brutality, and the state's well-earned reputation for violence would persist for generations to come." Matthew G. Schoenbachler, *Murder and Madness: The Myth of the Kentucky Tragedy* (Lexington: University Press of Kentucky, 2011), 17. Laws against dueling were found across the South but were frequently ignored. Virginia created anti-dueling laws "as early as 1776," Tennessee and North Carolina in 1802; Georgia in 1809; South Carolina in 1812; Louisiana in 1818; Alabama and Mississippi in 1830; Washington, DC, in 1839. Jack K. Williams, *Dueling in the Old South: Vignettes of Social History* (College Station: Texas A&M University Press, 1980), 66–67.

11. Smith, "Dueling," 77.

12. Robert V. Remini, *Henry Clay: Statesman for the Union* (New York: W. W. Norton, 1991), 53–55; David S. Heidler and Jeanne T. Heidler, *Henry*

Clay: The Essential American (New York: Random House, 2010), 71–73; James C. Klotter, *Henry Clay: The Man Who Would Be President* (New York: Oxford University Press, 2018), 65; Smith, "Dueling," 78; "Carl Schurz, *Life of Henry Clay,* 2 vols. (Boston: Houghton, Mifflin & Co., 1895), 1:51.

13. Recollections by Thomas Jessup of the Clay–Randolph duel, March 5, 1853, Henry Clay Memorial Foundation Papers, 96M2, University of Kentucky Special Collections, Lexington; Heidler and Heidler, *Henry Clay,* 197–99; Remini, *Henry Clay,* 294–95; Klotter, *Henry Clay,* 66–67; Williams, *Dueling in the Old South,* 58–59; Smith, "Dueling," 78; Franklin, *Militant South,* 51; "Mr. Clay's Corrective for Dueling," *Friend of Peace* 4 (January 5, 1827): 138.

14. Clay quoted in Smith, "Dueling," 80; H. Edward Richardson, *Cassius Marcellus Clay: Firebrand of Freedom* (Lexington: University Press of Kentucky, 1976), 35; Charles P. Roland, *Albert Sidney Johnston: Soldier of Three Republics* (Lexington: University Press of Kentucky, 2013), 107.

15. "Shaking Hands," *New York Telescope* 2 (March 25, 1826): 172.

16. Smith, "Dueling," 80; David Dary, *Frontier Medicine: From the Atlantic to the Pacific, 1492–1941* (New York: Alfred A. Knopf, 2008), 65; John D. Wright Jr., *Transylvania: Tutor to the West* (Lexington: University Press of Kentucky, 1980), 82.

17. Smith, "Dueling," 81; Ryan Chamberlain, *Pistols, Politics and the Press: Dueling in Nineteenth Century American Journalism* (Jefferson, NC: McFarland, 2009), 89; Catherine Clinton, *Mrs. Lincoln: A Life* (New York: HarperCollins, 2009), 21–22; Betty Boles Ellison, *The True Mary Todd Lincoln: A Biography* (Jefferson, NC: McFarland, 2014), 17; Randolph Hollingsworth, *Lexington, Queen of the Bluegrass* (Charleston, NC: Arcadia, 2004), 45; "George Prentice," *Harper's New Monthly Magazine,* January 1875, 198; "Kentucky Matters," *Ohio Farmer* 6 (June 20, 1857): 99; "Southern Crimes and Atrocities," *Liberator* 27 (June 26, 1857): 104.

18. "Youngsters in a Duel," *New York Sun,* January 31, 1896; "A Duel," *Frankfort Daily Commonwealth,* January 18, 1848; "An Old Time Duel on Indiana Soil," *Indianian* 3 (January 1899): 76–77.

19. Smith, "Dueling," 81; Collins and Collins, *History of Kentucky,* 2:768; Wyatt-Brown, *Southern Honor,* 356–57; William E. Railey, *History of Woodford County* (Frankfort: Published by the author, 1938), 309; Paul R. Shipman, "Reminiscences of Tom Marshall," *Galaxy* 17 (March 1874): 299; William Henry Perrin, ed. *County of Christian, Kentucky* (Chicago: F. A. Battey Publishing Co., 1884), 189.

20. "General Albert Sidney Johnston," in *The Encyclopedia of Northern Kentucky,* ed. Paul A. Tenkotte and James C. Claypool (Lexington: University Press of Kentucky, 2009), 495; Roland, *Albert Sidney Johnston,* 60–61; Jack D. Welsh, *Medical Histories of Confederate Generals* (Kent, OH: Kent State

University Press, 1995), 118. For details about the Johnston–Houston duel, see *Reminiscences of General Basil W. Duke, C. S. A.* (New York: Doubleday, Page, & Co., 1911), 106–8; and William Preston Johnston, *The Life of Gen. Albert Sidney Johnston* (New York: D. Appleton & Co., 1878), 74–80.

21. Francis Fisher Brown, *The Every-Day Life of Abraham Lincoln* (New York: G. P. Putnam & Sons, 1913), 93; Klotter, *Henry Clay,* 374; Steward, *Duels and the Roots of Violence in Missouri,* 126.

22. "Duelling—Again!" *Christian Watchman* 1 (August 21, 1819): 51; Lawrence M. Crutcher, *George Keats of Kentucky: A Life* (Lexington: University Press of Kentucky, 2012), 234. For the Rowan–Chambers duel, see Coleman, *Famous Kentucky Duels,* 3–16; and Stuart W. Sanders, "Ring Tells the Story of an 1801 Kentucky duel," *Maysville Ledger-Independent,* June 15, 2019.

23. Arthur B. Carter, *The Tarnished Cavalier: Major General Earl Van Dorn, C.S.A.* (Knoxville: University of Tennessee Press, 1999), 184–86; Robert G. Hartje, *Van Dorn: The Life and Times of a Confederate General* (Nashville: Vanderbilt University Press, 1967), 309–10, 314–15; Stuart W. Sanders, *Maney's Confederate Brigade at the Battle of Perryville* (Charleston: History Press, 2014), 139; Steward, *Duels and the Roots of Violence in Missouri,* 194–95; Jeffry D. Wert, "Lucius Marshall Walker," in *Historical Times Illustrated Encyclopedia of the Civil War,* ed. Patricia L. Faust (New York: Harper & Row, 1986), 798; Welsh, *Medical Histories of Confederate Generals,* 226; *The War of the Rebellion: A Compilation of the Official Records of the Union and Confederate Armies* (Washington, DC: GPO, 1880–1901), ser. 2, vol. 22, 1:525 (*OR;* unless noted, all citations to ser. 1); Richard F. Hamm, *Murder, Honor, and Law: Four Virginia Homicides from Reconstruction to the Great Depression* (Charlottesville: University of Virginia Press, 2003), 24–25.

24. Lorien Foote, *The Gentlemen and the Roughs: Violence, Honor, and Manhood in the Union Army* (New York: New York University Press, 2010), 98.

25. Leslie Combs to Lincoln, September 6, 1861, and Garrett Davis to Lincoln, January 7, 1862, both in Lincoln Papers, Library of Congress, transcribed and annotated by the Lincoln Studies Center, Knox College, Galesburg, IL, online at memory.loc.gov (Lincoln Papers, LC); *OR,* vol. 4:318, vol. 7:451.

26. R. W. Johnson, *A Soldier's Reminiscences in Peace and War* (Philadelphia: J. P. Lippincott, 1886), 248, 249; J. Montgomery Wright, "Notes of a Staff Officer at Perryville," *Battles and Leaders of the Civil War,* ed. Robert Underwood Johnson and Clarence Clough Buel, repr. ed., 4 vols. (Secaucus, NJ: Castle Books, 1887), 3:60n.

27. Wright, "Notes of a Staff Officer at Perryville," 60n, 61n; Don Carlos Buell, "East Tennessee and the Campaign of Perryville," in Johnson and Buel, *Battles and Leaders of the Civil War,* 3:43n; Cole's version quoted in C. C. Gilbert, "Bragg's Invasion of Kentucky, Chapter 3," *Southern Bivouac* 4

(November 1885): 338. In his biography of Governor Morton, A. James Fuller writes that the shooting of Nelson "had been a matter of honor, if not quite a duel." A. James Fuller, *Oliver P. Morton and the Politics of the Civil War and Reconstruction* (Kent, OH: Kent State University Press, 2017), 116.

28. Gilbert, "Bragg's Invasion of Kentucky," 337, 338; Donald A. Clark, "Major General William 'Bull' Nelson," in *The Encyclopedia of Northern Kentucky*, ed. Tenkotte and Claypool, 648; Buell, "East Tennessee," 43n; Wright, "Notes of a Staff Officer at Perryville," 61n; Foote, *Gentlemen and the Roughs*, 89. For the shooting of Bull Nelson, see Stuart W. Sanders, "The Murder of Bull Nelson," *Civil War Quarterly*, Early Spring 2015, 52–59, 98.

29. Robert M. Ireland, "The Problem of Concealed Weapons in Nineteenth-Century Kentucky," *Register of the Kentucky Historical Society* 91 (Autumn 1993): 377, 385, 371–72. Ireland notes "the connection between the decline of the duel and the rise of the habit of carrying concealed deadly weapons" (370). For what happened to postwar Kentuckians who endured public shame for refusing to duel, see Klotter, *Kentucky Justice*. As Klotter explains, Richard Reid committed suicide after being whipped and refusing to respond to the attack with violence. Also see Robert M. Ireland, "The Suicide of Judge Richard Reid: Politics and Honor Run Amok," *Filson Club History Quarterly* 71 (April 1997): 144–45.

9. His Blood Is on His Own Head

1. "To the Public," *Tri-Weekly Commonwealth*, May 21, 1862; "The Last Duel Fought in Kentucky," *Louisville Courier-Journal*, March 12, 1877.

2. "Last Duel," *Courier-Journal*; "To the Public," *Tri-Weekly Commonwealth*; J. Winston Coleman Jr., *Famous Kentucky Duels* (Lexington: Henry Clay Press, 1969), 112, 113, 114. Like Metcalfe regarding his conflict with Casto, Alexander Hamilton believed his duel with Aaron Burr was "impossible . . . to avoid." Quoted in Joanne B. Freeman, *Affairs of Honor: National Politics in the New Republic* (New Haven: Yale University Press, 2001), 164. Metcalfe dueling to avoid future trouble reflected Southern honor culture. As one South Carolinian wrote, "the practice of duelling is a bad one, but a necessary evil, and must some time be adopted in order to avoid a worse one." Metcalfe was fighting Casto to eliminate future challenges, a "worse" evil. John Hope Franklin, *The Militant South: 1800–1861* (Chicago: University of Illinois Press, 2002), 49. For Union soldiers, dueling was a violation of three Articles of War: the 25th, 26th, and 28th Articles. See Lorien Foote, *The Gentlemen and the Roughs: Violence, Honor, and Manhood in the Union Army* (New York: New York University Press, 2010), 94, 95, 97.

3. Metcalfe's response from Casto and Metcalfe duel correspondence, Filson Historical Society, Louisville; "Last Duel," *Courier-Journal*; and

Coleman, *Famous Kentucky Duels*, 113–14; "To the Public," *Tri-Weekly Commonwealth*; newspaper clippings, J. Winston Coleman Scrapbooks, vol. 19:57, Transylvania University Special Collections and Archives.

4. "To the Public," *Tri-Weekly Commonwealth*; Coleman, *Famous Kentucky Duels*, 114, 115.

5. "Col. T. A. Respess, City's Oldest Citizen Died Late Tuesday," *Maysville Daily Public Ledger*, March 19, 1919; "Col. Thomas A. Respess 89 Years Old Today," *Maysville Daily Public Ledger*, March 10, 1915; *Annual Report of the Miami University to the Forty-Second General Assembly, for the Year 1845* (N.p.: n.p., n.d.), 22; 1860 US Federal Census, Maysville, Mason County, available at Ancestry.com.

6. "To the Public," *Tri-Weekly Commonwealth*; Coleman, *Famous Kentucky Duels*, 115, 116, 117; "Last Duel," *Courier-Journal*. The rules of the Casto–Metcalfe duel were similar to those for an 1861 duel that was to be fought between Indiana legislators Gideon C. Moody and Horace Heffren, Newport, Kentucky, with rifles at seventy-five yards. *Indiana State Sentinel*, February 20, 1861. See also Stuart W. Sanders, "Politics Bad Now? In 1861, Indiana Politicians Nearly Dueled," *Shelbyville (IN) News*, March 4, 2020.

7. "To the Public," *Tri-Weekly Commonwealth*; Coleman, *Famous Kentucky Duels*, 114n5, 117; "Letter from Kentucky," *Caledonian* (St. Johnsbury, VT), May 23, 1862; "Last Duel," *Courier-Journal*.

8. Earl J. Coates and Dean S. Thomas, *An Introduction to Civil War Small Arms* (Gettysburg: Thomas Publications, 1990), 31; Caroline R. Miller, "Casto–Metcalfe Duel," in *The Encyclopedia of Northern Kentucky*, ed. Paul A. Tenkotte and James C. Claypool (Lexington: University Press of Kentucky, 2009), 165; Charles Edward Chapel, *Guns of the Old West: An Illustrated Guide* (Mineola, NY: Dover, 2002), 200; Thomas Read, *The Original Iron Brigade* (Lanham, MD: Fairleigh Dickinson University Press, 2011), 32; Joseph C. Bilby, *Civil War Firearms: The Historical Background, Tactical Use, and Modern Collecting and Shooting* (Pennsylvania: Combined Books, 1996), 189, 180–81, 109; *Duty, Honor, and Country: The Civil War Experiences of Captain William P. Black, Thirty-Seventh Illinois Infantry*, ed. Michael E. Banasik (Iowa City: Camp Pope Bookshop, 2006), 25n1; Glenn Tucker, *Chickamauga: Bloody Battle in the West* (Dayton, OH: Morningside, 1992), 351, 352; Williamson Murray and Wayne Wei-Siang Hsieh, *A Savage War: A Military History of the Civil War* (Princeton, NJ: Princeton University Press, 2016), 343; Peter Cozzens, *This Terrible Sound: The Battle of Chickamauga* (Chicago: University of Illinois Press, 1992), 419, 436.

9. "Fatal Duel," *Richmond Daily Dispatch*, November 2, 1863.

10. "To the Public," *Tri-Weekly Commonwealth*; newspaper clippings, J. Winston Coleman Scrapbooks, vol. 19:59.

11. "To the Public," *Tri-Weekly Commonwealth*.

12. Coleman, *Famous Kentucky Duels*, 117–18, 119; "Letter from Kentucky," *Caledonian*; Miller, "Casto–Metcalfe Duel," 165; "Last Duel," *Courier-Journal*; Lewis Collins and Richard H. Collins, *History of Kentucky*, 2 vols. (Covington: Collins & Co., 1882), 1:584, 2:547; Thomas S. Ward, "Dover," in Tenkotte and Claypool, *Encyclopedia of Northern Kentucky*, 279.

13. "To the Public," *Tri-Weekly Commonwealth*; Coleman, *Famous Kentucky Duels*, 115; "Last Duel," *Louisville Courier-Journal*; 1860 US Federal Census, Nicholas County, District 2, accessed via Ancestry.com on September 14, 2016; Capt. Samuel G. Rogers, Compiled Service Record, 18th Kentucky Infantry, Company I, available at Fold3.com; 1860 US Federal Census—Slave Schedule, Nicholas County, District 1, available at Ancestry.com.

14. "Letter from Kentucky," *Caledonian*.

15. "Duel of Other Days," *Maysville Evening Bulletin*, December 8, 1903; "Last Duel," *Courier-Journal*; "Letter from Kentucky," *Caledonian*.

16. Coleman, *Famous Kentucky Duels*, 119; "To the Public," *Tri-Weekly Commonwealth*; "Last Duel," *Courier-Journal*.

17. "Last Duel," *Courier-Journal*; "Letter from Kentucky," *Caledonian*; "Old Killings Recalled," *Hazel Green (KY) Herald*, May 23, 1895; Coleman, *Famous Kentucky Duels*, 119. Coleman writes that the property was a farm owned by Lewis Long.

18. "Last Duel," *Courier-Journal*; "Letter from Kentucky," *Caledonian*.

19. "To the Public," *Tri-Weekly Commonwealth*; "Last Duel," *Courier-Journal*.

20. "To the Public," *Tri-Weekly Commonwealth*; *Lexington Observer and Reporter*, May 10, 1862; "Old Killings Recalled," *Hazel Green Herald*; Coleman, *Famous Kentucky Duels*, 120.

21. "Last Duel," *Courier-Journal*; "To the Public," *Tri-Weekly Commonwealth*; *Lexington Observer and Reporter*, May 10, 1862.

22. "To the Public," *Tri-Weekly Commonwealth*.

23. "Last Duel," *Courier-Journal*; "Letter from Kentucky," *Caledonian*.

24. "Last Duel," *Courier-Journal*; "To the Public," *Tri-Weekly Commonwealth*; Coleman, *Famous Kentucky Duels*, 120; "Letter from Kentucky," *Caledonian*.

25. "Letter from Kentucky," *Caledonian*; "Last Duel," *Courier-Journal*. Another version of Metcalfe's remarks was "Gentleman, this fight was forced on me; I did not know the man even by sight, and never spoke to him; I bore him no ill will, and gave him no cause of quarrel against me." "To the Public," *Tri-Weekly Commonwealth*.

26. "To the Public," *Tri-Weekly Commonwealth*; Coleman, *Famous Kentucky Duels*, 119, 120; "Letter from Kentucky," *Caledonian*.

27. "Letter from Kentucky," *Caledonian*; "Fatal Duel in Kentucky," *Portsmouth Daily Times*, May 10, 1862.

28. Collins and Collins, *History of Kentucky*, 1:584.

29. "Last Duel," *Courier-Journal*; "Letter from Kentucky," *Caledonian*.

30. Coleman, *Famous Kentucky Duels*, 120; "Fatal Duel in Kentucky," *Portsmouth Daily Times*; "Another Arrival of Rebel Sympathizers," *Cincinnati Daily Press*, October 10, 1861.

31. Miller, "Casto–Metcalfe Duel," 165; Coleman, *Famous Kentucky Duels*, 120, 121n14.

32. Donald A. Clark, *The Notorious "Bull" Nelson: Murdered Civil War General* (Carbondale: Southern Illinois University Press, 2013), 163; "William Nelson," *Louisville Courier Journal*, September 11, 1895; "A Strange Man," *Louisville Courier-Journal*, January 29, 1880. For Kentucky's postwar Confederate turn, see Anne E. Marshall, *Creating a Confederate Kentucky: The Lost Cause and Civil War Memory in a Border State* (Chapel Hill: University of North Carolina Press, 2013).

33. "Administrator's Notice," *Maysville Dollar Weekly Bulletin*, June 26, 1862. News of the duel was reported widely. The *Guardian* in London, England, even ran a short notice about Metcalfe shooting Casto in its June 3, 1862, edition.

34. "Fatal Duel," *Woodstock Sentinel*, May 21, 1862; "The Union in Kentucky," *Frankfort Tri-Weekly Commonwealth*, May 21, 1862.

35. General Lucius Desha Civil War Diary, 1997Ms454, University of Kentucky Special Collections, Lexington. Union soldiers later camped on Desha's farm and confiscated his corn to feed their mules and horses. Lt. David McKinney wrote his sister, "We are encamped on the farm of Gen. Desha, who is a prisoner at Camp Chase Columbus Ohio." McKinney to "Dear Sister," October 16, 1862, David McKinney Letters, Filson Historical Society.

36. Thornton F. Marshall et al. to Thomas E. Bramlette, February 22, 1864, Office of the Governor, Thomas E. Bramlette, Governor's Official Correspondence File, Petitions for Pardons, Remissions, and Respites, 1863–67, BR9–314 to BR9–315, Kentucky Department for Libraries and Archives, Frankfort, accessed via *Civil War Governors of Kentucky*, http://discovery.civilwargovernors.org/document/KYR-0001-004-0513.

37. Thornton F. Marshall et al. to James F. Robinson, August 26, 1863, and Isaac Nelson and Thomas A. Respess to Thomas E. Bramlette, September 1, 1863, both in Office of the Governor, Thomas E. Bramlette: Governor's Official Correspondence File, Petitions for Pardons, Remissions, and Respites, 1863–1867, BR8–103, KDLA, accessed via *Civil War Governors of Kentucky: Digital Documentary Edition*, Kentucky Historical Society, http://discovery.civilwargovernors.org/document/KYR-0001-029-0547, http://discovery.civilwargovernors.org/document/KYR-0001-004-00710071.

38. May 11, 1862, Journal by Ellen Kenton McGaughey Wallace, transcribed by James T. Killebrew, Kentucky Historical Society, Frankfort.

10. Doomed to Exile

1. "Secessionists Footing the Bills," *Highland Weekly News,* May 1, 1862; J. Winston Coleman Jr., *Famous Kentucky Duels* (Lexington: Henry Clay Press, 1969), 121; *Ebensburg (PA) Democrat and Sentinel,* June 11, 1862; *The War of the Rebellion: A Compilation of the Official Records of the Union and Confederate Armies* (Washington, DC: GPO, 1880–1901), vol. 16, 1:752 (*OR*; unless noted, all citations to ser. 1); "From Kentucky," *New York Times,* May 15, 1862.

2. Coleman, *Famous Kentucky Duels,* 121; *OR*, vol. 16, 1:760, 756; Kenneth A. Hafendorfer, *The Battle of Richmond, Kentucky* (Louisville: KH Press, 2006), 47; John D. McAulay, *Carbines of the U.S. Cavalry, 1861–1905* (Lincoln, RI: Andrew Mowbray, 1996), 17; Janet B. Hewett, ed., *Supplement to the Official Records of the Union and Confederate Armies:* part 2, *Record of Events* (Wilmington, NC: Broadfoot, 1996), vol. 21, ser. 33:763 (*S-OR*).

3. *S-OR,* vol. 21, ser. 33:764; Leonidas Metcalfe to Jeremiah T. Boyle, July 21, 1862, John Metcalfe Family Papers, SC1273, Kentucky Historical Society, Frankfort.

4. William A. Penn, *Kentucky Rebel Town: The Civil War Battles of Cynthiana and Harrison County* (Lexington: University Press of Kentucky, 2016), 133; "Secessionists Footing the Bills," *Highland Weekly News*; "Footing the Bills," *Gallipolis (OH) Journal*, August 28, 1862; "Assessing Secessionists to Pay Damages," *Wheeling Daily Intelligencer,* August 25, 1862; "Paid His Assessment," *Dakota County Herald (Dakota City, NE),* November 13, 1913.

5. Lewis Collins and Richard H. Collins, *History of Kentucky,* 2 vols. (Covington: Collins & Co., 1882), 1:129; *Military History of Kentucky* (Frankfort: State Journal, 1939), 201; D. Warren Lambert, *When the Ripe Pears Fell: The Battle of Richmond, Kentucky* (Richmond: Madison County Historical Society, 1995), 15; "Another 'Beast,'" *Western Democrat* (Charlotte, NC), September 9, 1862.

6. Thomas Speed, *The Union Regiments of Kentucky* (Louisville: Courier-Journal Job Printing Co., 1897), 185, 188; *Report of the Adjutant General of the State of Kentucky* (Frankfort: Kentucky Yeoman, 1866), 1:208, 180; *S-OR,* vol. 21, ser. 33:763, 764; Leonidas Metcalfe Compiled Service Record, Seventh Kentucky Union Infantry, available at Fold3.com; Lambert, *When the Ripe Pears Fell,* 15; *OR*, vol. 16, 2:230, 236; Dennis W. Belcher, *The Cavalry of the Army of the Cumberland* (Jefferson, NC: McFarland, 2016), 69; *The National Almanac and Annual Record for the Year 1864* (Philadelphia: George W. Childs, 1864), 370.

7. James Lee McDonough, *War in Kentucky: From Shiloh to Perryville* (Knoxville: University of Tennessee Press, 1994), 81. For additional information about the 1862 Kentucky campaign, see Kenneth W. Noe, *Perryville: This*

Grand Havoc of Battle (Lexington: University Press of Kentucky, 2001), 27–42; Stuart W. Sanders, "The Kentucky Campaign and the Battle of Perryville," *Blue and Gray*, Holiday 2005, 7–9; Thomas Lawrence Connelly, *Army of the Heartland* (Baton Rouge: Louisiana State University Press, 1967), 188–91; Earl J. Hess, *Banners to the Breeze: The Kentucky Campaign, Corinth, and Stones River* (Lincoln: University of Nebraska Press, 2000), 57–84; Gerald J. Prokopowicz, *All for the Regiment: The Army of the Ohio, 1861–1862* (Chapel Hill: University of North Carolina Press, 2001), 136–58.

8. *OR,* vol. 16, 2:353, 435; Hafendorfer, *Battle of Richmond,* 47; Leonidas Metcalfe et al. to S. B. Brown, August 21, 1862, Office of the Governor, James F. Robinson: Governor's Official Correspondence File, Military Correspondence, 1862–1863, R2-17, Kentucky Department for Libraries and Archives, Frankfort, accessed via *Civil War Governors of Kentucky: Digital Documentary Edition,* Kentucky Historical Society, http://discovery.civilwargovernors .org/document/KYR-0001-027-0021; Frank Moore, ed., *The Rebellion Record: A Dairy of American Events,* 12 vols. (New York: G. P. Putnam, 1863), 5:590. For the Union retreat, see Brian D. McKnight, *Contested Borderland: The Civil War in Appalachian Kentucky and Virginia* (Lexington: University Press of Kentucky, 2006), 87–88. For a Union soldier's description of the retreat from the Cumberland Gap, see Letter from Thomas F. Leech, November 2, 1862, Thomas F. Leech Letters, SC 173, Kentucky Historical Society, Frankfort.

9. Kenneth A. Hafendorfer, *They Died by Twos and Tens: The Confederate Cavalry in the Kentucky Campaign of 1862* (Louisville: KH Press, 1995), 216, 217; Hafendorfer, *Battle of Richmond,* 47, 48, 49; Lambert, *When the Ripe Pears Fell,* 14, 16, 15; *OR,* vol. 16, 1:885; Howell Carter, *A Cavalryman's Reminiscences of the Civil War,* repr. ed. (New Orleans: American Printing Co., 1979), 35; Moore, *Rebellion Record,* 5:590. Description of Big Hill from author's correspondence with Phillip Seyfrit, Battle of Richmond Association, December 16, 2016.

10. Hafendorfer, *Twos and Tens,* 217; Moore, *Rebellion Record,* 5:590; *OR,* vol. 16, 1:885; Lambert, *When the Ripe Pears Fell,* 16; *S-OR,* vol. 21, ser. 33:764; Carter, *Cavalryman's Reminiscences of the Civil War,* 35.

11. Moore, *Rebellion Record,* 5:591, 420; Hafendorfer, *Battle of Richmond,* 50, 52; Carter, *Cavalryman's Reminiscences of the Civil War,* 35; Lambert, *When the Ripe Pears Fell,* 17; Hafendorfer, *Twos and Tens,* 217; Coleman, *Famous Kentucky Duels,* 122.

12. Moore, *Rebellion Record,* 5:590, 591; Hafendorfer, *Twos and Tens,* 220–21; John David Smith and William Cooper Jr., eds., *A Union Woman in Civil War Kentucky: The Diary of Frances Peter* (Lexington: University Press of Kentucky, 2000), 28n1; Hafendorfer, *Battle of Richmond,* 53–54, 49, 55; Lambert, *When the Ripe Pears Fell,* 17, 18; *OR,* vol. 16, 1:886; Carter, *Cavalryman's Reminiscences of the Civil War,* 35; *S-OR,* vol. 21, ser. 33:764, 761.

13. *OR,* vol. 16, 1:885, 884; Lambert, *When the Ripe Pears Fell,* 21, 17; *S-OR,* vol. 21, ser. 33:764; Coleman, *Famous Kentucky Duels,* 121; unidentified newspaper clipping from the *Daily Gazette,* September 16, 1862, John Metcalfe Family Papers, SC1273, Kentucky Historical Society (KHS), Frankfort; Ann Clay to Brutus Clay, August 1862, *Voices from the Century Before: The Odyssey of a Nineteenth Century Kentucky Family,* ed. Mary Clay Berry (New York: Arcade, 1994), 297; "A Blue Grass Belle Reports on the Civil War," Martha Wheeler Hathaway's diary transcription, Hathaway Family Papers, 59M113, UK. Maj. Gen. Horatio G. Wright said that the Seventh Kentucky "was cut to pieces." *OR,* vol. 16, 2:413.

14. Frances Peter, August 29, 1862, *Union Woman in Civil War Kentucky,* 28. Although the Seventh Kentucky Cavalry crumbled, some men still wanted to serve with the regiment. On September 10, 1862, James Sudduth informed Governor Robinson that he wanted to "serve my bleeding country in any position" but "would prefer the command of the Cavalry lately under the command of Col. Metcalf." James Sudduth to James F. Robinson, September 10, 1862, Office of the Governor, James F. Robinson: Appointments by the Governor, Military Appointments, 1862–1863, R2-156 to R2-157, KDLA, accessed via *Civil War Governors of Kentucky,* http://discovery.civilwargovernors .org/document/KYR-0001-028-0053.

15. J. S. Scott to "Commanding Officer, Federal Forces, Richmond, Ky.," August 23, 1862, John Metcalfe Family Papers, SC1273, KHS; Moore, *Rebellion Record,* 5:591; Lambert, *When the Ripe Pears Fell,* 18; Hafendorfer, *Twos and Tens,* 221; Hafendorfer, *Battle of Richmond,* 56–57.

16. For the Battle of Richmond, see *OR,* vol. 16, 1:907–52; McDonough, *War in Kentucky,* 129–46; Hafendorfer, *Battle of Richmond;* Lambert, *When the Ripe Pears Fell;* Donald A. Clark, *The Notorious "Bull" Nelson: Murdered Civil War General* (Carbondale: Southern Illinois University Press, 2013), 133–36.

17. Hafendorfer, *Battle of Richmond,* 100–102, 357; *S-OR,* vol. 21, ser. 33:764; *OR,* vol. 16, 1:909, 915; September 5, 1862, *Bluegrass Confederate: The Headquarters Diary of Edward O. Guerrant,* ed. William C. Davis and Meredith L. Swentor (Baton Rouge: Louisiana State University Press, 1999), 139. In his report after the Battle of Richmond, one Confederate colonel referred to Metcalfe as "the notorious Metcalf." *OR,* vol. 16, 1:949.

18. Moore, *Rebellion Record,* 5:590, 420; Carter, *Cavalryman's Reminiscences of the Civil War,* 35; *OR,* vol. 16, 1:884; Coleman, *Famous Kentucky Duels,* 122; Belcher, *Cavalry of the Army of the Cumberland,* 69; Metcalfe Compiled Service Record, available at Fold3.com; "The Last Duel Fought in Kentucky," *Louisville Courier-Journal,* March 12, 1877; *Report of the Adjutant General of the State of Kentucky,* 1:180. Because both Colonel Metcalfe and Lieutenant Colonel Oden resigned, command of the regiment passed down to a major. "The Battles Near Richmond, Ky.," *Indiana State Sentinel* (Indianapolis), September 8, 1862.

By September 28, 1862, the Seventh Kentucky Cavalry was still considered "disorganized." *OR*, vol. 16, 2:552. Later, Metcalfe's widow, the remarried Sarah Brewington, sued the federal government because Metcalfe had not been paid as colonel of the Seventh Kentucky, as he had not been formally mustered into the unit. In 1904, she received $83.80 for his service. See "Sarah E. Brewington, Widow, v. The United States," *Cases Decided in the Court of Claims of the United States, at the Term of 1903–4* (Washington, DC: GPO, 1904), 39:399–405.

19. Confederate cavalry in Mason County noted in William H. Wadsworth to James F. Robinson, September 16, 1862, Office of the Governor, James F. Robinson: Governor's Official Correspondence File, Military Correspondence, 1862–1863, R2-67 to R2-68, KDLA, accessed via *Civil War Governors of Kentucky*, http:// discovery.civilwargovernors.org/document /KYR-0001-027-0041.

20. "How to Dispose of Kentucky Slaves—Col. Metcalfe's Views," *Belmont Chronicle*, September 25, 1862. One newspaper reported that lawsuits brought against Metcalfe "for acts done under military orders in the line of duty as a soldier," threats against him, and the fact he was "ostracised" at home, forced him to move to Ohio. "Treatment of Kentucky Soldiers at Home," *Evansville Journal*, June 11, 1868. Lincoln first suggested compensated emancipation in March 1862. Four months later, he again offered it to border state representatives. Armstead L. Robinson, *Bitter Fruits of Bondage: The Demise of Slavery and the Collapse of the Confederacy, 1861–1865* (Charlottesville: University of Virginia Press, 2005), 176; Christopher Phillips, *The Civil War in the Border South* (Santa Barbara: Praeger, 2013), 71; Lowell H. Harrison, *Lincoln of Kentucky* (Lexington: University Press of Kentucky, 2000), 227.

21. "N——! N——!! N——!!!" *Gallipolis (OH) Journal*, August 28, 1862.

22. "N——! N——!! N——!!!" *Gallipolis Journal*.

23. "N——! N——!! N——!!!" *Gallipolis Journal*. Metcalfe had made these arguments as early as August 4, 1862. The *New York Times* noted that Metcalfe condemned "sympathizing scoundrels in Kentucky who profess to do nothing" and wanted to remove slavery, which was "the cause of this war." The *Times* also said that he supported compensated emancipation. "Affairs in Kentucky," August 4, 1862.

24. "How to Dispose of Kentucky Slaves," *Belmont Chronicle*.

25. For the Battle of Perryville, see Noe, *Perryville*; Stuart W. Sanders, *Perryville under Fire: The Aftermath of Kentucky's Largest Civil War Battle* (Charleston, SC: History Press, 2012); and McDonough, *War in Kentucky*.

26. "Affairs in Kentucky," *Hancock (Findlay, OH) Jeffersonian*, January 2, 1863.

27. "Affairs in Kentucky," *Hancock Jeffersonian*.

28. "Affairs in Kentucky," *Hancock Jeffersonian*.

29. Caroline R. Miller, "Casto–Metcalfe Duel," in *The Encyclopedia of Northern Kentucky*, ed. Paul A. Tenkotte and James C. Claypool (Lexington: University Press of Kentucky, 2009), 165; Metcalfe from Leonidas Metcalfe to Jesse E. Peyton, April 20, 1864, Lincoln Papers, LC; Victor B. Howard, *Black Liberation in Kentucky: Emancipation and Freedom, 1862–1884* (Lexington: University Press of Kentucky, 1983), 69–70.

30. Coleman, *Famous Kentucky Duels*, 122; "Last Duel," *Louisville Courier-Journal*; "Treatment of Kentucky Union Soldiers at Home," *Evansville Journal*; *Louisville Daily Courier*, June 10, 1868; Genealogy of the Metcalfe Family Papers, Metcalfe Family Papers; *Louisville Daily Courier*, June 8, 1868; Brad Asher, *The Most Hated Man in Kentucky: The Lost Cause and the Legacy of Union General Stephen Burbridge* (Lexington: University Press of Kentucky, 2021).

31. "The Rebel Spirit in Kentucky," *Cleveland (TN) Weekly Herald*, July 28, 1876; "Murdered for the Flag in Kentucky," *Carson (NV) Daily Appeal*, August 15, 1876.

11. History Is Written in Blood

1. Lewis Collins and Richard H. Collins, *History of Kentucky*, 2 vols. (Covington: Collins & Co., 1882), 1:342; *Journal of the House of Representatives of the Commonwealth of Kentucky, Begun and Held in the Town of Frankfort, on Monday, the Second Day of September, in the Year of our Lord 1861* (Frankfort: Yeoman Office, 1861), 545; "General News," *New York Times* January 1, 1862; Berry Craig and Dieter C. Ullrich, *Unconditional Unionist: The Hazardous Life of Lucian Anderson, Kentucky Congressman* (Jefferson, NC: McFarland, 2016), 75; Berry Craig, *Kentucky Confederates: Secession, Civil War, and the Jackson Purchase* (Lexington: University Press of Kentucky, 2014), 156, 166.

2. Edwin Porter Thompson, *History of the Orphan Brigade* (Cincinnati: Caxton, 1868), 46; "General News," *New York Times*; *Journal of the House of Representatives of the Commonwealth of Kentucky*, September 1861 session, 545; Craig, *Kentucky Confederates*, 168; George W. Ewing, Confederate Applications for Presidential Pardons, 1865–1867, available at Ancestry.com; Edward Coffman, *The Story of Logan County* (Nashville: Parthenon, 1962), 47; US Pardons and Amnesty Proclamations, 1865–1869, (September 1865–August 1866), 17:477, available at Ancestry.com; J. H. Battle, W. H. Perrin, and G. C. Kniffin, *Kentucky: A History of the State*, 2nd ed. (Louisville: F. A. Battey Publishing Co., 1885), 841.

3. Eastham Tarrant, *The Wild Riders of the First Kentucky Cavalry* (Louisville: R. H. Carothers, 1894), 37; Lindsey Apple, *The Family Legacy of Henry Clay: In the Shadow of a Kentucky Patriarch* (Lexington: University Press of Kentucky, 2011), 115, 113, 119; George W. Ranck, *History of Lexington, Kentucky:*

Its Early Annals and Recent Progress (Cincinnati: Robert Clarke & Co., 1872), 214, 390; "Death of Hon. James B. Clay," *New York Times*, January 28, 1864; *Death of Hon. James B. Clay, Taken from the True Presbyterian, February 4th, Louisville, Ky., 1864* (N.p.: n.p., 1864), 1, 2; Collins and Collins, *History of Kentucky*, 1:114, 130; James B. Clay to Richard Pindell, 1864, Henry Clay Memorial Foundation Papers, 96M2, University of Kentucky Special Collections, Lexington.

4. James A. Ramage, "Charles Slaughter Morehead," in *Kentucky's Governors*, ed. Lowell H. Harrison (Lexington: University Press of Kentucky, 2004), 77; William C. Harris, *Lincoln and the Border States: Preserving the Union* (Lawrence: University Press of Kansas, 2011), 112; Chapman Coleman, *The Life of John J. Crittenden*, 2 vols. (Philadelphia: J. P. Lippincott & Co., 1873), 2:348.

5. "Obituary," *Telegraph and Telephone Age* 29 (June 1, 1911), 394; Richard A. Schwarzlose, *The Nation's Newsbrokers:* vol. 1 of 2, *The Formative Years: From Pretelegraph to 1865* (Evanston, IL: Northwestern University Press, 1989), 248; "Martin W. Barr Dies," *Washington Herald*, May 12, 1911; "Funeral of War Veteran," *Washington Evening Star*, May 12, 1911.

6. "Col. R. T. Durrett," *Louisville Courier-Journal*, September 17, 1913; "Death Claims Col. Durrett," *Louisville Courier-Journal*, September 17, 1913; Fannie Porter Dickey, *Blades O' Bluegrass* (Louisville: John P. Morton & Co., 1892), 306; James R. Bentley, "Reuben Thomas Durrett," in *The Encyclopedia of Louisville*, ed. John E. Kleber (Lexington: University Press of Kentucky, 2001), 260; Thomas D. Clark, "Reuben T. Durrett and His Kentuckiana Interests and Collection," *Filson Club History Quarterly* 56 (October 1982): 354–56; "Gen. Castleman's Gift to Col. Roosevelt," *Montgomery Times*, May 30, 1910; James T. White to Reuben Durrett, "Dear Sir" letter, October 1, 1891, Reuben T. Durrett Added Papers, Correspondence, 1891, Filson Historical Society, Louisville.

7. William A. Penn, *Kentucky Rebel Town: The Civil War Battles of Cynthiana and Harrison County* (Lexington: University Press of Kentucky, 2016), 240; "Veteran Editor Dead," *Maysville Daily Public Ledger*, November 30, 1907; "A Rebel Editor Shot," *Brownlow's Knoxville Whig*, December 4, 1867; "News Items," *Evansville Journal*, November 28, 1867.

8. *Evansville Journal* (February 4, 1868; "Kentucky Knowledge," *Semi-Weekly South Kentuckian* (Hopkinsville), May 29, 1885; "Veteran Editor Dead," *Maysville Daily Public Ledger*, 4; *Owingsville (KY) Outlook* April 23, 1896; "Indications," *Maysville Evening Bulletin*, April 20, 1896.

9. "Dead at Maysville," *Louisville Courier-Journal*, March 21, 1891. For a list of some of the law books Stanton authored, see *Catalogue of the Library of the Chicago Law Institute* (Chicago: Chicago Law Institute, 1887), 115; and Talbot H. Wallis, *Catalogue of the California State Library* (Sacramento: James J. Ayers, 1886), 406.

10. John C. Underwood, *Report of the Proceedings Incidental to the Erection and Dedication of the Confederate Monument* (Chicago: William Johnston Printing Co., 1896), 85; "The J. B. Gordon Monument Association," *Confederate Veteran* 13 (June 1903): 244–45; George Francis James, ed., *The Logan Monument Memorial* (Chicago: University of Chicago Press, 1898), "Forrester," *Bourbon News* (Paris, KY), November 21, 1913; George Forrester Compiled Service Record, 3rd Kentucky Cavalry, available at Fold3.com.

11. "Death of James H. Hall, Sr.," *Louisville Courier-Journal*, February 10, 1886; "Eagle Plow Works," in *The Encyclopedia of Northern Kentucky*, ed. Paul A. Tenkotte and James C. Claypool (Lexington: University Press of Kentucky, 2008), 288; E. Polk Johnson, *A History of Kentucky and Kentuckians*, 3 vols. (Chicago: Lewis Publishing Co., 1912), 3:1283.

12. 1860 US Federal Census, Maysville, Mason County, available at Ancestry.com; Collins and Collins, *History of Kentucky*, 1:145; James Louis Head, *The Atonement of John Brooks: The Story of the True Johnny "Reb" Who Did Not Come Marching Home* (Geneva, FL: Heritage Press, 2001), 203–4; James M. Prichard, *Embattled Capital: Frankfort, Kentucky, in the Civil War* (Frankfort: Frankfort Heritage Press, 2014), 153–55; Benjamin Franklin Cooling, *To the Battles of Franklin and Nashville and Beyond* (Knoxville: University of Tennessee Press, 2011), 250; "William Hunt," *Maysville Evening Bulletin*, January 15, 1892.

13. "Death of Capt. Isaac Nelson," *Maysville Daily Public Ledger*, April 26, 1892; "Proved Fatal," *Maysville Evening Bulletin*, April 26, 1892.

14. "Col. T. A. Respess, City's Oldest Citizen Died Late Tuesday," *Maysville Daily Public Ledger*, March 19, 1919; "Then and Now," *Maysville Daily Evening Bulletin*, March 13, 1882; "The May Court," *Maysville Daily Evening Bulletin*, May 22, 1883; "Col. Thomas A. Respess 89 Years Old Today," *Maysville Daily Public Ledger*, March 10, 1915; "Two Witnesses Survive," *Louisville Courier-Journal*, March 19, 1916; "Colonel Respess Buried Thursday Morning," *Maysville Daily Public Ledger*, March 20, 1919.

15. Rogers Compiled Service Record, Eighteenth Kentucky Infantry, available at Fold3.com.

16. "Double Tragedy," *Maysville Daily Evening Bulletin*, September 28, 1883; *Maysville Daily Evening Bulletin*, October 1, 3, 1883; "Rogers Fratricide," *Bourbon News* (Paris, KY), October 2, 1883. For the trial and additional information about the case, see *Maysville Daily Evening Bulletin*, October 12, 1883; *Semi-Weekly Bourbon News* (Paris, KY), October 12, November 16, 1883; *Maysville Daily Evening Bulletin*, November 16, 1883; "Circuit Court Proceedings," *Maysville Daily Evening Bulletin*, October 15, 1885; *Maysville Daily Evening Bulletin*, October 20, 1883; "Notes of Current Events," *Stanford (KY) Semi-Weekly Interior Journal*, October 27, 1885; "Notes of Current Events," *Stanford (KY) Semi-Weekly Interior Journal*, November 18, 1884.

17. 1870 US Federal Census, Robertson County, and 1880 US Federal Census, Carlisle, Nicholas County, both available at Ancestry.com; "Stocks and Crops," *Maysville Evening Bulletin,* October 10, 1889, April 28, 1894, October 3, 1883, February 16, 1900.

18. Kentuckians, like many Southerners, frequently carried weapons before and after the Civil War. Historian John Hope Franklin wrote that this practice flourished because enslavers and overseers carried weapons to punish enslaved people and to protect themselves from slaves. Thus, the practice of carrying weapons became commonplace across Southern society, and this prevalence of arms led to more violence. John Hope Franklin, *The Militant South: 1800–1861* (Chicago: University of Illinois Press, 2002), 69. Joanne B. Freeman and Dickson D. Bruce also note the links between slavery and violence. See Joanne B. Freeman, *The Field of Blood: Violence in Congress and the Road to Civil War* (New York: Farrar, Straus & Giroux, 2018), 70; and Dickson D. Bruce, *Violence and Culture in the Antebellum South* (Austin: University of Texas Press, 1979), 7. When examining Kentucky's high murder rates after the Civil War, Robert Ireland gives "the impact of liquor, concealed weapons, and the code of honor" as contributing factors. Robert M. Ireland, "Homicide in Nineteenth Century Kentucky," *Register of the Kentucky Historical Society* 81 (Spring 1983): 136.

19. Bruce, *Violence and Culture,* 42–43, 67.

20. Dick Steward, *Duels and the Roots of Violence in Missouri* (Columbia: University of Missouri Press, 2000), 135–36. Ireland notes that "supporters of the duel submitted that with its decline came an increase in street fights." Ireland, "Homicide in Nineteenth Century Kentucky," 143.

21. Stella Pickett Hardy, *Colonial Families of the Southern States of America* (Baltimore: Southern Book Co., 1958), 243; "Thomas M. Green," *Louisville Daily Journal,* September 28, 1868; *Central Kentucky Gazette,* April 10, 1867; "Candidates for Congress," *Central Kentucky Gazette,* April 10, 1867; "A Death Shot," *Louisville Courier-Journal,* November 17, 1887; "Yields to Death," *Louisville Courier-Journal,* April 8, 1904.

22. "Killed by a Newspaper Man," *Washington Evening Star,* November 16, 1887; *Big Sandy News,* November 24, 1887; "A Terrible Tragedy," *Maysville Evening Bulletin,* November 17, 1887; "Terrible Tragedy," *Lexington Press,* November 17, 1887; "The Killing of Baldwin," *Louisville Courier-Journal,* December 2, 1887; "A Death Shot," *Louisville Courier-Journal*; "The Baldwin Killing," *Louisville Courier-Journal,* November 25, 1887.

23. "A Death Shot," *Louisville Courier-Journal*; "Col. Green's Trial," *Louisville Courier-Journal,* November 29, 1887; "Col. Green's Trial," *Louisville Courier-Journal,* December 4, 1887; "literally jammed" from "Green's Trial," *Louisville Courier-Journal,* December 1, 1887; "Yields to Death," *Louisville Courier-Journal*; John Wilson Townsend, *Kentucky in American Letters, 1784–1912,* 2 vols. (Cedar Rapids, IA: Torch Press, 1913), 1:312.

12. Two Young Bloods

1. Jack K. Williams, *Dueling in the Old South: Vignettes of Social History* (College Station: Texas A&M University Press, 1980), 78–81; Richard F. Hamm, *Murder, Honor, and Law: Four Virginia Homicides From Reconstruction to the Great Depression* (Charlottesville: University of Virginia Press, 2003), 60. One example of a formal postwar duel occurred at Shanghai, Mississippi in 1870, when businessman Ed T. Freeman shot and killed Edwin F. Hamlin, "a rising young lawyer." One report said that after the duel, "strong men stood around, men who had dared death on many a battlefield. They wept like children." "The Late Duel in Mississippi," *Kentucky Advocate* (Danville), September 9, 1870.

2. Among the last duels in Kentucky was a fight between two Paris residents, Isaac Hanson and Noah S. Alexander, who fought with pistols at ten paces in April 1867. The men missed four times; on the fifth, Alexander was slightly wounded and Hanson suffered a wound in the hip. Hanson was the brother of Roger Hanson, who before the war had been injured in a duel near Vevay, Indiana. Isaac Hanson and Alexander did not use traditional dueling pistols. Instead, they fired six-shot Colt Navy revolvers. "Various Items," *Brooklyn Daily Eagle*, May 7, 1867; "Bad Shooting," *New Orleans Times-Picayune*, May 10, 1867.

3. "Scraps and Facts," *Yorkville* (SC) *Enquirer*, March 8, 1866.

4. "Our Governor's Sons," *Hartford Herald*, May 22, 1895; "Auspicious Occurrences," *Friend of Peace* 4 (January 5, 1827): 126; Charles J. Bussey, "Joseph Desha," in *Kentucky's Governors: 1792–1985*, ed. Lowell H. Harrison (Lexington: University Press of Kentucky, 2004), 31.

5. "Desha–Kimbrough Duel," in *The Kentucky Encyclopedia*, ed. John E. Kleber (Lexington: University Press of Kentucky, 1992), 265; William A. Penn, *Kentucky Rebel Town: The Civil War Battles of Cynthiana and Harrison County* (Lexington: University Press of Kentucky, 2016), 248; "Duel after the War," *Maysville Evening Bulletin*, May 19, 1902; J. Winston Coleman, "The Code Duello in Ante-Bellum Kentucky," in *A Kentucky Sampler: Essays from the Filson Club History Quarterly, 1926–1979*, ed. Lowell Harrison and Nelson L. Dawson (Lexington: University Press of Kentucky, 1977), 131; J. Winston Coleman Jr., *Famous Kentucky Duels* (Lexington: Henry Clay Press, 1969), 132, 123, 125; *The B. O. Gaines History of Scott County*, 2 vols. Georgetown, KY: B. O. Gaines, 1905), 2:435.

6. Albert D. Kirwan, ed., *Johnny Green of the Orphan Brigade: The Journal of a Confederate Soldier* (Lexington: University Press of Kentucky, 1984), 66n3; Gaines, *History of Scott County*, 2:435, 434; Edwin Porter Thompson, *History of the Orphan Brigade* (Cincinnati: Caxton Publishing, 1868), 491; Coleman, *Famous Kentucky Duels*, 123.

7. Thompson, *Orphan Brigade,* 491–92, 493; Coleman, *Famous Kentucky Duels,* 124; Kirwan, *Johnny Green,* 67n3; Joseph Desha Compiled Service Record, Ninth Kentucky Infantry, available at Fold3.com; Penn, *Kentucky Rebel Town,* 8, 75, 83; Joseph Desha to his brothers, Cave and Lucius Desha, August 25, 1861, Capt. Joseph Desha letter, SC 78, Kentucky Historical Society, Frankfort.

8. *Johnny Green,* 67, 6n3; Thompson, *Orphan Brigade,* 197, 494, 726, 220; "Final Roll Call," *Louisville Courier-Journal,* May 9, 1902; Coleman, *Famous Kentucky Duels,* 124, 125; Desha Compiled Service Record; "Duel after the War," *Maysville Evening Bulletin.*

9. "Final Roll Call," *Louisville Courier-Journal;* Thompson, *Orphan Brigade,* 494; Desha to brothers, Cave and Lucius Desha.

10. Coleman, *Famous Kentucky Duels,* 125; 1860 US Federal Census, Harrison County, District 2, and 1860 US Federal Census—Slave Schedule, Harrison County, both available at Ancestry.com.

11. US National Home for Disabled Volunteer Soldiers Register, Johnson City, TN, available at Ancestry.com; Coleman, *Famous Kentucky Duels,* 125; Alexander Kimbrough Compiled Service Record, 4th Kentucky Infantry, available at Fold3.com; Coleman, "Code Duello in Ante-Bellum Kentucky," 131.

12. "Desha–Kimbrough Duel," 265; Coleman, "Code Duello in Ante-Bellum Kentucky," 131; Coleman, *Famous Kentucky Duels,* 126; Penn, *Kentucky Rebel Town,* 248; Gaines, *History of Scott County,* 2:435.

13. Gaines, *History of Scott County,* 2:435; "Desha–Kimbrough Duel," 265; Gary R. Matthews, *Basil Wilson Duke: The Right Man in the Right Place* (Lexington: University Press of Kentucky, 2005), 215; "Pistols and Coffee," *Louisville Daily Courier,* February 21, 1866.

14. Gaines, *History of Scott County,* 2:435; "Desha–Kimbrough Duel," 265; Coleman, *Famous Kentucky Duels,* 126, 128, 130, 123; Coleman, "Code Duello in Ante-Bellum Kentucky," 131; Penn, *Kentucky Rebel Town,* 248; "Duel after the War," *Maysville Evening Bulletin.*

15. Coleman, *Famous Kentucky Duels,* 129, 130; "Desha–Kimbrough Duel," 265; Gaines, *History of Scott County,* 2:435; "Duel after the War," *Maysville Evening Bulletin;* Matthews, *Basil Duke,* 215; Coleman, "Code Duello in Ante-Bellum Kentucky," 132; Thomas Marshall Green, *Historic Families of Kentucky* (Cincinnati: Robert Clarke & Co., 1889), 65; Thompson, *Orphan Brigade,* 440–42. McDowell also described in Ephraim McDowell Anderson, *Memoirs: Historical and Personal* (St. Louis: Times Printing Co., 1868), 379.

16. Coleman, *Famous Kentucky Duels,* 127, 123, 128, 127n8; "Desha–Kimbrough Duel," 265; Gaines, *History of Scott County,* 2:435, 434; "Duel after the War," *Maysville Evening Bulletin;* Penn, *Kentucky Rebel Town,* 248;

Coleman, "Code Duello in Ante-Bellum Kentucky," 131–32, 133n32. One man who toured the Duke farm said the dueling ground where Desha and Kimbrough fought was "well defined by two large forest trees." By 1940, however, only one tree remained. From "The Old James K. Duke Farm, Scott County, Ky., Birthplace of Gen. Basil W. Duke," Mss.AM847j, Filson Historical Society, Louisville.

17. "Scraps and Facts," *Yorkville Enquirer,* 2; Coleman, *Famous Kentucky Duels,* 129, 130; Coleman, "Code Duello in Ante-Bellum Kentucky," 132; *Cleveland Daily Leader,* April 5, 1866; Gaines, *History of Scott County,* 2:435.

18. Coleman, "Code Duello in Ante-Bellum Kentucky," 132; Coleman, *Famous Kentucky Duels,* 131.

19. Gaines, *History of Scott County,* 2:435; "Desha–Kimbrough Duel," 265.

20. Coleman, *Famous Kentucky Duels,* 131; Gaines, *History of Scott County,* 2:435; Coleman, "Code Duello in Ante-Bellum Kentucky," 132; "Duel after the War," *Maysville Evening Bulletin*; *Memphis Public Ledger,* March 27, 1866; "Southern News," *St. Cloud (MN) Democrat,* April 5, 1866; Penn, *Kentucky Rebel Town,* 248.

21. Gaines, *History of Scott County,* 2:435; Coleman, *Famous Kentucky Duels,* 131, 132; "From Cincinnati," *Louisville Daily Courier,* April 21, 1866, 4; "Duel after the War," *Maysville Evening Bulletin.*

22. Coleman, *Famous Kentucky Duels,* 133.

23. Coleman, *Famous Kentucky Duels,* 133, 134; US National Home for Disabled Volunteer Soldiers Register; 1910 US Federal Census, Malibu, District 0288, Los Angeles County, California, accessed via Ancestry.com on October 20, 2016; "Desha–Kimbrough Duel," 265.

24. Penn, *Kentucky Rebel Town,* 248; Warren Smith from Gaines, *History of Scott County,* 2:435; "Desha–Kimbrough Duel," 265; Coleman, *Famous Kentucky Duels,* 132, 133; "Final Roll Call," *Louisville Courier-Journal,* May 9, 1902; "Duel after the War," *Maysville Evening Bulletin*; "Crosses of Honor," *Louisville Courier-Journal,* January 18, 1902.

25. Coleman, *Famous Kentucky Duels,* 134; "Desha–Kimbrough Duel," 265; Coleman, "Code Duello in Ante-Bellum Kentucky, 132; "Duel after the War," *Maysville Evening Bulletin.*

Conclusion

1. *Maysville Daily Public Ledger,* May 9, 1892; "Paintings," *Maysville Evening Bulletin,* June 10, 1892.

2. "Dover," *Maysville Daily Public Ledger,* May 11, 1892; author's correspondence with Sue Ellen Grannis, curator, Gateway Museum Center, September 7, 2016.

3. Author's correspondence with Grannis; author's correspondence with Paul Tierney, park naturalist, Carter Caves State Resort Park, December 14, 2016.

4. Jack K. Williams, *Dueling in the Old South: Vignettes of Social History* (College Station: Texas A&M University Press, 1980), 80. Edward L. Ayers notes that postwar violence among upper classes was not by any means confined to Kentucky bluebloods; rather, violence was found across the South, and few antagonists were convicted of crimes. Edward L. Ayers, *Vengeance and Justice: Crime and Punishment in the Nineteenth-Century American South* (Oxford: Oxford University Press, 1984), 10. Robert M. Ireland recognizes "the decline of the duel and the rise of the habit of carrying concealed deadly weapons." Robert M. Ireland, "The Problem of Concealed Weapons in Nineteenth-Century Kentucky," *Register of the Kentucky Historical Society* 91 (Autumn 1993): 370. For information about Kentucky laws concerning concealed weapons, see 372–74. Dick Steward contends that Missouri followed a similar pattern of the formal duel being replaced by spontaneous violence, which evolved into the Western-type gunfight. Dick Steward, *Duels and the Roots of Violence in Missouri* (Columbia: University of Missouri Press, 2000), 5.

5. "After Thirteen Years," *Louisville Courier Journal,* September 8, 1879. Richard Hamm writes, "Even as the duel disappeared, the lure of honor grew stronger for many white southern men. . . . Indeed, the culture of honor became more deadly as guns became more widely available." Richard F. Hamm, *Murder, Honor, and Law: Four Virginia Homicides from Reconstruction to the Great Depression* (Charlottesville: University of Virginia Press, 2003), 62.

6. Hambleton Tapp and James C. Klotter, *Kentucky: Decades of Discord, 1865–1900* (Frankfort: Kentucky Historical Society, 1977), 377, 378, 383, 384; Anne E. Marshall, *Creating a Confederate Kentucky: The Lost Cause and Civil War Memory in a Border State* (Chapel Hill: University of North Carolina Press, 2013), 56. Marshall argues that violence perpetrated by the Ku Klux Klan and similar groups was the "natural outgrowth of the pervasive and intense guerrilla activity that had plagued the state during the war." This organized violence "became a way to assert conservative values, Democratic politics, and, most of all, white supremacy" (57, 58, 60). For racial violence during this period, see George C. Wright, *Racial Violence in Kentucky, 1865–1940* (Baton Rouge: Louisiana State University Press, 1990). For an examination of Kentucky's reputation during the twentieth century, see Anthony Harkins, "Colonels, Hillbillies, and Fightin': Twentieth-Century Kentucky in the National Imagination," *Register of the Kentucky Historical Society* 113 (Spring–Summer 2015): 421–52.

7. Kentuckians' carrying of concealed weapons did not begin after the Civil War. Ireland notes that in the 1830s, legislators "blamed over one-half of the commonwealth's murders on such carrying." Ireland, "Problem of

Concealed Weapons," 374, 375, 376. Members of the state's 1850 Constitutional Convention also recognized the dangers of concealed weapons, noting that they caused more deaths than duels. In 1854, the legislature passed a law against concealed weapons, excluding only the "ordinary pocket knife." Ireland writes that legal exemptions for self-defense kept the practice going in Kentucky, despite laws to the contrary (375).

8. "The Harrodsburg Tragedy," *Louisville Courier-Journal*, November 29, 1873; "The Harrodsburg Tragedy," *Louisville Courier-Journal*, December 6, 1873; "The Harrodsburg Tragedy," *Louisville Courier-Journal*, December 22, 1873. For an overview of the shooting, see L. F. Johnson, *Famous Kentucky Tragedies and Trials* (Louisville: Baldwin Law Book Company, 1916), 191–204.

9. "Harrodsburg," *Louisville Courier-Journal*, January 5, 1874.

10. "Arrest of Prentice and Durrett," *New-York Daily Tribune*, July 23, 1857; "Prentice Is Challenged, but Backs Out," *New York Herald*, July 25, 1857; "The Editorial Affray at Louisville," *Washington Evening Star*, July 25, 1857; "A Deplorable Tragedy," *Breckenridge News* (Cloverport, KY), April 2, 1879; James C. Klotter, *Kentucky Justice, Southern Honor, and American Manhood: Understanding the Life and Death of Richard* Reid (Baton Rouge: Louisiana State University Press, 2003), 38–39. For an overview of Elliott's murder, see Robert M. Ireland, "The Buford-Elliott Tragedy and the Traditions of Kentucky Criminal Justice," *Filson Club History Quarterly* 66 (July 1992): 395–420.

11. "Gen. McPherson's Death," *Belmont Chronicle* (St. Clairsville, OH), May 15, 1879.

12. Broadside, "From the Proceedings of the Mass Meetings of the Women of Louisville, Held Tuesday, February 6, 1900," Filson Historical Society, Louisville.

13. "Prominent Men Engage in Street Fight," *Bourbon News* (Paris, KY), July 9, 1907; "Lawyer Carries Pistol," *Mt. Sterling Advocate*, July 10, 1907; *Maysville Daily Public Ledger*, July 30, 1908.

14. Johnson, *Famous Kentucky Tragedies*, 289–91; "Stabbed Him to Death," *New York Times*, November 9, 1889. For Goodloe's biography, see *Society of the Army of the Cumberland, Twenty-First Reunion, Toledo, Ohio, 1890* (Cincinnati: Robert Clarke & Co., 1891), 290–92.

15. Johnson, *Famous Kentucky Tragedies*, 289–90; "Stabbed Him to Death," *New York Times*.

16. "Stabbed Him to Death," *New York Times*; Johnson, *Famous Kentucky Tragedies*, 284; Lewis Collins and Richard H. Collins, *History of Kentucky*, 2 vols. (Covington: Collins & Co., 1882), 1:49; William H. Townsend, *Lincoln and the Bluegrass: Slavery and Civil War in Kentucky* (Lexington: University Press of Kentucky, 1955), 84.

17. "Terrible Tragedy," *Maysville Evening Bulletin*, November 9, 1889; "Foes to the Death," *Aurora (IL) Daily Express*, November 9, 1889; "Stabbed Him to Death," *New York Times*; Johnson, *Famous Kentucky Tragedies*, 282, 285.

18. Johnson, *Famous Kentucky Tragedies*, 282, 285, 287; "Foes to the Death," *Aurora Daily Express*, 2; "Stabbed Him to Death," *New York Times*; "Little Hope for Goodloe," *New York Times*, November 10, 1889.

19. Johnson, *Famous Kentucky Tragedies*, 283, 287, 288, 291; "Stabbed Him to Death," *New York Times*; "Little Hope for Goodloe," *New York Times*.

20. "Little Hope for Goodloe," *New York Times*; Johnson, *Famous Kentucky Tragedies*, 288.

21. Reporter from "A Kentucky Tragedy," *Watchman and Southron* (Sumter, SC), April 17, 1895.

22. *Bourbon News* (Paris, KY), May 11, 1883.

23. Tapp and Klotter, *Kentucky*, 400; "A Day's Record of Deeds of Violence in Kentucky," *Arizona Weekly Journal-Miner* (Prescott), October 26, 1892.

24. James C. Klotter, *William Goebel: The Politics of Wrath* (Lexington: University Press of Kentucky, 1977), 100–102; Lowell H. Harrison and James C. Klotter, *A New History of Kentucky* (Lexington: University Press of Kentucky, 1997), 277, 280; Suzanne Marshall, *Violence in the Black Patch of Kentucky and Tennessee* (Columbia: University of Missouri Press, 1994), 86; Newspaper Clippings, Charles A. Hardin Papers, 87M38, University of Kentucky Special Collections, Lexington. For statistical information about Kentucky's changing murder rate, see Robert M. Ireland, "Homicide in Nineteenth Century Kentucky," *Register of the Kentucky Historical Society* 81 (Spring 1983): 134.

25. "Duel of Other Days," *Maysville Evening Bulletin*, December 8, 1903.

26. Bertram Wyatt-Brown, *Southern Honor: Ethics and Behavior in the Old South* (Oxford: Oxford University Press, 2007), 359; "The Last Duel Fought in Kentucky," *Louisville Courier-Journal*, March 12, 1877; "Old Killings Recalled," *Hazel Green (KY) Herald*, May 23, 1895.

Index